THE MAN WHO GREW YOUNG

ALSO BY DANIEL QUINN:

AFTER DACHAU

ISHMAEL

THE STORY OF B

PRIVIDENCE: THE STORY OF A FIFTY-YEAR VISION QUEST

MY ISHMAEL: A SEQUEL

BEYOND CIVILIZATION: HUMANITY'S NEXT GREAT ADVENTURE

PUBLISHED IN THE UNITED STATES OF AMERICA
CONTEXT BOOKS, NEW YORK.
DISTRIBUTED BY PUBLISHERS GROUP WEST

WWW.CONTEXTBOOKS.COM

COVER DESIGN: ARCHIE FERGUSON

CONTEXT BOOKS
368 BROADWAY
SUITE 314
NEW YORK, NY 10013

LIBRARY OF CONGRESS CONTROL NUMBER: 2001090596

ISBN 1-893956-17-2
ISBN 1-893956-19-9

9 8 7 6 5 4 3 2 1

MANUFACTURED IN THE UNITED STATES OF AMERICA

This book is dedicated to my teachers,
some mislaid, some departed, but none forgotten:

Dr. Leonard J. Eslick, whose honors course devoted
to Plato's *Republic* showed me what a text can do.
Thomas Merton, who was wise enough to see
that I was a likelier poet than a monk.
Francis Squibb, who taught me how to write prose.
Ruth C. Hunt, the best boss I ever had, by many miles.
Michael Carden, who helped me see what was going on.
The assorted murderers, thieves, armed robbers, con men,
arsonists, and street hustlers of the Stateville Penitentiary
Writers Workshop, who taught me more about American
social realities than I could teach them about writing.
Ada Saichy, who insisted I would be my own teacher.
Richard V. Perry, who made me see that, except
with evening wear, black shoes must be shunned.
Steve Teske, a dear man but hard to find.
Bill Hearst, great friend and loyal student.
Gayanne DeVry, whose friendship, patience, and
artistry have contributed immeasurably to my life.
Alan D. Thornhill, Ph.D., friend and colleague.
David Lawrence, brilliant designer and delightful person,
who died an early victim of AIDS but made his mother happy
by promising never to use any mayonnaise but Hellman's.

THE MAN WHO

GREW YOUNG

DANIEL QUINN

ILLUSTRATIONS BY TIM ELDRED

CONTEXT BOOKS · NEW YORK 2001

PREFACE

THE LURE OF THE IMPOSSIBLE

I think it's fair to say that the role of the artist is to attempt the impossible—to paint what cannot be painted, sculpt what cannot be sculpted, write what cannot be written. In fact, any artist who shuns the impossible and settles for what is easily accomplished is not really much of an artist.

In 1978 I started writing a book that was completely impossible. It didn't occur to me at the time that it was impossible, and in fact I finished it in about six months (or thought I had). I sent it to a literary agent, who found it fascinating—but thought it would be impossible to sell. I took his word for it and decided to write it a different way . . . which proved to be impossible. After a thousand pages, I could see no end in sight. I threw away this second version and wrote a third; after penning a thousand pages (and in those days I *did* use a pen), there was still no end in sight. I started a fourth version that bore no resemblance to the first three. When it was close enough to being finished to show to someone, I sent it to a different literary agent, who found it fascinating—but thought it would be impossible to sell.

Since I was finding it difficult to produce a version that actually reached a satisfactory conclusion, I decided to issue the fifth version in parts, and simply to write as many parts as were needed. The first three parts were brilliant—the best writing I'd ever done—and, publishing and distributing them myself, I achieved quite an impressive local underground following in the Santa Fe area. But the fourth part would not come, though I worked on it for months. Like the previous ones, the fifth version was a failure.

Nevertheless, it gave me an idea of how I might go about writing a sixth version, which, amazingly, I actually finished. Quite confident now, I sent it off to the same agent who had found the first version fascinating. He didn't find the sixth version fascinating, however. He thought it was drivel. Even worse, he told me I was wasting my evident talent on this material, because nothing I could ever do with it would make it publishable.

By this time seven years had passed, and I was ready for a vacation. I decided to spend it tackling something that was easily accomplished, which turned out to be a novel called *Dreamer*. It wasn't a bad novel, merely a possible one. My agent immediately recognized it as marketable, and it was sold, published, praised briefly, and forgotten, as such books generally are.

I went back to work on version six of my impossible book, cutting it in half to produce a seventh version that I thought I might be able to sell myself to one publisher or another. No one was interested.

There remained an eighth version to be written, which I needn't describe at length here, because it won the largest prize ever given to a single work of fiction and went on to become an international bestseller in twenty languages. This was *Ishmael*, a book my agent had assured me was impossible to write. He wasn't far wrong (after all, it had taken me about a dozen years to write it), but I fired him all the same.

A bout four years after finishing *Ishmael* I conceived another impossible novel. In this novel, our universe had come to an end—and had begun retracing its steps backwards through time. When it reached a point roughly corresponding to the year 2040 of our own era, the hero of my novel (a man named Adam Taylor) would be born. The novel would open when he was about thirty years old.

I found, however, that it was impossible to write a novel about someone living backwards in time. I should say that it was impossible *for me* to write a novel about someone living backwards in time. Perhaps another writer could do it.

I put the idea away. After all, I had plenty of other impossible novels to work on.

I tinkered with one called *The Holy*, which I'd started in about 1989 (and which my agent confidently assured me was impossible). I tinkered with it, but it remained impossible. I went on to other projects.

Then one day in 1995 I got a call from a stranger, Michael Taylor of Boyle-Taylor Productions. He explained that, having read and been impressed by *Ishmael,* he wondered if I had a screenplay he could look at with an eye to production.

I said, "You mean a screenplay of *Ishmael.*"

"No," he said, "I don't really think it's possible to do *Ishmael* as a feature film. I was wondering if you had something else entirely."

I told him I didn't at the moment but that I *could* have something else. "I have a story idea that won't work as a novel, but it *would* work as a film."

He told me that if I wrote it as a script he'd be glad to have a look at it.

I spent the next few months writing a screenplay about a man living backwards in time. It opened this way:

EXT. — A COUNTRY CEMETERY — DAY

The film begins with a long shot of that most ordinary of film-opening scenes, the grave-side service, attended by all the usual people: the husband of the deceased (ADAM TAYLOR), the mother of the deceased (HELEN CRANE), a MINISTER, and a handful of friends: DOUG, HARRY, JENNIFER, PAUL, TERESA. The film runs for some time before we begin to see that this is not the ordinary grave-side service after all. The casket, instead of being lowered *into* the grave, is being drawn up *out* of the grave. The flowers on the casket, instead of falling *from* the mourners' hands, leap up *into* the mourners' hands. By now it should be clear that this is a burial scene in reverse motion.

The minister opens his prayer book and begins to read aloud—unintelligibly (since it's in reverse). When he's finished, he closes his book, looks around, nods, and the mourners begin to back away from the grave toward their cars. Adam, a man in his late thirties, is the last to leave. Finally he too begins to back away toward the cars. After a few steps he looks over his shoulder, and his eyes meet those of Mrs. Crane. He turns back to the grave site and the camera turns with him, producing a blur pan. When it ends, we're seeing the scene from Adam's point of view. He and the others are no longer backing toward their cars, they're walking in the normal way. From his point of view (and therefore from ours), the action of the film is taking place in forward motion (and continues to do so from this point on).

Echoing the verdict given on the first version of the book that ultimately became *Ishmael*, Michael Taylor told me that *The Man Who Grew Young* was fascinating—but would never be produced as a film. As I had in the other case, I took his word for it.

It might have been left at that if not for a further intervention by *Ishmael*. Always a wonderful matchmaker, this book brought me into contact with Tim Eldred, a young Californian who wanted to know if he could mount a not-for-profit dramatic reading of it. As we discussed it, I learned that he was a comic-book artist, and he sent me some published samples of his work. Seeing these, I realized that, even if *The Man Who Grew Young* couldn't be a film, it could certainly be a graphic novel. After reading the screenplay, Tim eagerly agreed to work with me on it.

And work it was—far more than I imagined—most of it being done by Tim, of course, since the scenario (my contribution) was already in place. In reality, Tim single-handedly turned *The Man Who Grew Young* into a film-on-paper, donning every film-making hat in turn—casting director, costume-designer, property-master, location manager, set-decorator, lighting director, director of "photography," and director. That he did his work with extraordinary brilliance is evident at a glance, and no author could be happier than I am with this astonishing realization of my concept.

Having said all this, I must hurry on. An impossible screenplay is awaiting my attention—and after that two of the most impossible novels I've ever dreamed of.

I can hardly wait to get at them!

(And, by the way, that other "impossible" novel, *The Holy*, will be published by Context Books in the fall of 2002.)

Daniel Quinn
Houston, May 2001

PART ONE

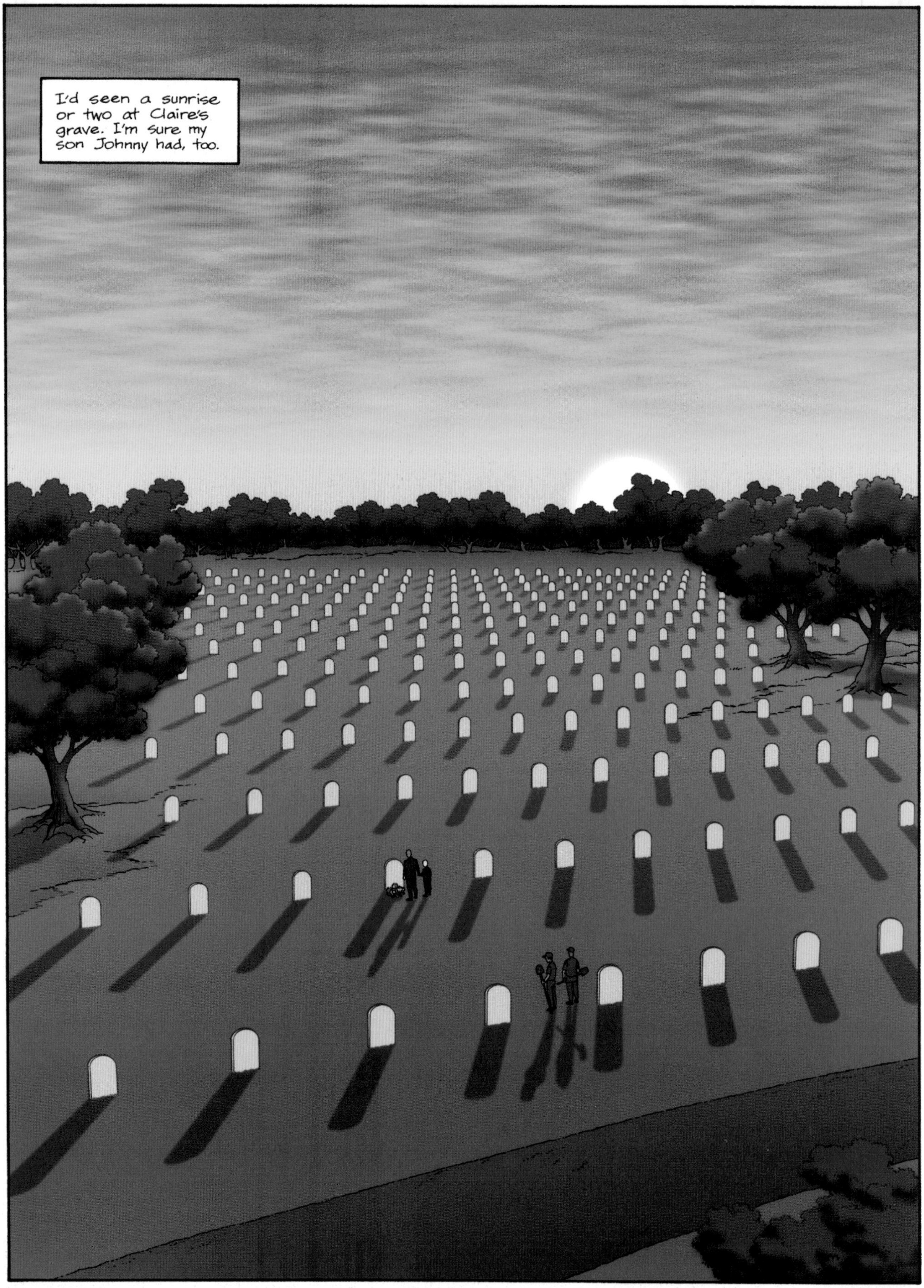
I'd seen a sunrise or two at Claire's grave. I'm sure my son Johnny had, too.

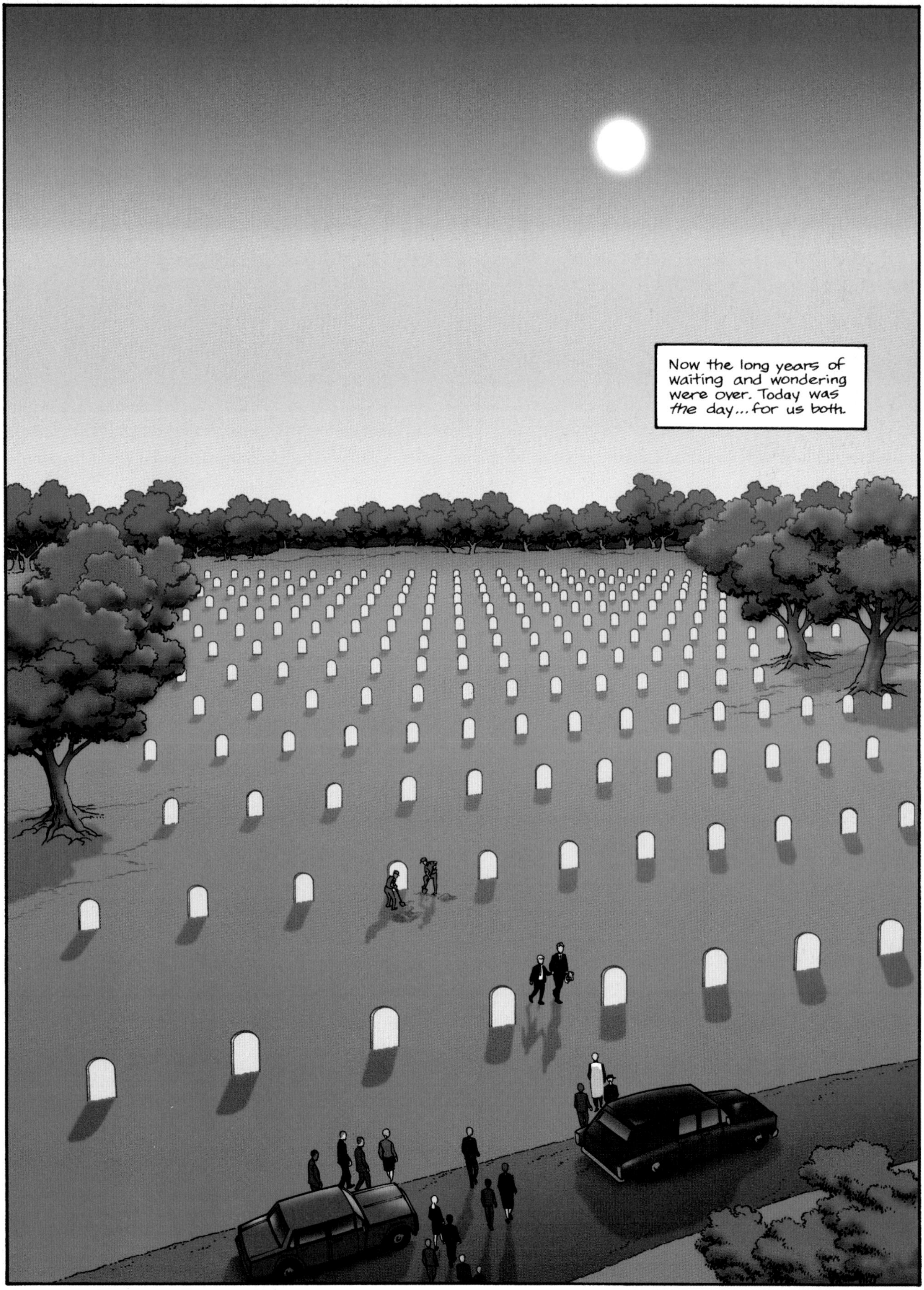
Now the long years of waiting and wondering were over. Today was *the* day...for us both.

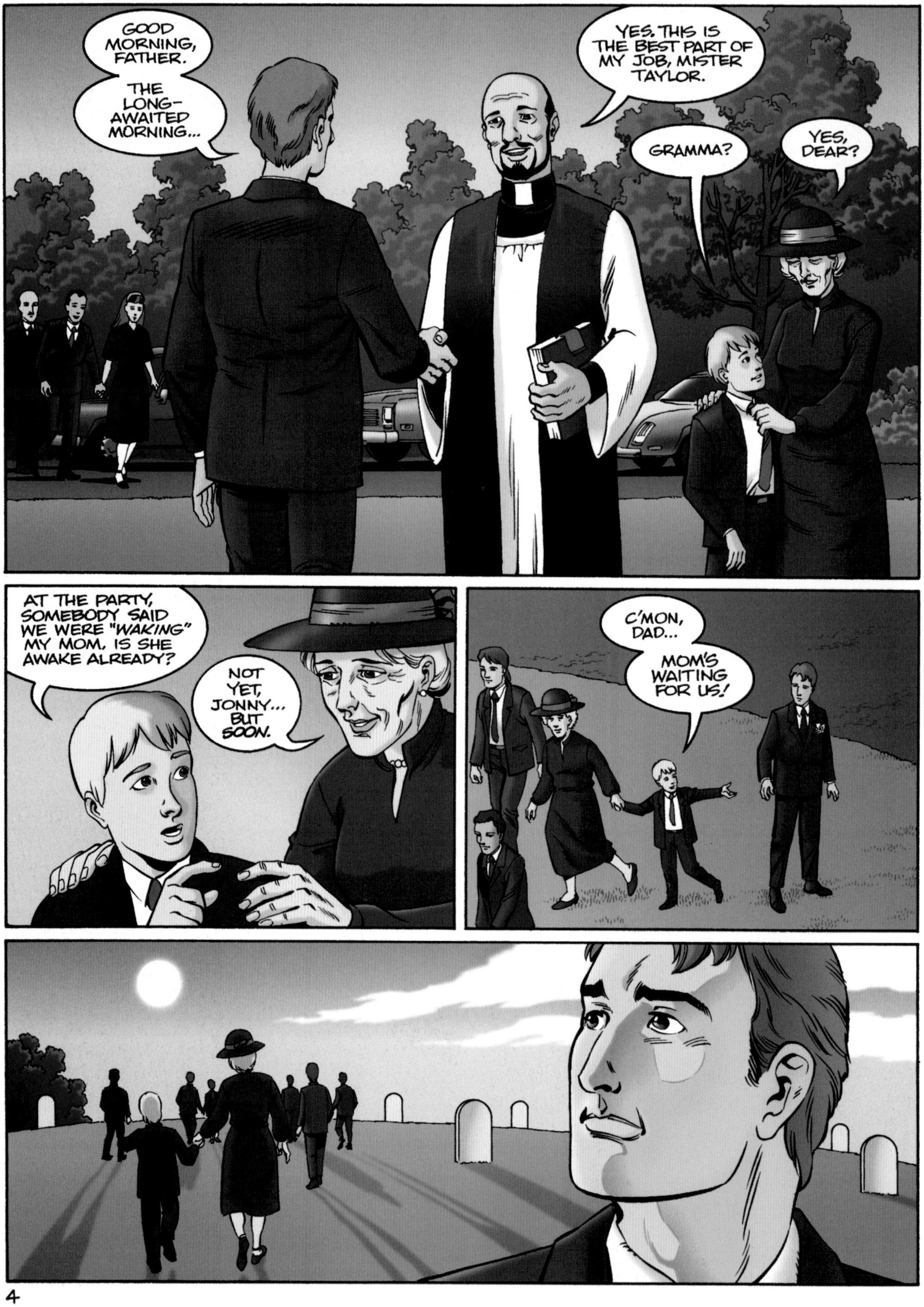
GOOD MORNING, FATHER.
THE LONG-AWAITED MORNING...
YES. THIS IS THE BEST PART OF MY JOB, MISTER TAYLOR.
GRAMMA?
YES, DEAR?
AT THE PARTY, SOMEBODY SAID WE WERE "WAKING" MY MOM. IS SHE AWAKE ALREADY?
NOT YET, JONNY... BUT SOON.
C'MON, DAD...
MOM'S WAITING FOR US!

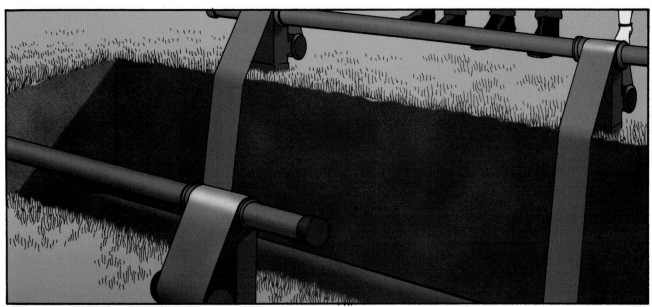

FROM MOTHER OF EARTH TO MOTHER OF FLESH...

It happens to all, someday. But this was the first time for me...getting ready to meet someone who was just a name, even if she was the mother of my son.

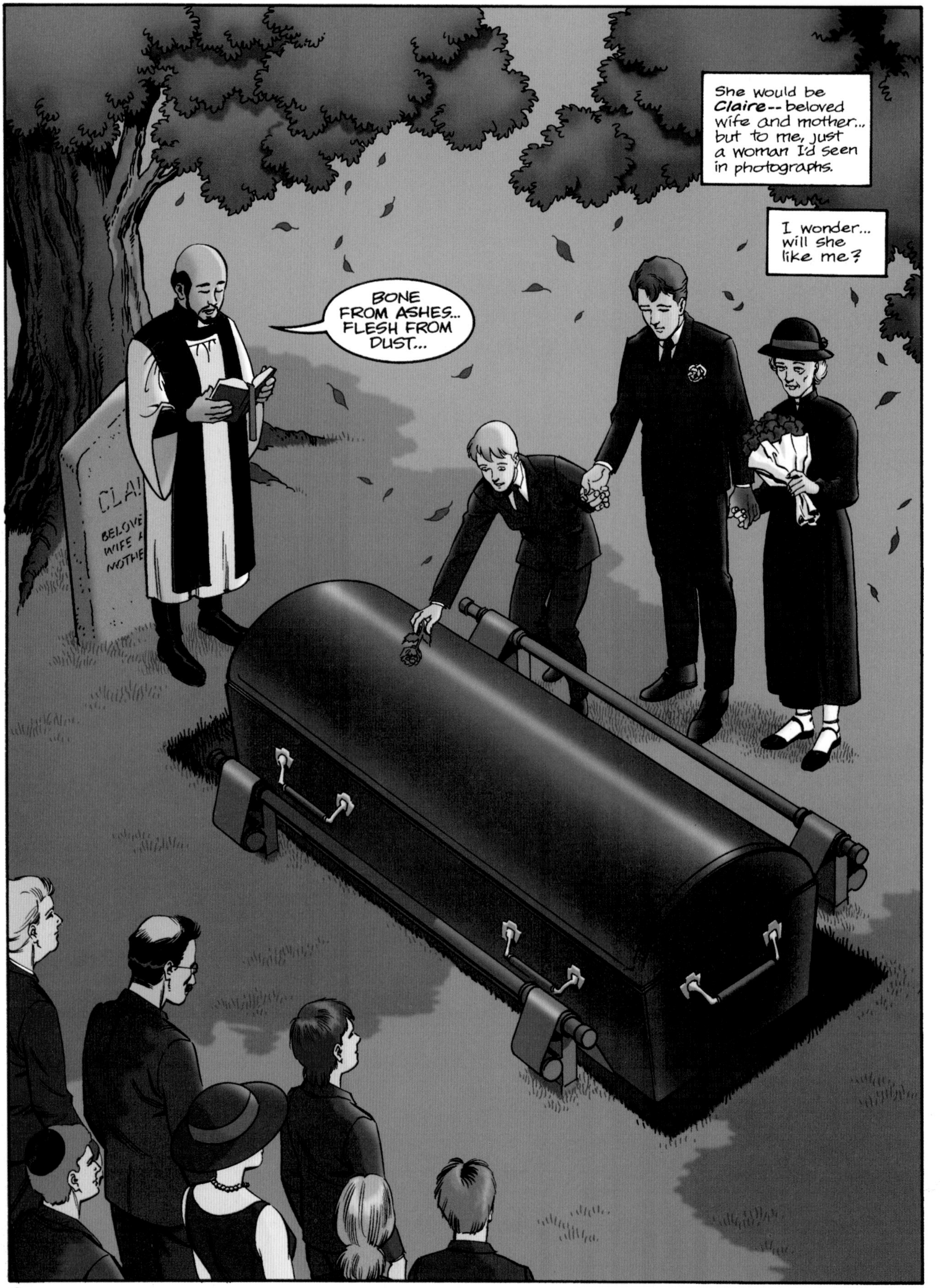
She would be Claire-- beloved wife and mother... but to me, just a woman I'd seen in photographs.
I wonder... will she like me?
BONE FROM ASHES... FLESH FROM DUST...
CLAI
BELOVE
WIFE A
MOTHE

I'd have to keep everyone calm during the steps to come... the service at the church, the lying-in-state at the funeral home...

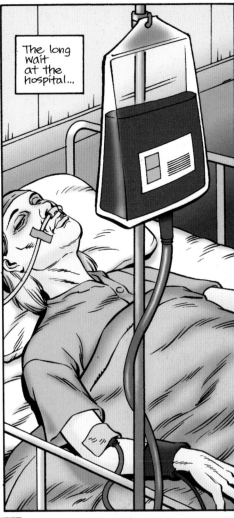

The long wait at the hospital...

Finally, the doctor told us we could go in.

Everyone had warned us not to expect too much of her. After all, at this point she didn't know either of us from Adam.

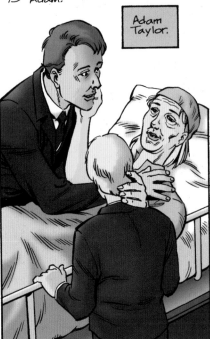

Everyone enjoyed making this little joke, because my name IS Adam.

Adam Taylor.

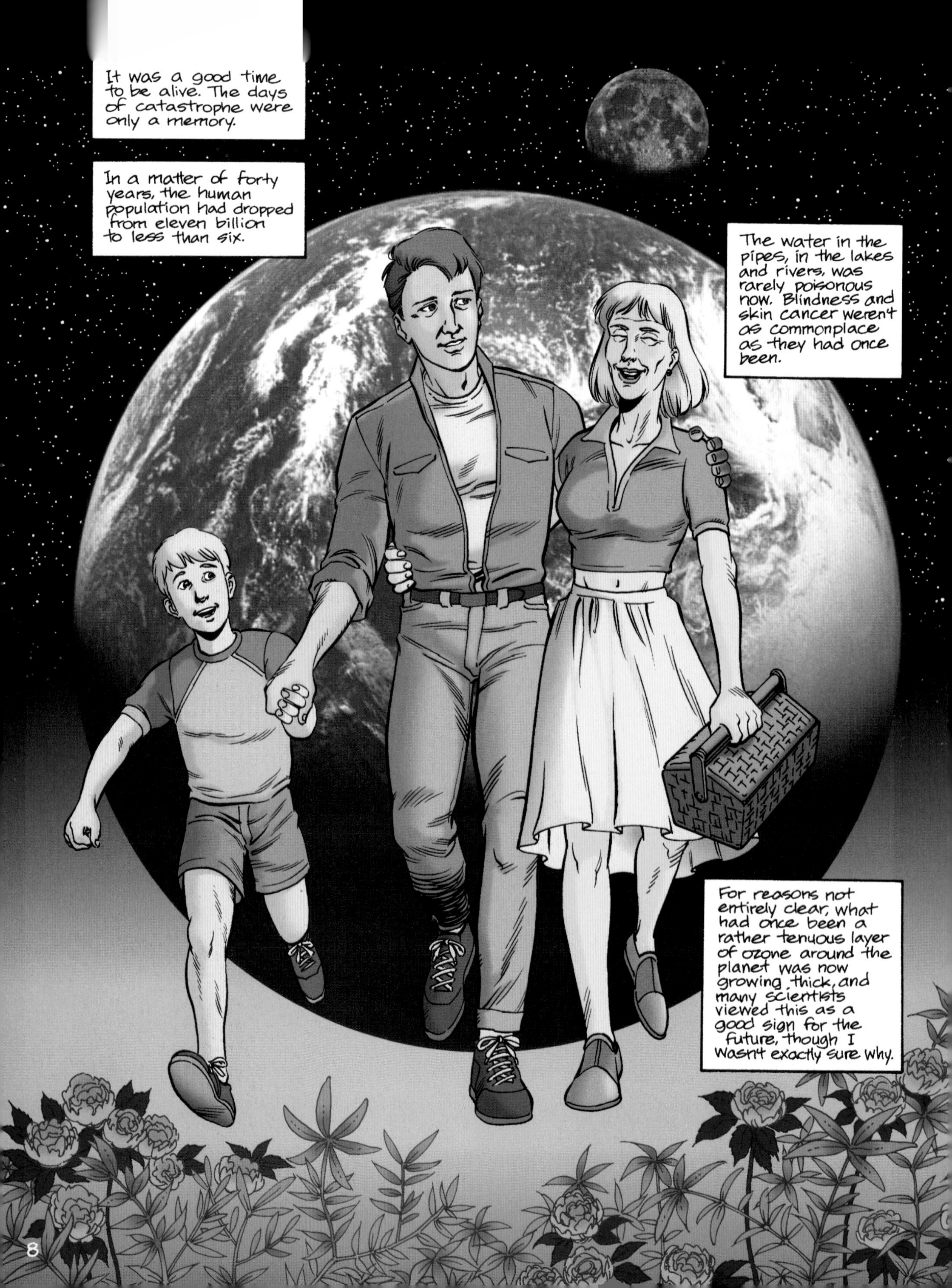
It was a good time to be alive. The days of catastrophe were only a memory.
In a matter of forty years, the human population had dropped from eleven billion to less than six.
The water in the pipes, in the lakes and rivers, was rarely poisonous now. Blindness and skin cancer weren't as commonplace as they had once been.
For reasons not entirely clear, what had once been a rather tenuous layer of ozone around the planet was now growing thick, and many scientists viewed this as a good sign for the future, though I wasn't exactly sure why.

At the newspaper, we'd recently gotten rid of our computer system, to everyone's relief.

I think we all felt more valuable relying on our own brains and muscles.

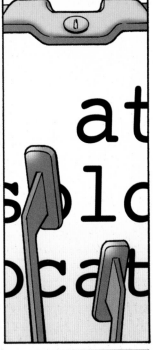

Every year, the planet was growing greener. Scientists said this explained why the air was getting cleaner. Or partly explained it.

Of course, factories were running day and night, and that helped.

Every year, billions of tons of fossil fuel were going into the ground.

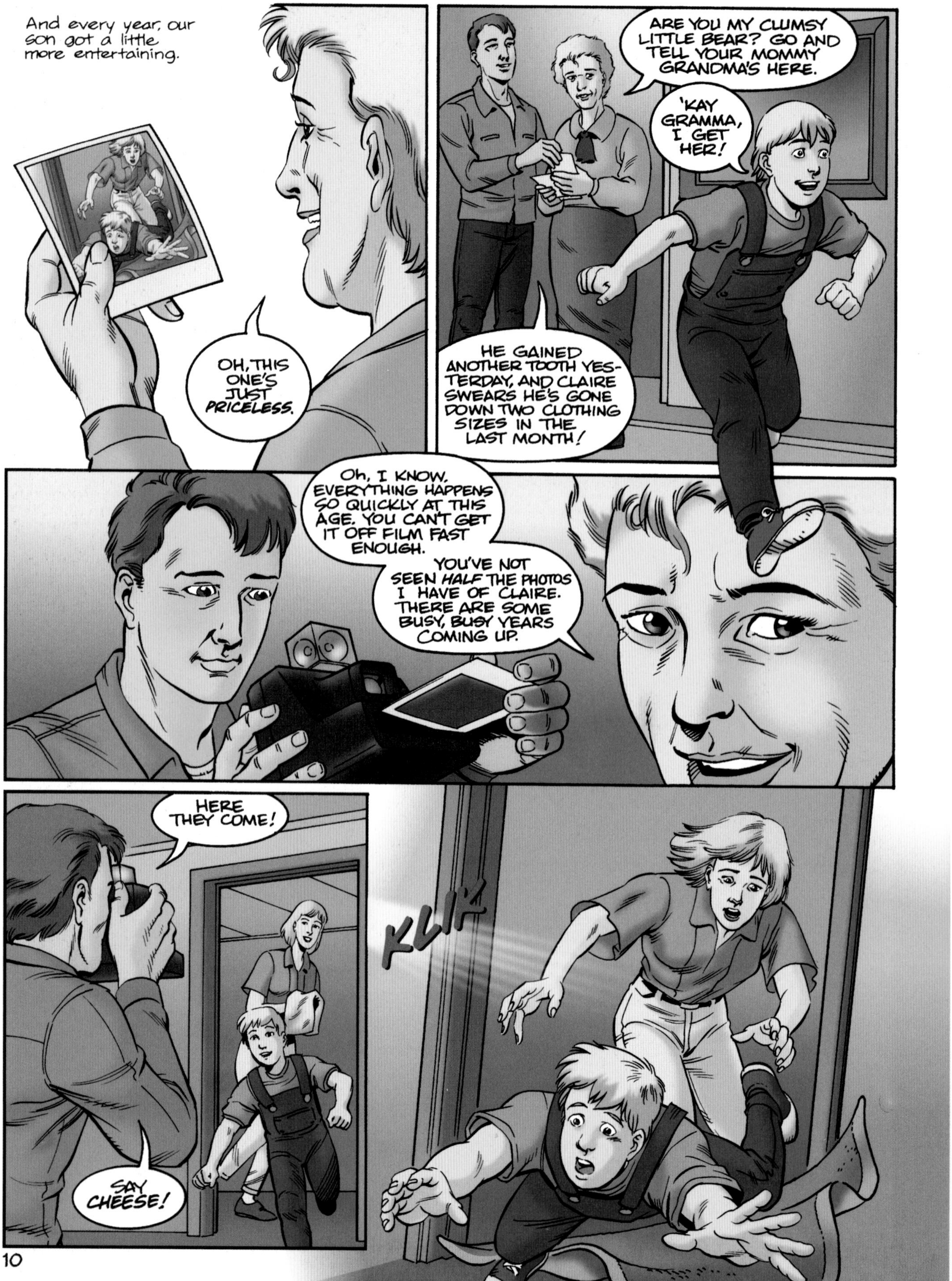
And every year, our son got a little more entertaining.
OH, THIS ONE'S JUST PRICELESS.
ARE YOU MY CLUMSY LITTLE BEAR? GO AND TELL YOUR MOMMY GRANDMA'S HERE.
'KAY GRAMMA, I GET HER!
HE GAINED ANOTHER TOOTH YESTERDAY, AND CLAIRE SWEARS HE'S GONE DOWN TWO CLOTHING SIZES IN THE LAST MONTH!
Oh, I KNOW. EVERYTHING HAPPENS SO QUICKLY AT THIS AGE. YOU CAN'T GET IT OFF FILM FAST ENOUGH.
YOU'VE NOT SEEN HALF THE PHOTOS I HAVE OF CLAIRE. THERE ARE SOME BUSY, BUSY YEARS COMING UP.
HERE THEY COME!
SAY CHEESE!
KLIK

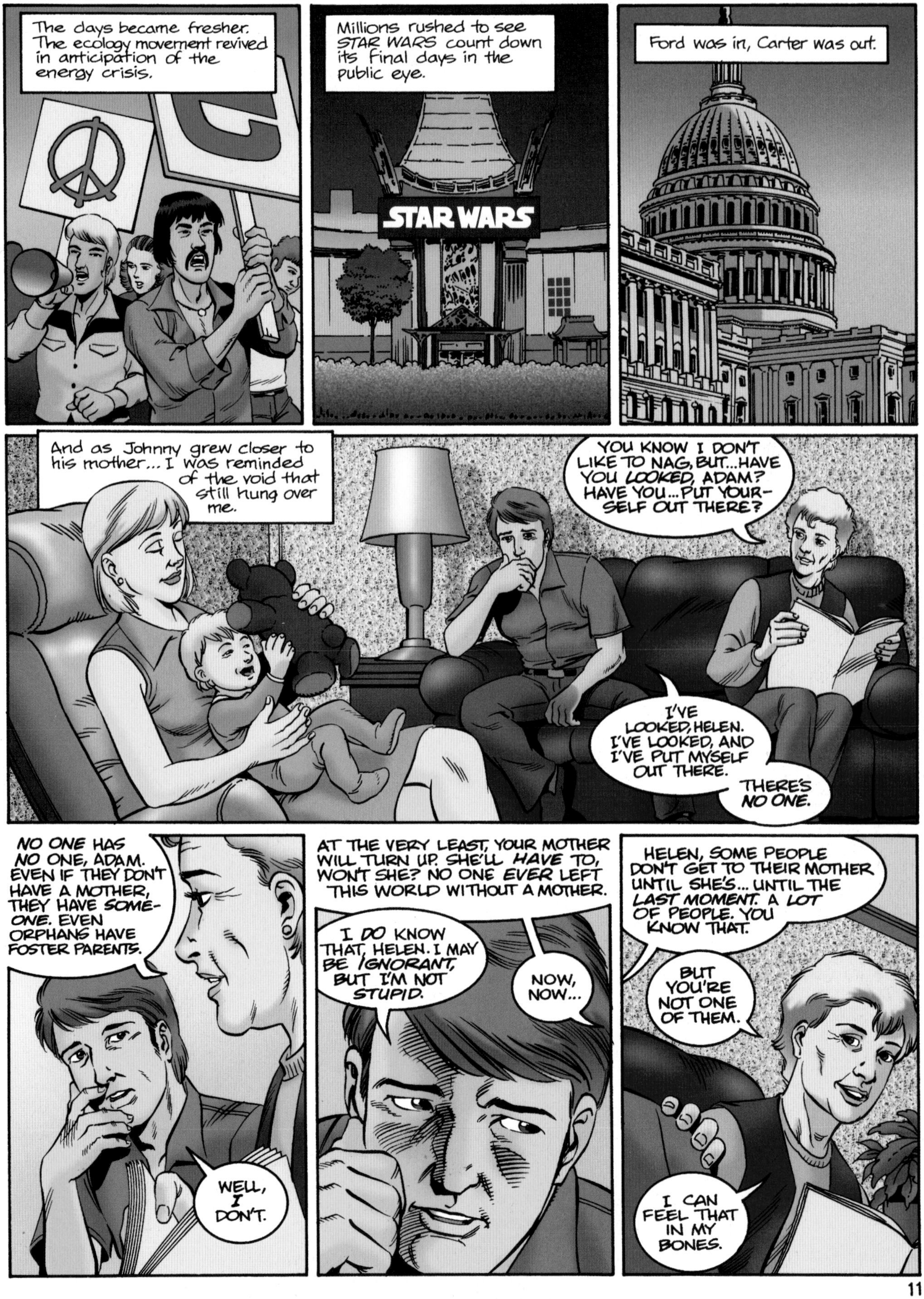
The days became fresher. The ecology movement revived in anticipation of the energy crisis.
Millions rushed to see STAR WARS count down its final days in the public eye.
STAR WARS
Ford was in, Carter was out.
And as Johnny grew closer to his mother... I was reminded of the void that still hung over me.
YOU KNOW I DON'T LIKE TO NAG, BUT...HAVE YOU LOOKED, ADAM? HAVE YOU...PUT YOURSELF OUT THERE?
I'VE LOOKED, HELEN. I'VE LOOKED, AND I'VE PUT MYSELF OUT THERE.
THERE'S NO ONE.
NO ONE HAS NO ONE, ADAM. EVEN IF THEY DON'T HAVE A MOTHER, THEY HAVE SOMEONE. EVEN ORPHANS HAVE FOSTER PARENTS.
WELL, I DON'T.
AT THE VERY LEAST, YOUR MOTHER WILL TURN UP. SHE'LL HAVE TO, WON'T SHE? NO ONE EVER LEFT THIS WORLD WITHOUT A MOTHER.
I DO KNOW THAT, HELEN. I MAY BE IGNORANT, BUT I'M NOT STUPID.
NOW, NOW...
HELEN, SOME PEOPLE DON'T GET TO THEIR MOTHER UNTIL SHE'S... UNTIL THE LAST MOMENT. A LOT OF PEOPLE. YOU KNOW THAT.
BUT YOU'RE NOT ONE OF THEM.
I CAN FEEL THAT IN MY BONES.

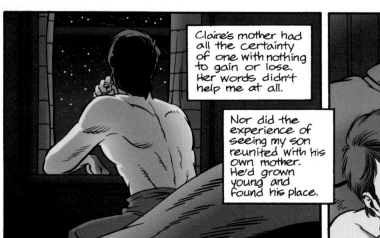

Claire's mother had all the certainty of one with nothing to gain or lose. Her words didn't help me at all.

Nor did the experience of seeing my son reunited with his own mother. He'd grown young and found his place.

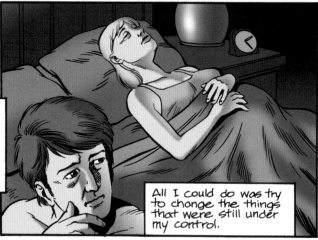

All I could do was try to change the things that were still under my control.

Without Johnny, we didn't need all the space in that house...

...so Claire and I found a nice apartment.

KITCHEN

BOOKS

I'd long ago given back my job at the paper, so we had to do without a formal honeymoon.

Nevertheless, our final day of marriage was beautiful. All of our friends helped us to celebrate the love we'd shared.

...AND DO YOU, CLAIRE, RELEASE THIS MAN FROM HIS VOWS OF MATRIMONY...

Then began our days of closure.

WHAT HAPPENED TO YOUR HAND? DO YOU MIND IF I ASK?

NOTHING HAPPENED TO IT...

...OR AT LEAST NOTHING THAT I KNOW OF. IT'S JUST A BIRTH-MARK.

DOES IT BOTHER YOU?

NO, NOT AT ALL. I THINK IT'S SORT OF SEXY.

A BIRTHMARK?

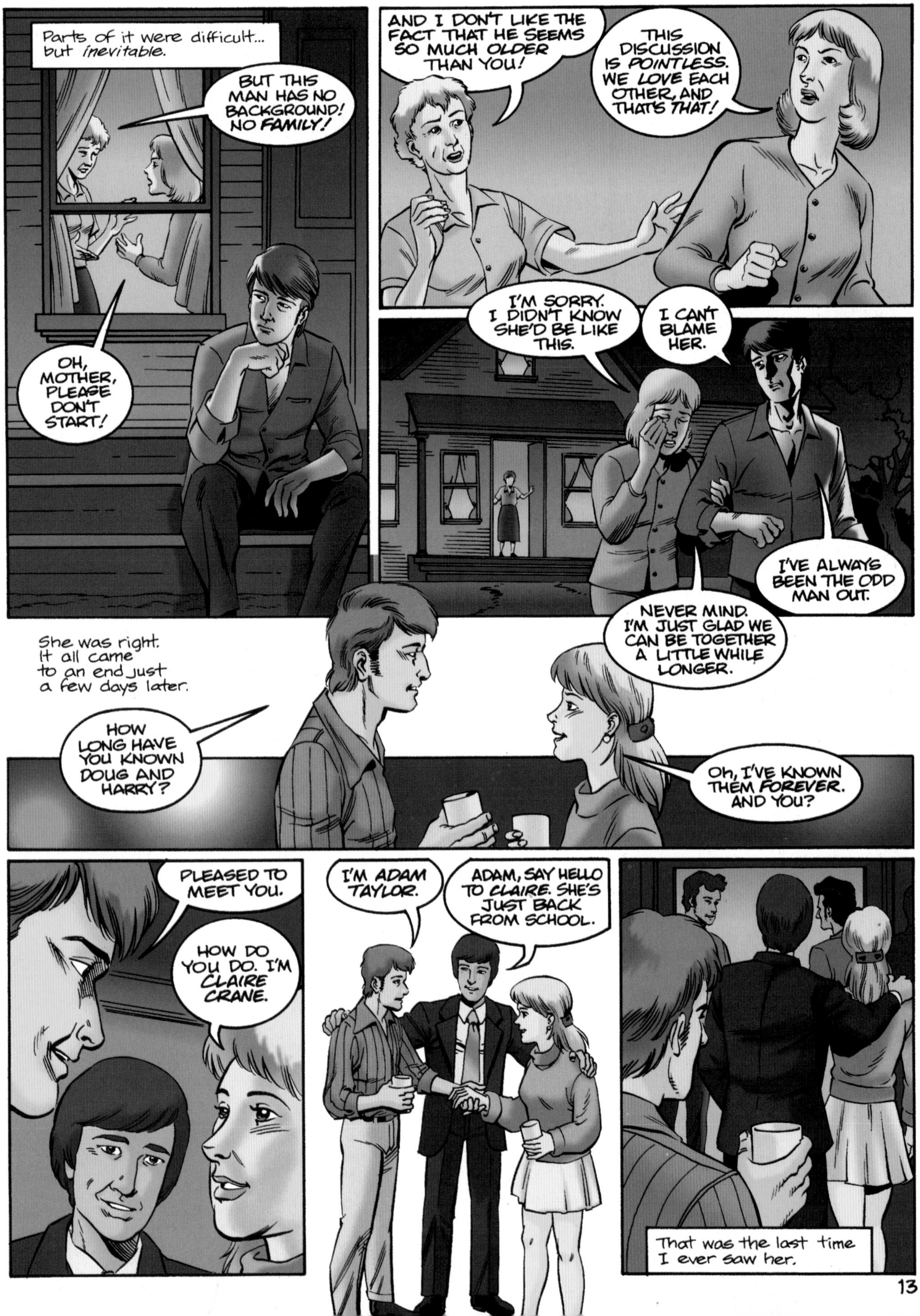
Parts of it were difficult... but *inevitable.*
BUT THIS MAN HAS NO BACKGROUND! NO *FAMILY!*
OH, MOTHER, PLEASE DON'T START!
AND I DON'T LIKE THE FACT THAT HE SEEMS SO MUCH *OLDER* THAN YOU!
THIS DISCUSSION IS *POINTLESS.* WE *LOVE* EACH OTHER, AND THAT'S *THAT!*
I'M SORRY. I DIDN'T KNOW SHE'D BE LIKE THIS.
I CAN'T BLAME HER.
I'VE ALWAYS BEEN THE ODD MAN OUT.
NEVER MIND. I'M JUST GLAD WE CAN BE TOGETHER A LITTLE WHILE LONGER.
She was right. It all came to an end just a few days later.
HOW LONG HAVE YOU KNOWN DOUG AND HARRY?
Oh, I'VE KNOWN THEM *FOREVER.* AND YOU?
PLEASED TO MEET YOU.
HOW DO YOU DO. I'M *CLAIRE CRANE.*
I'M *ADAM TAYLOR.*
ADAM, SAY HELLO TO *CLAIRE.* SHE'S JUST BACK FROM SCHOOL.
That was the last time I ever saw her.

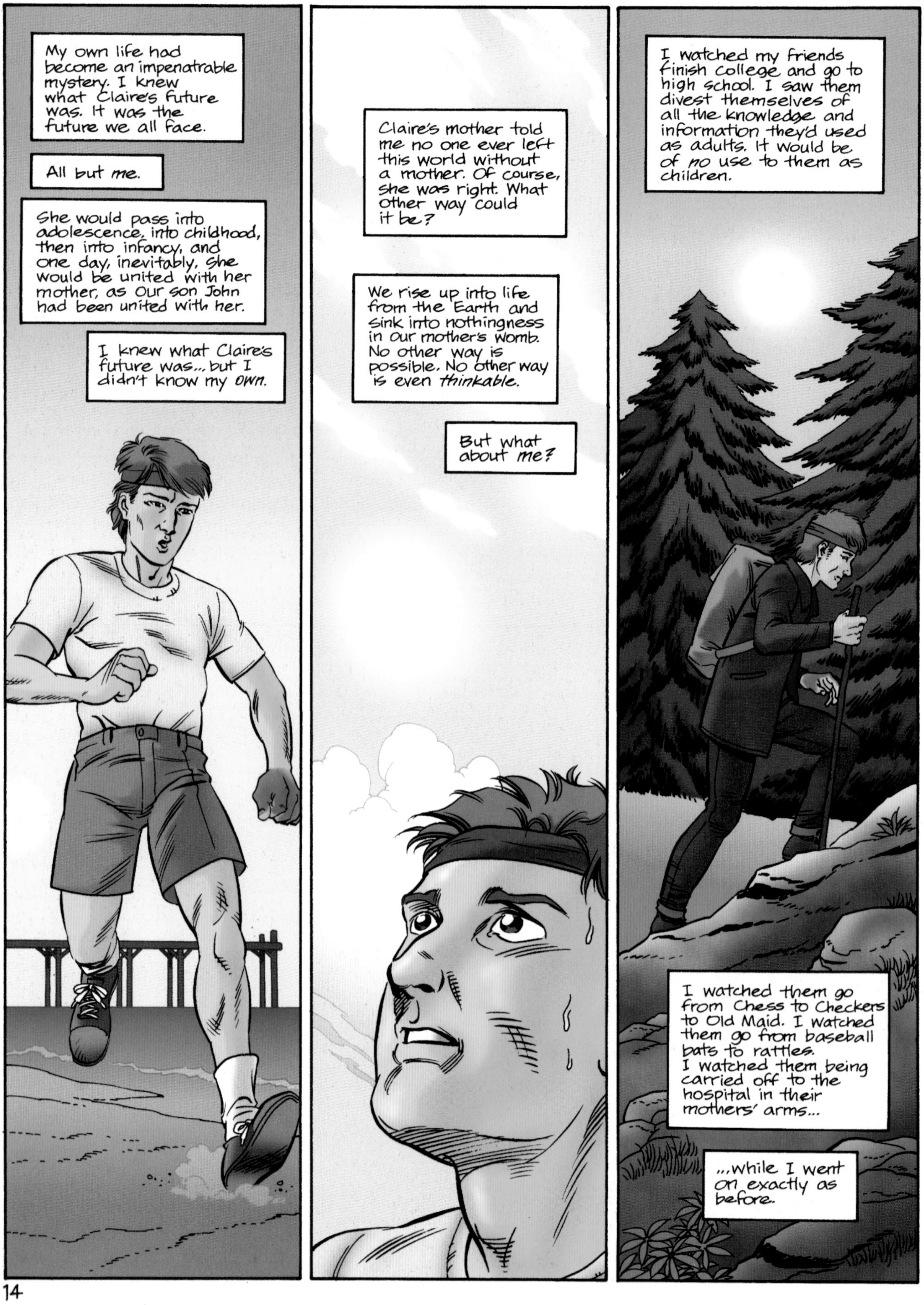
My own life had become an impenatrable mystery. I knew what Claire's future was. It was the future we all face.
All but *me*.
She would pass into adolescence, into childhood, then into infancy, and one day, inevitably, she would be united with her mother, as our son John had been united with her.
I knew what Claire's future was... but I didn't know my *own*.
Claire's mother told me no one ever left this world without a mother. Of course, she was right. What other way could it be?
We rise up into life from the Earth and sink into nothingness in our mother's womb. No other way is possible. No other way is even *thinkable*.
But what about *me*?
I watched my friends finish college and go to high school. I saw them divest themselves of all the knowledge and information they'd used as adults. It would be of *no* use to them as children.
I watched them go from Chess to Checkers to Old Maid. I watched them go from baseball bats to rattles. I watched them being carried off to the hospital in their mothers' arms...
...while I went on exactly as before.

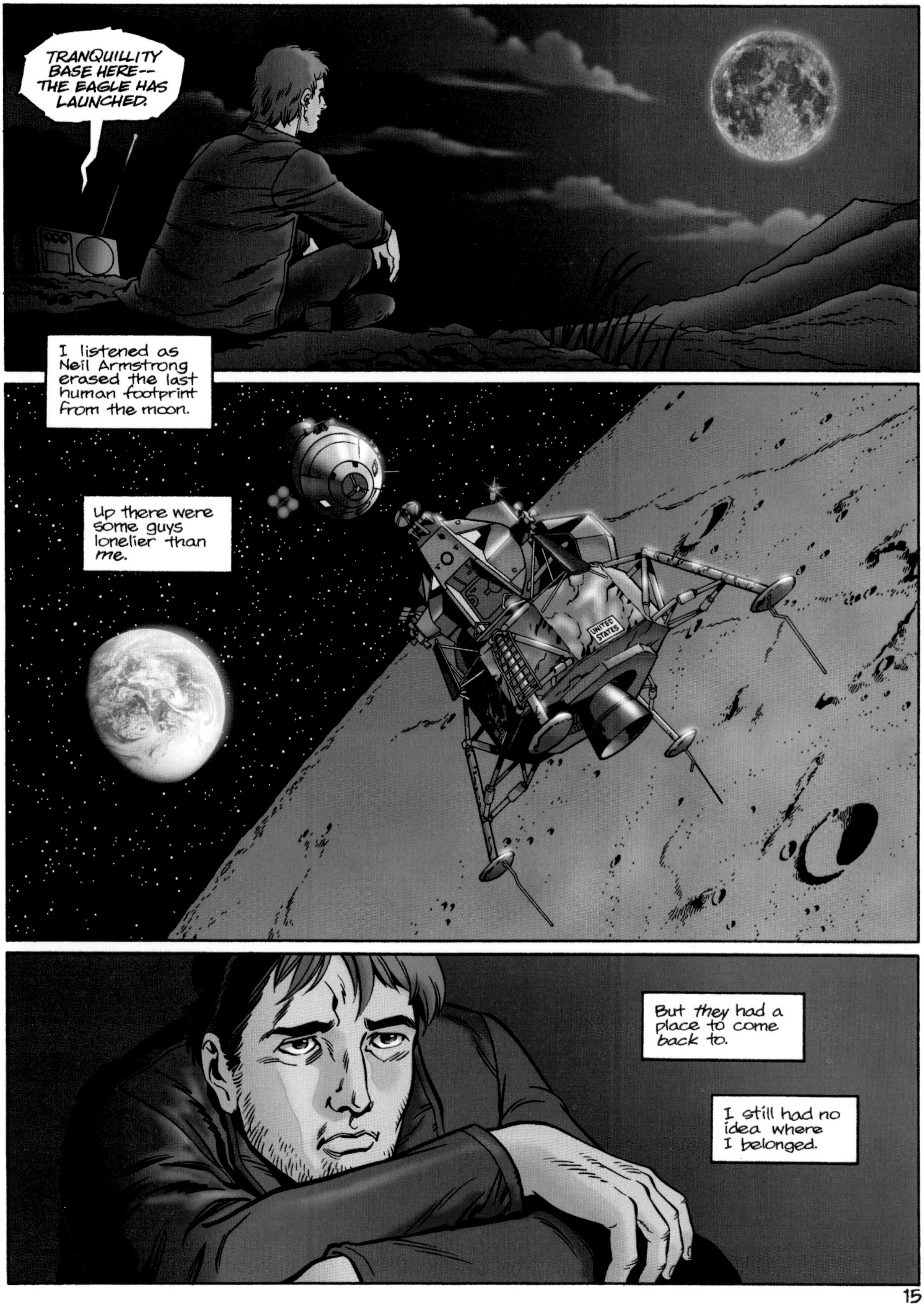
TRANQUILLITY BASE HERE-- THE EAGLE HAS LAUNCHED.
I listened as Neil Armstrong erased the last human footprint from the moon.
Up there were some guys lonelier than me.
UNITED STATES
But *they* had a place to come back to.
I still had no idea where I belonged.

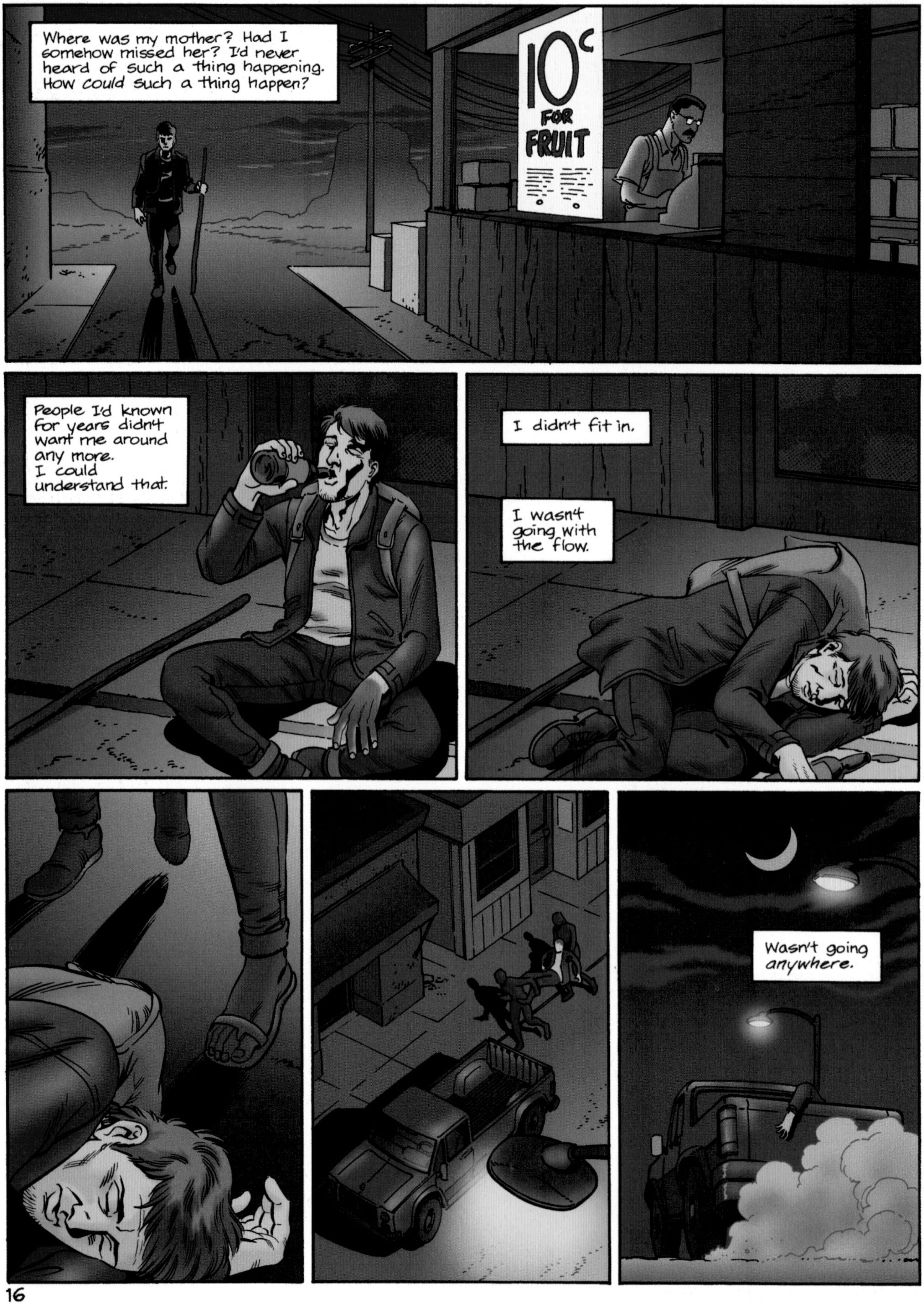
Where was my mother? Had I somehow missed her? I'd never heard of such a thing happening. How could such a thing happen?
10¢ FOR FRUIT
People I'd known for years didn't want me around any more. I could understand that.
I didn't fit in.
I wasn't going with the flow.
Wasn't going *anywhere.*

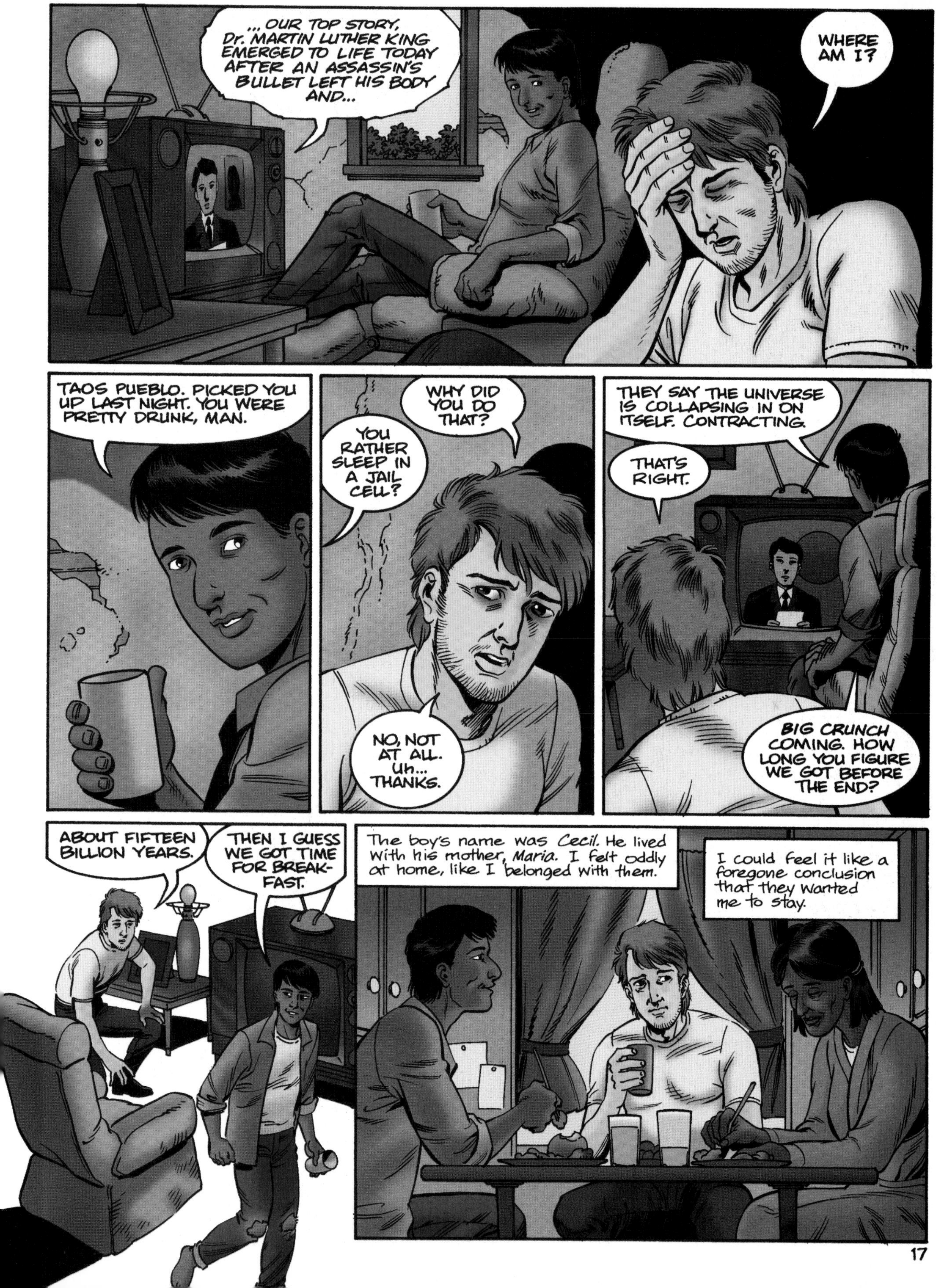
...OUR TOP STORY, Dr. MARTIN LUTHER KING EMERGED TO LIFE TODAY AFTER AN ASSASSIN'S BULLET LEFT HIS BODY AND...
WHERE AM I?
TAOS PUEBLO. PICKED YOU UP LAST NIGHT. YOU WERE PRETTY DRUNK, MAN.
WHY DID YOU DO THAT?
YOU RATHER SLEEP IN A JAIL CELL?
NO, NOT AT ALL. Uh... THANKS.
THEY SAY THE UNIVERSE IS COLLAPSING IN ON ITSELF. CONTRACTING.
THAT'S RIGHT.
BIG CRUNCH COMING. HOW LONG YOU FIGURE WE GOT BEFORE THE END?
ABOUT FIFTEEN BILLION YEARS.
THEN I GUESS WE GOT TIME FOR BREAK-FAST.
The boy's name was Cecil. He lived with his mother, Maria. I felt oddly at home, like I belonged with them.
I could feel it like a foregone conclusion that they wanted me to stay.

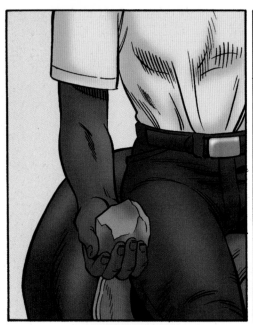

OVER THERE IN THAT ARROYO, I THINK.

HERE WE ARE.

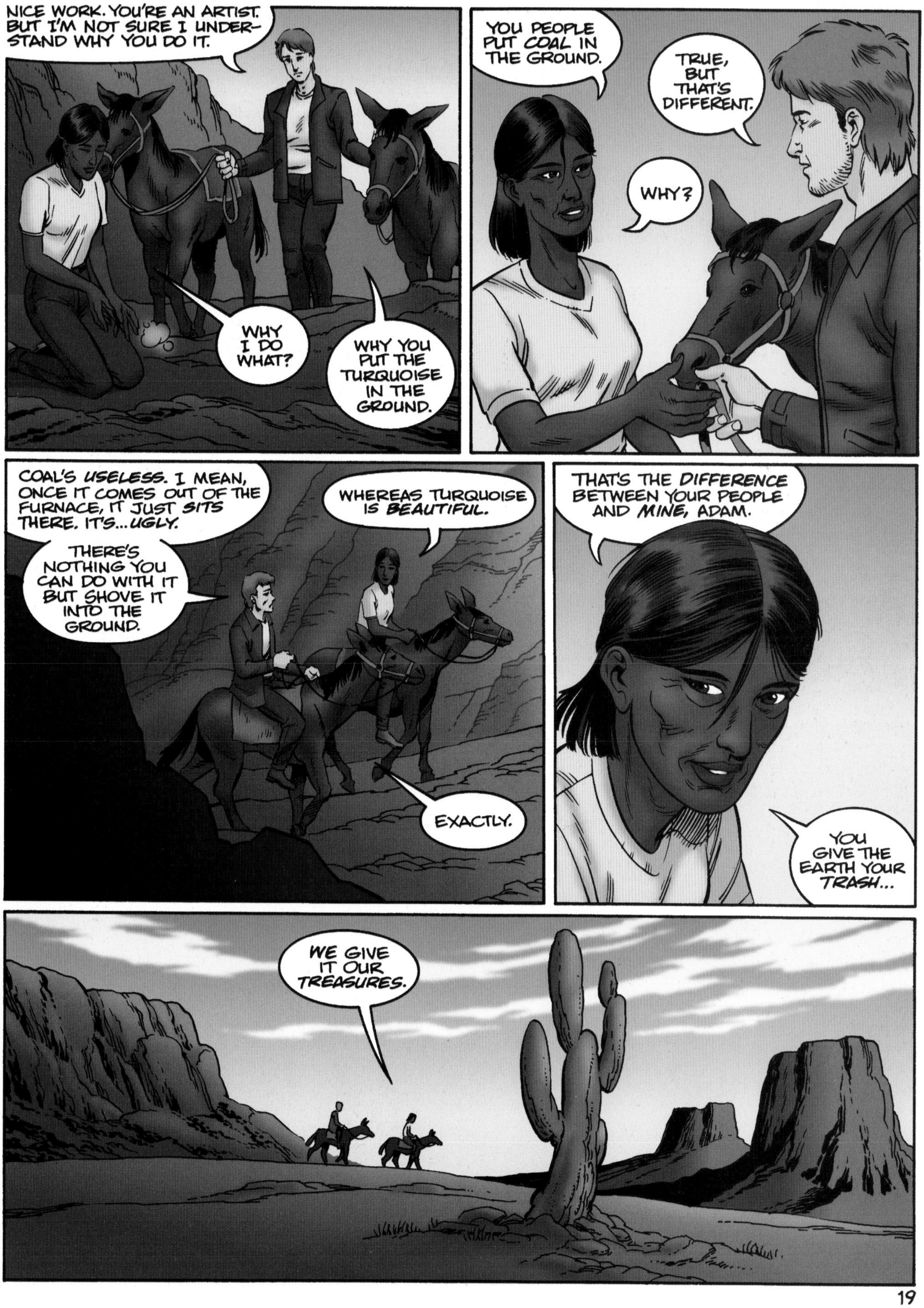
NICE WORK. YOU'RE AN ARTIST. BUT I'M NOT SURE I UNDERSTAND WHY YOU DO IT.
WHY I DO WHAT?
WHY YOU PUT THE TURQUOISE IN THE GROUND.
YOU PEOPLE PUT COAL IN THE GROUND.
TRUE, BUT THAT'S DIFFERENT.
WHY?
COAL'S USELESS. I MEAN, ONCE IT COMES OUT OF THE FURNACE, IT JUST SITS THERE. IT'S...UGLY.
THERE'S NOTHING YOU CAN DO WITH IT BUT SHOVE IT INTO THE GROUND.
WHEREAS TURQUOISE IS BEAUTIFUL.
EXACTLY.
THAT'S THE DIFFERENCE BETWEEN YOUR PEOPLE AND MINE, ADAM.
YOU GIVE THE EARTH YOUR TRASH...
WE GIVE IT OUR TREASURES.

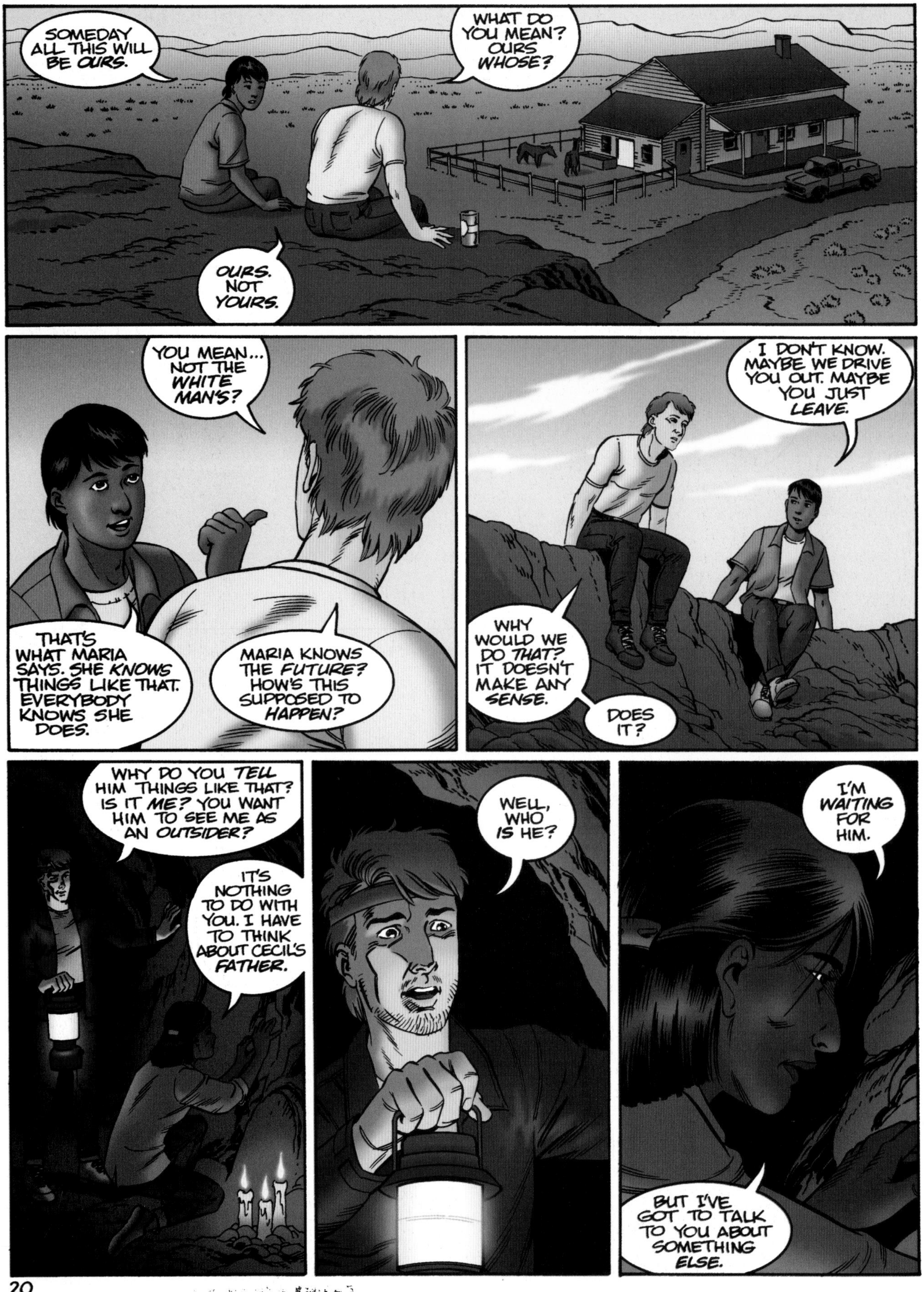
SOMEDAY ALL THIS WILL BE *OURS*.
WHAT DO YOU MEAN? OURS *WHOSE?*
OURS. NOT *YOURS.*
YOU MEAN... NOT THE *WHITE MAN'S?*
THAT'S WHAT MARIA SAYS. SHE *KNOWS* THINGS LIKE THAT. EVERYBODY KNOWS SHE DOES.
MARIA KNOWS THE *FUTURE?* HOW'S THIS SUPPOSED TO *HAPPEN?*
I DON'T KNOW. MAYBE WE DRIVE YOU OUT. MAYBE YOU JUST *LEAVE.*
WHY WOULD WE DO *THAT?* IT DOESN'T MAKE ANY SENSE.
DOES IT?
WHY DO YOU *TELL* HIM THINGS LIKE THAT? IS IT *ME?* YOU WANT HIM TO SEE ME AS AN *OUTSIDER?*
IT'S NOTHING TO DO WITH YOU. I HAVE TO THINK ABOUT CECIL'S *FATHER.*
WELL, WHO *IS* HE?
I'M *WAITING* FOR HIM.
BUT I'VE GOT TO TALK TO YOU ABOUT SOMETHING *ELSE.*

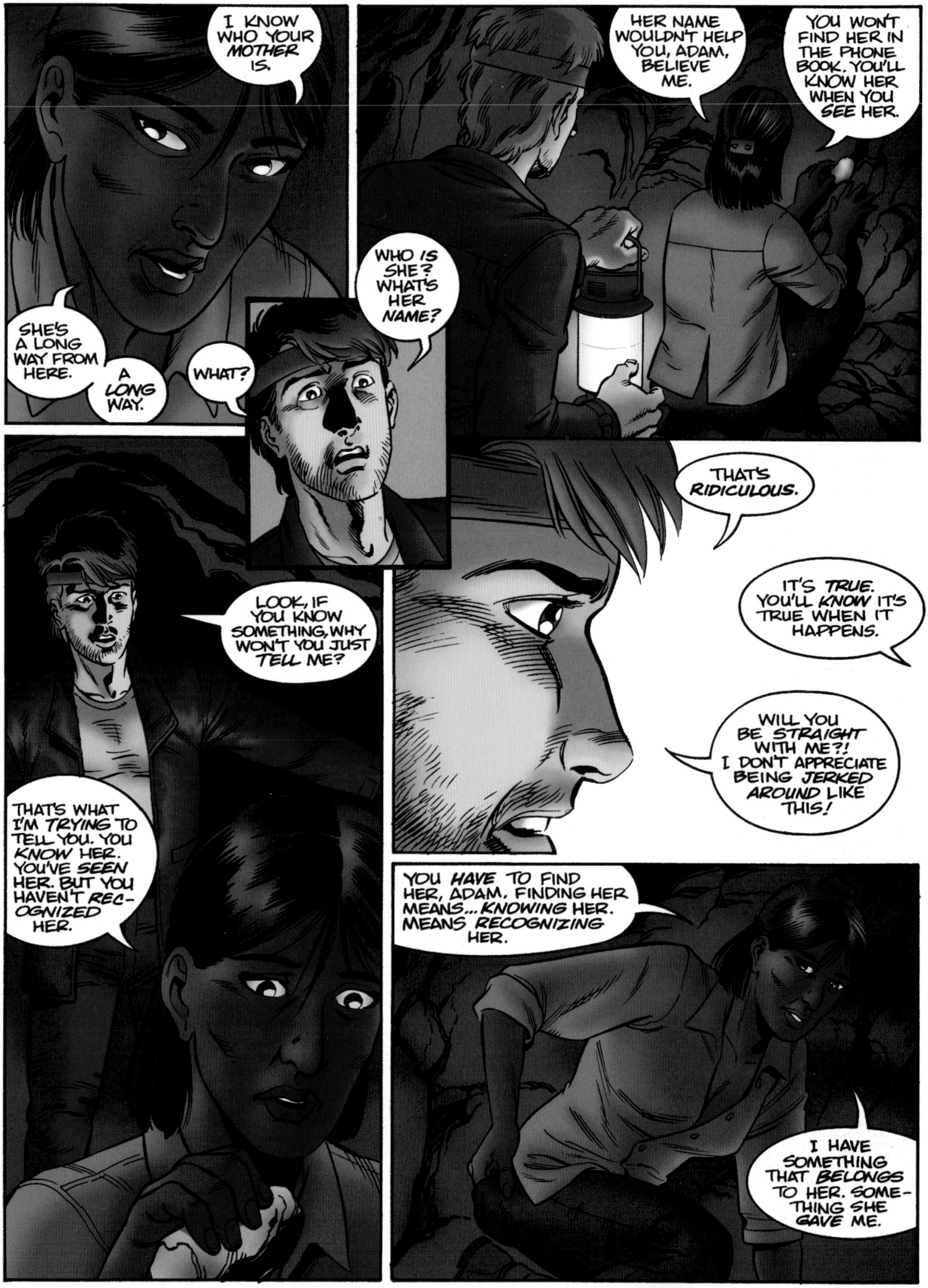
I KNOW WHO YOUR MOTHER IS.
HER NAME WOULDN'T HELP YOU, ADAM, BELIEVE ME.
YOU WON'T FIND HER IN THE PHONE BOOK. YOU'LL KNOW HER WHEN YOU SEE HER.
WHO IS SHE? WHAT'S HER NAME?
SHE'S A LONG WAY FROM HERE.
A LONG WAY.
WHAT?
THAT'S RIDICULOUS.
IT'S TRUE. YOU'LL KNOW IT'S TRUE WHEN IT HAPPENS.
LOOK, IF YOU KNOW SOMETHING, WHY WON'T YOU JUST TELL ME?
WILL YOU BE STRAIGHT WITH ME?! I DON'T APPRECIATE BEING JERKED AROUND LIKE THIS!
THAT'S WHAT I'M TRYING TO TELL YOU. YOU KNOW HER. YOU'VE SEEN HER. BUT YOU HAVEN'T RECOGNIZED HER.
YOU HAVE TO FIND HER, ADAM. FINDING HER MEANS... KNOWING HER. MEANS RECOGNIZING HER.
I HAVE SOMETHING THAT BELONGS TO HER. SOMETHING SHE GAVE ME.

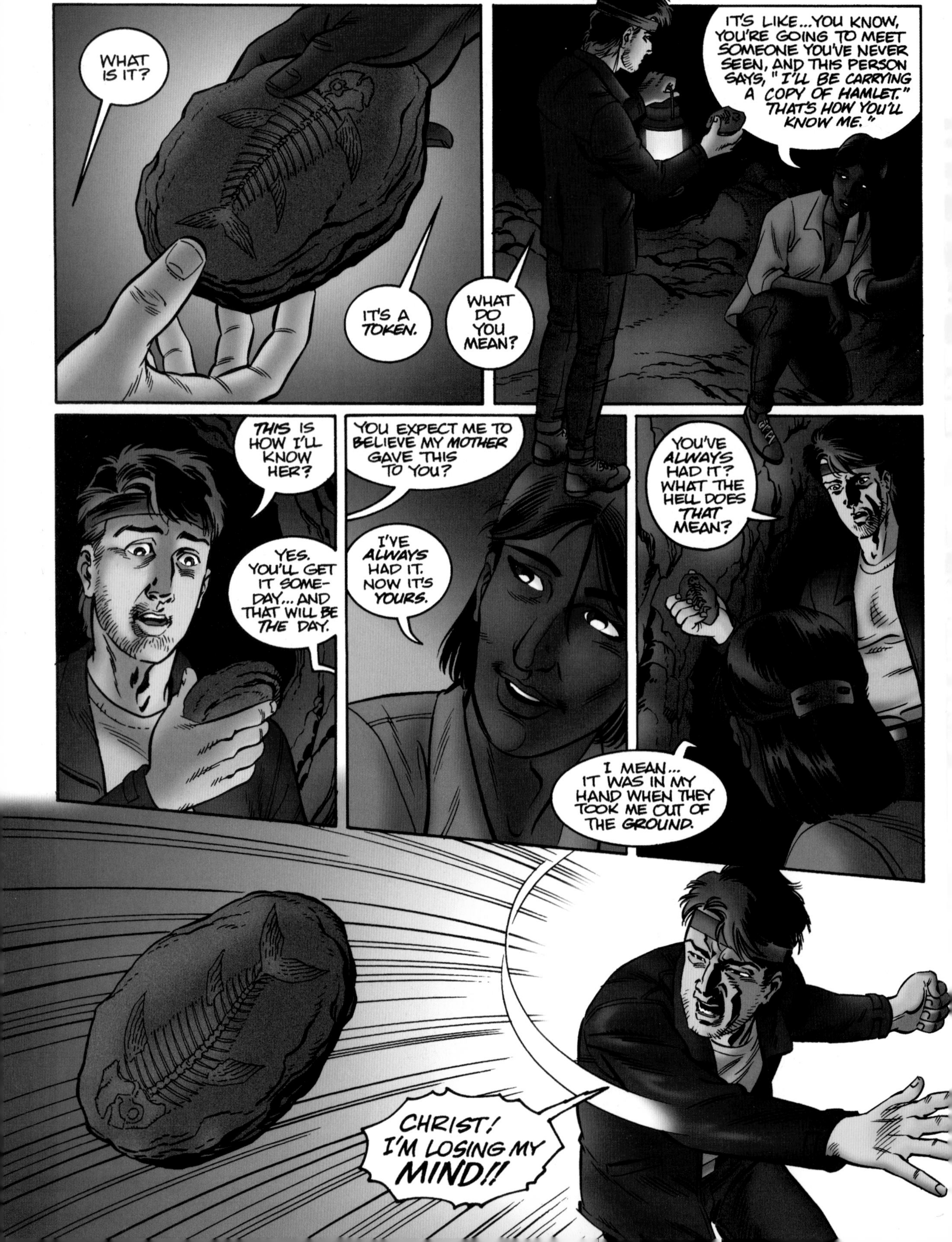
WHAT IS IT?
IT'S A *TOKEN.*
WHAT DO YOU MEAN?
IT'S LIKE...YOU KNOW, YOU'RE GOING TO MEET SOMEONE YOU'VE NEVER SEEN, AND THIS PERSON SAYS, "*I'LL BE CARRYING A COPY OF HAMLET.*" *THAT'S HOW YOU'LL KNOW ME.*"
THIS IS HOW I'LL KNOW HER?
YES. YOU'LL GET IT SOME-DAY... AND THAT WILL BE *THE* DAY.
YOU EXPECT ME TO BELIEVE MY *MOTHER* GAVE THIS TO YOU?
I'VE *ALWAYS* HAD IT. NOW IT'S *YOURS.*
YOU'VE *ALWAYS* HAD IT? WHAT THE HELL DOES *THAT* MEAN?
I MEAN... IT WAS IN MY HAND WHEN THEY TOOK ME OUT OF THE *GROUND.*
CHRIST! I'M LOSING MY *MIND!!*

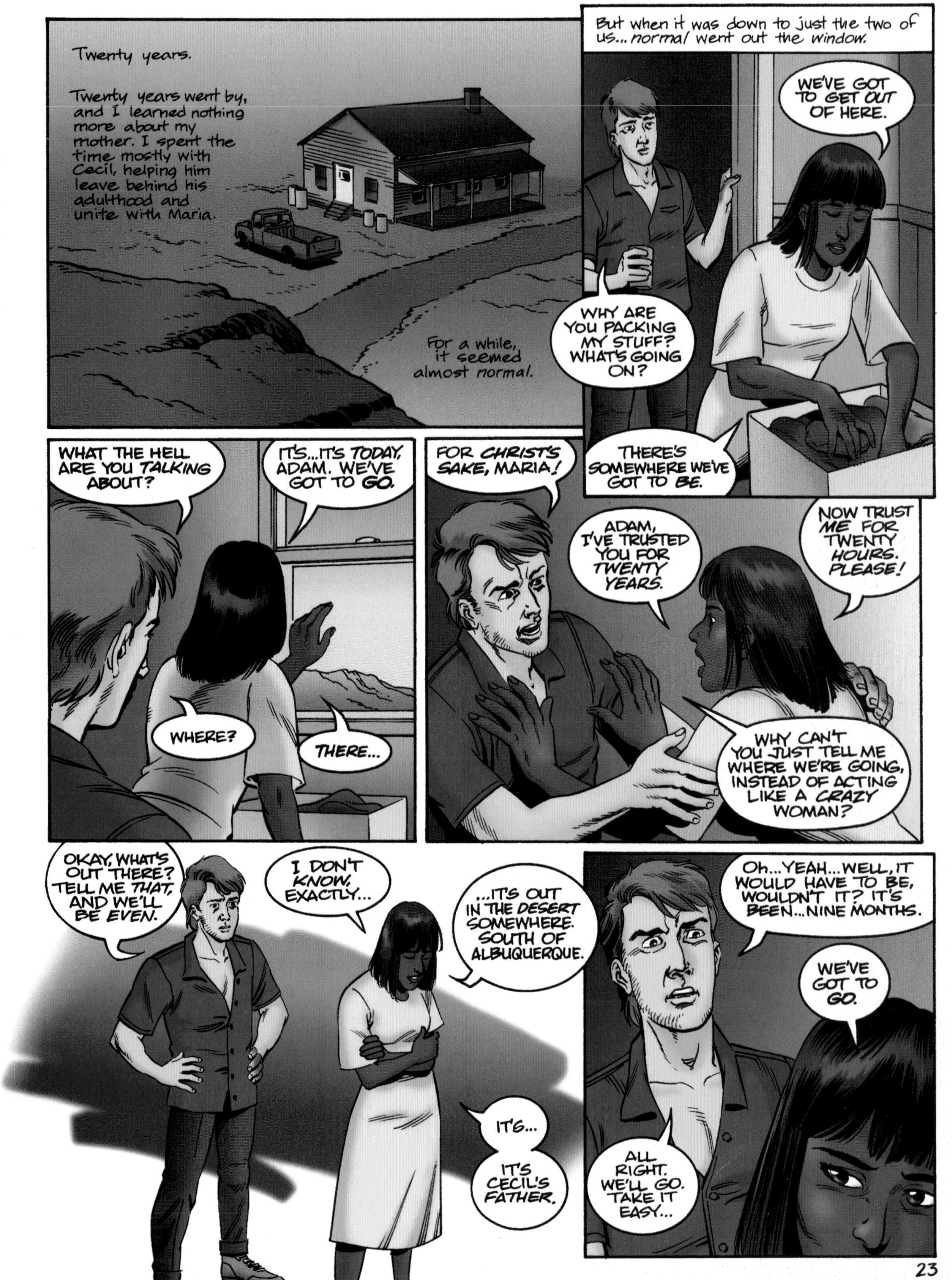

Twenty years.
Twenty years went by, and I learned nothing more about my mother. I spent the time mostly with Cecil, helping him leave behind his adulthood and unite with Maria.
For a while, it seemed almost normal.
But when it was down to just the two of us... normal went out the window.
WE'VE GOT TO GET OUT OF HERE.
WHY ARE YOU PACKING MY STUFF? WHAT'S GOING ON?
THERE'S SOMEWHERE WE'VE GOT TO BE.
WHAT THE HELL ARE YOU TALKING ABOUT?
IT'S...IT'S TODAY, ADAM. WE'VE GOT TO GO.
WHERE?
THERE...
FOR CHRIST'S SAKE, MARIA!
ADAM, I'VE TRUSTED YOU FOR TWENTY YEARS.
NOW TRUST ME FOR TWENTY HOURS. PLEASE!
WHY CAN'T YOU JUST TELL ME WHERE WE'RE GOING, INSTEAD OF ACTING LIKE A CRAZY WOMAN?
OKAY, WHAT'S OUT THERE? TELL ME THAT, AND WE'LL BE EVEN.
I DON'T KNOW, EXACTLY...
...IT'S OUT IN THE DESERT SOMEWHERE. SOUTH OF ALBUQUERQUE.
IT'S...
IT'S CECIL'S FATHER.
Oh...YEAH...WELL, IT WOULD HAVE TO BE, WOULDN'T IT? IT'S BEEN...NINE MONTHS.
WE'VE GOT TO GO.
ALL RIGHT. WE'LL GO. TAKE IT EASY...

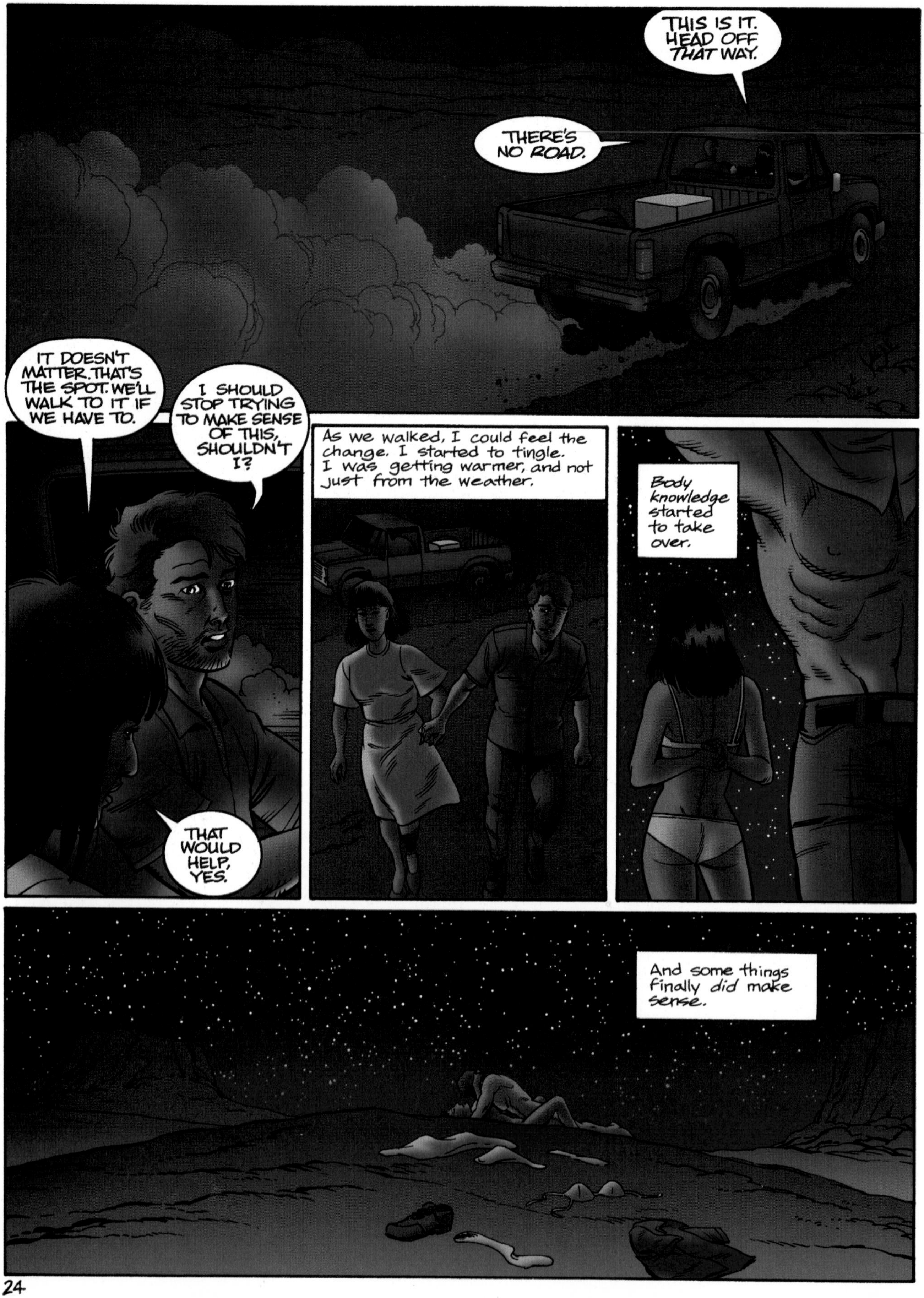
THIS IS IT. HEAD OFF THAT WAY.
THERE'S NO ROAD.
IT DOESN'T MATTER. THAT'S THE SPOT. WE'LL WALK TO IT IF WE HAVE TO.
I SHOULD STOP TRYING TO MAKE SENSE OF THIS, SHOULDN'T I?
THAT WOULD HELP, YES.
As we walked, I could feel the change. I started to tingle. I was getting warmer, and not just from the weather.
Body knowledge started to take over.
And some things finally did make sense.

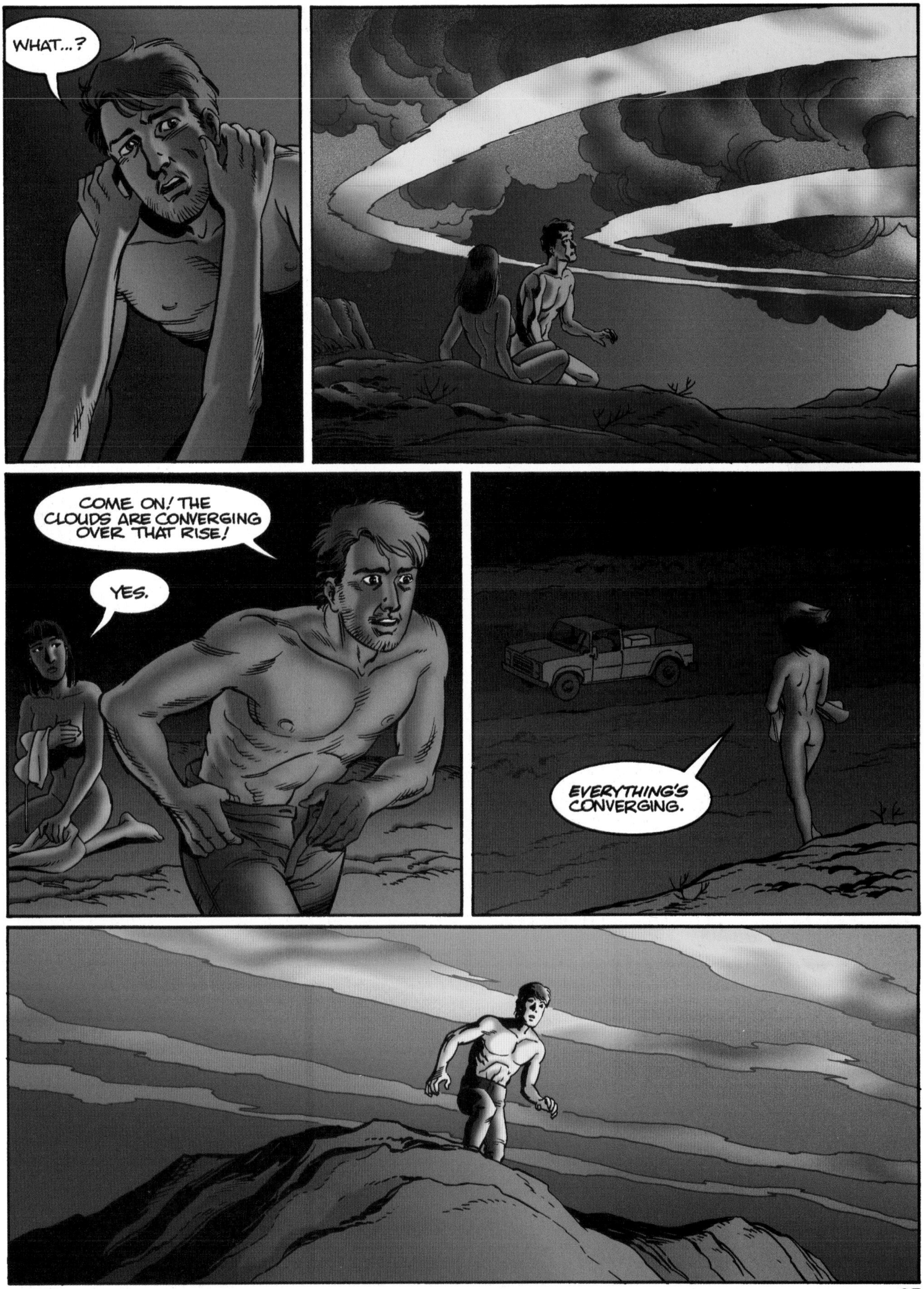
WHAT...?
COME ON! THE CLOUDS ARE CONVERGING OVER THAT RISE!
YES.
EVERYTHING'S CONVERGING.

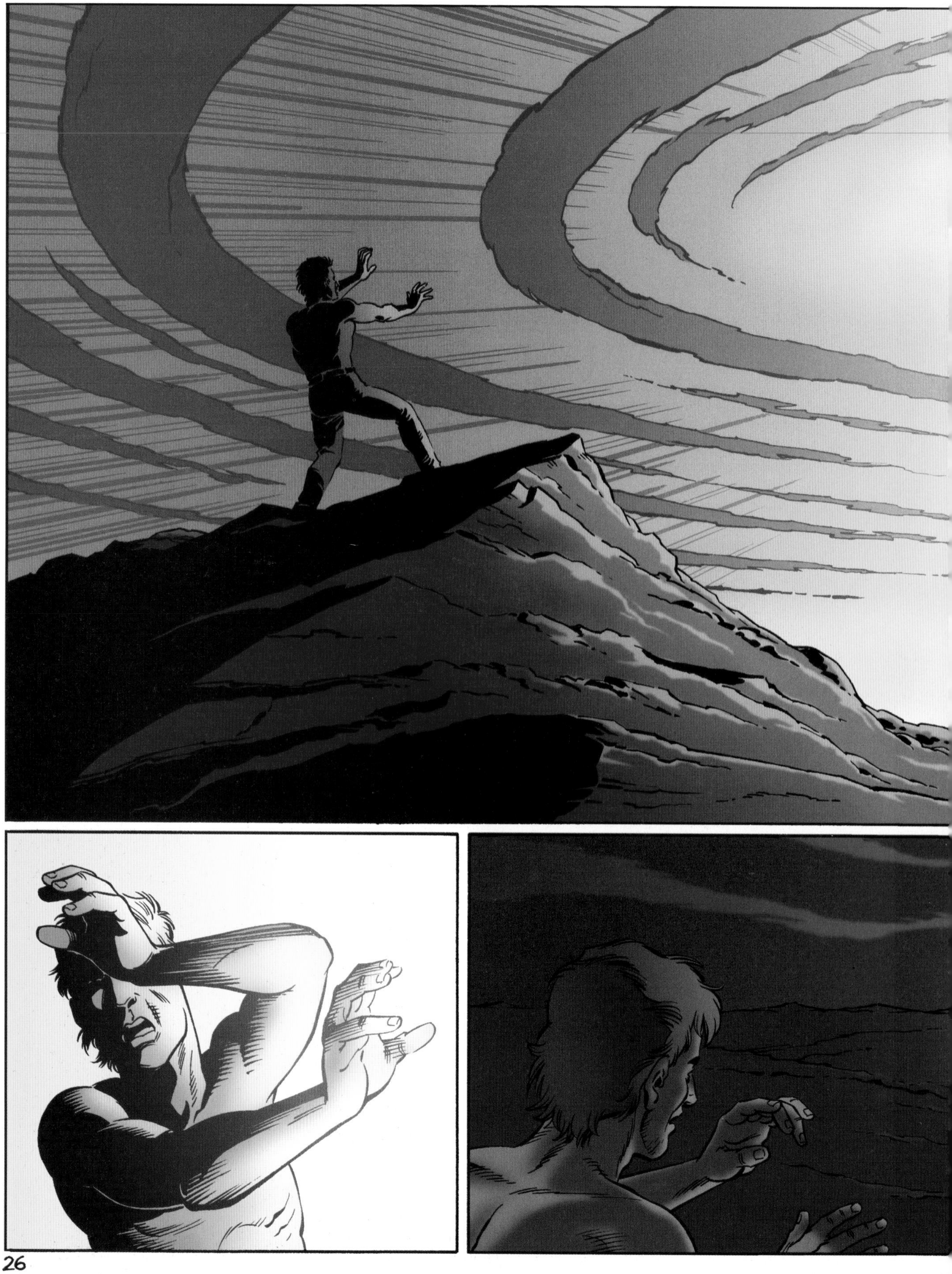

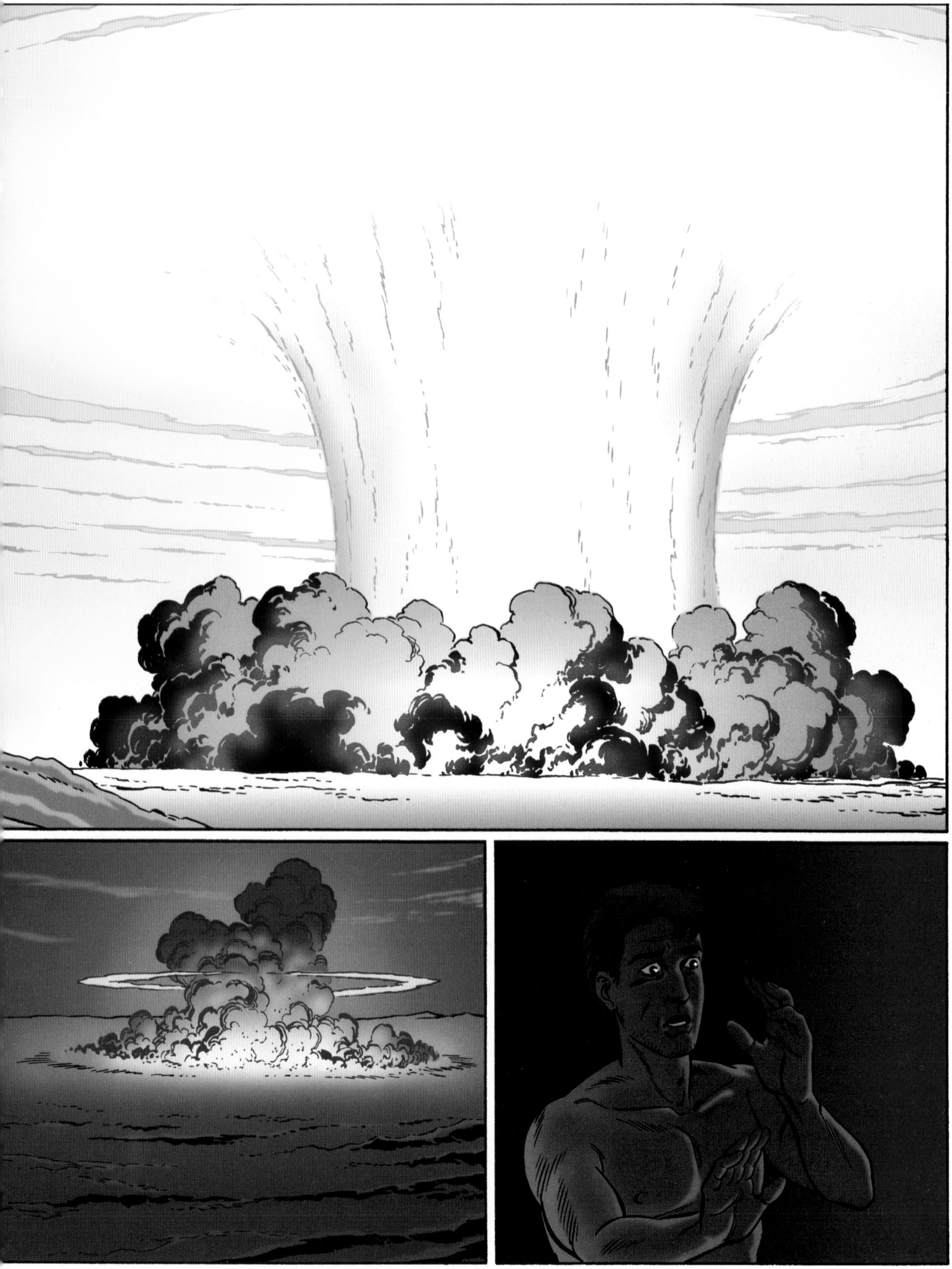

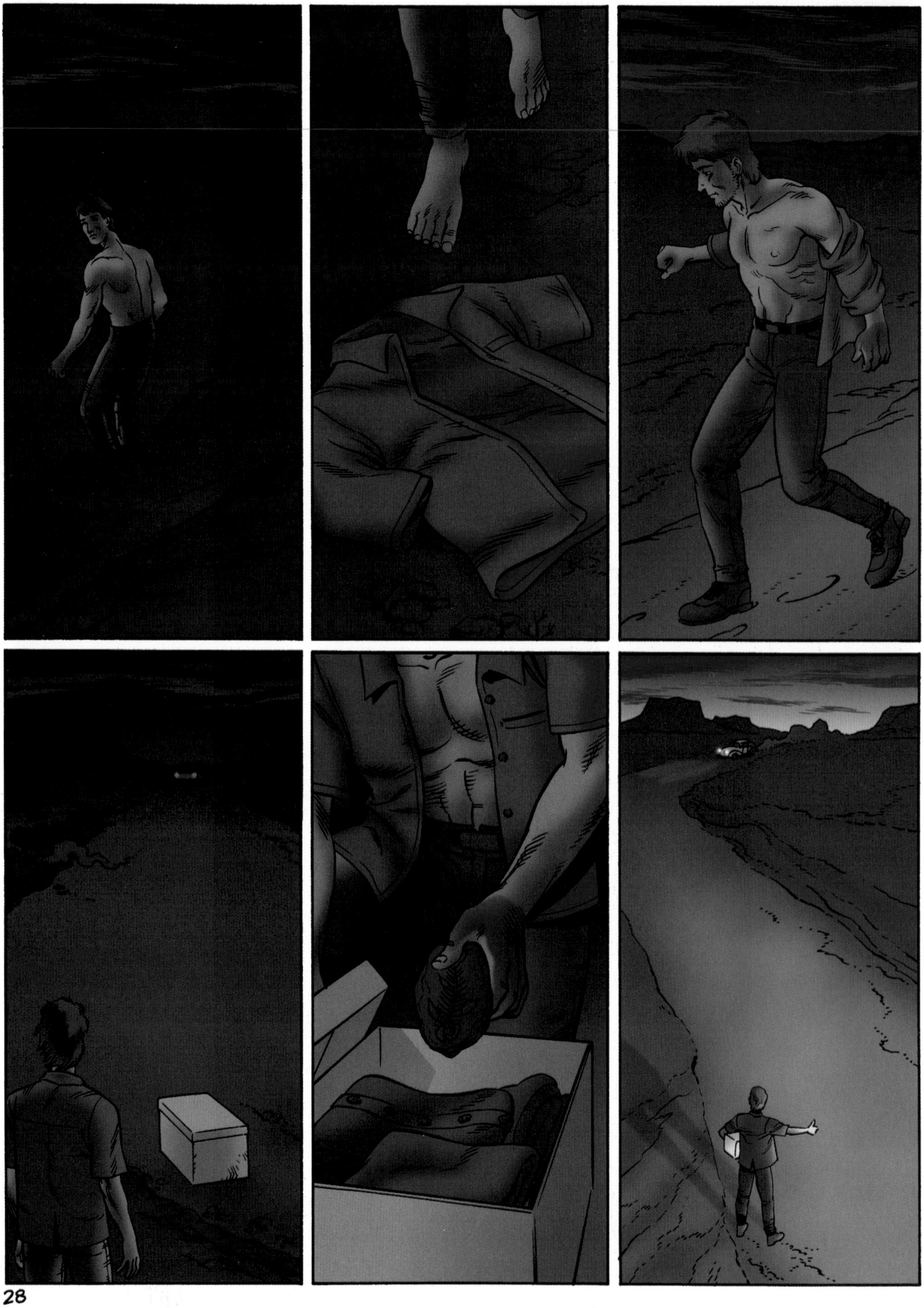

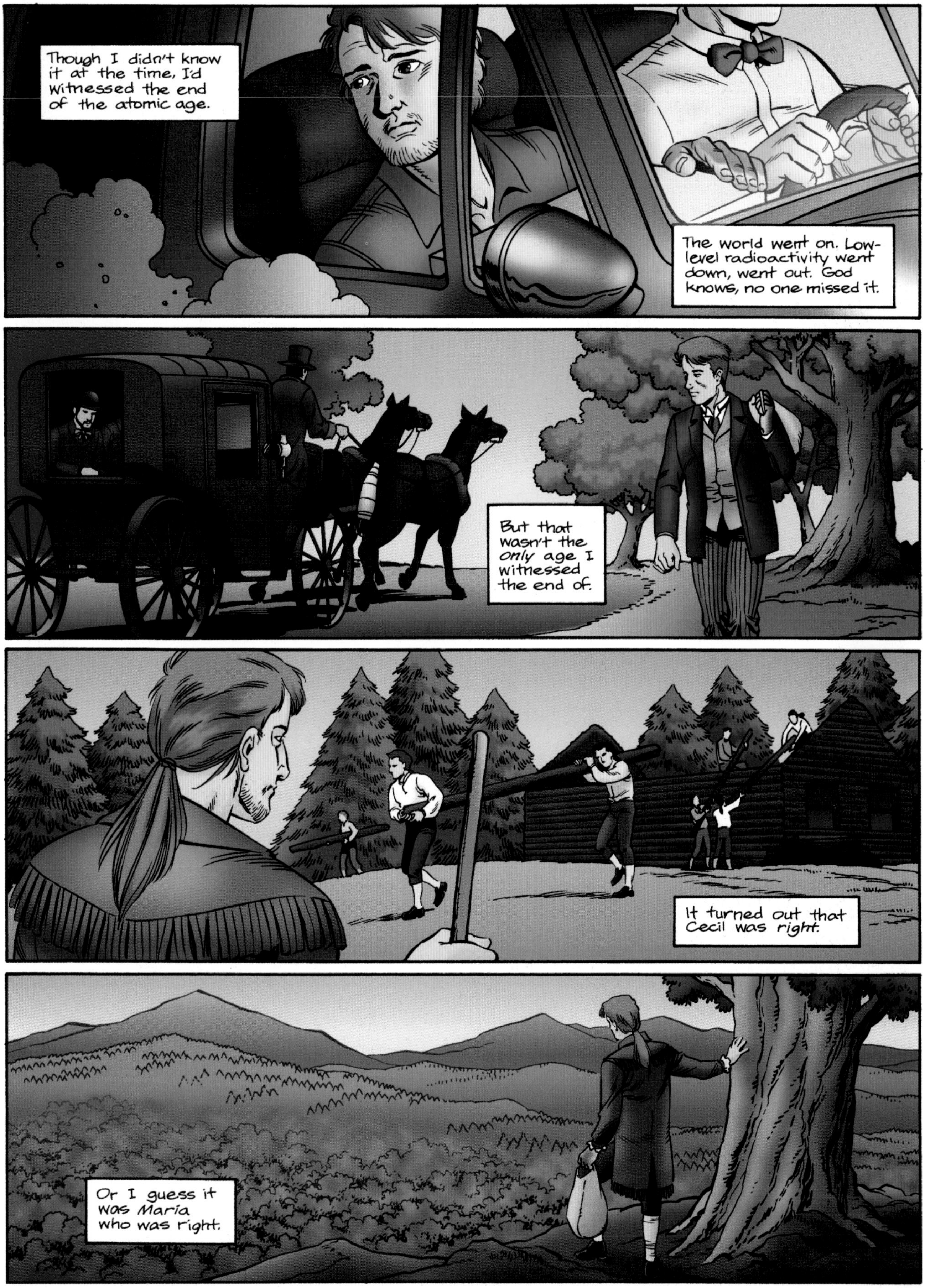
Though I didn't know it at the time, I'd witnessed the end of the atomic age.
The world went on. Low-level radioactivity went down, went out. God knows, no one missed it.
But that wasn't the *only* age I witnessed the end of.
It turned out that Cecil was *right*.
Or I guess it was *Maria* who was right.

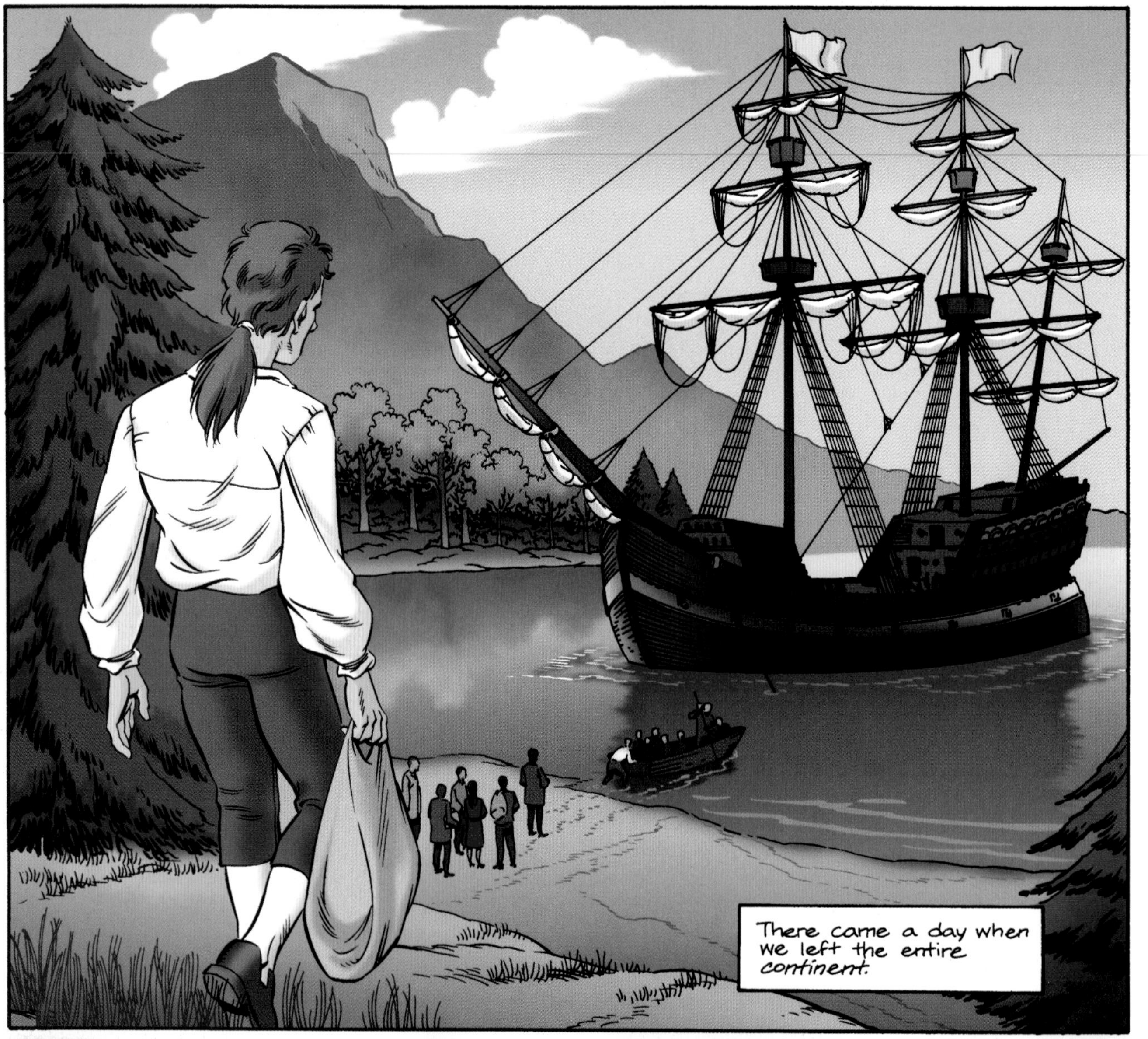
There came a day when we left the entire *continent.*

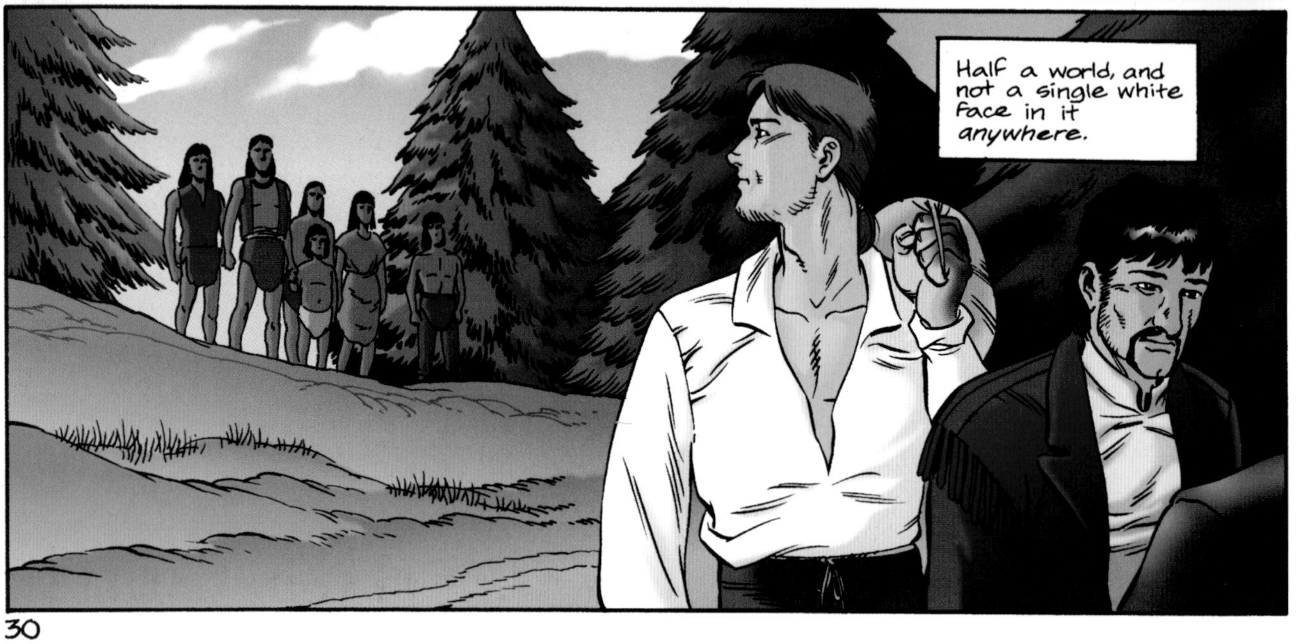
Half a world, and not a single white face in it *anywhere.*

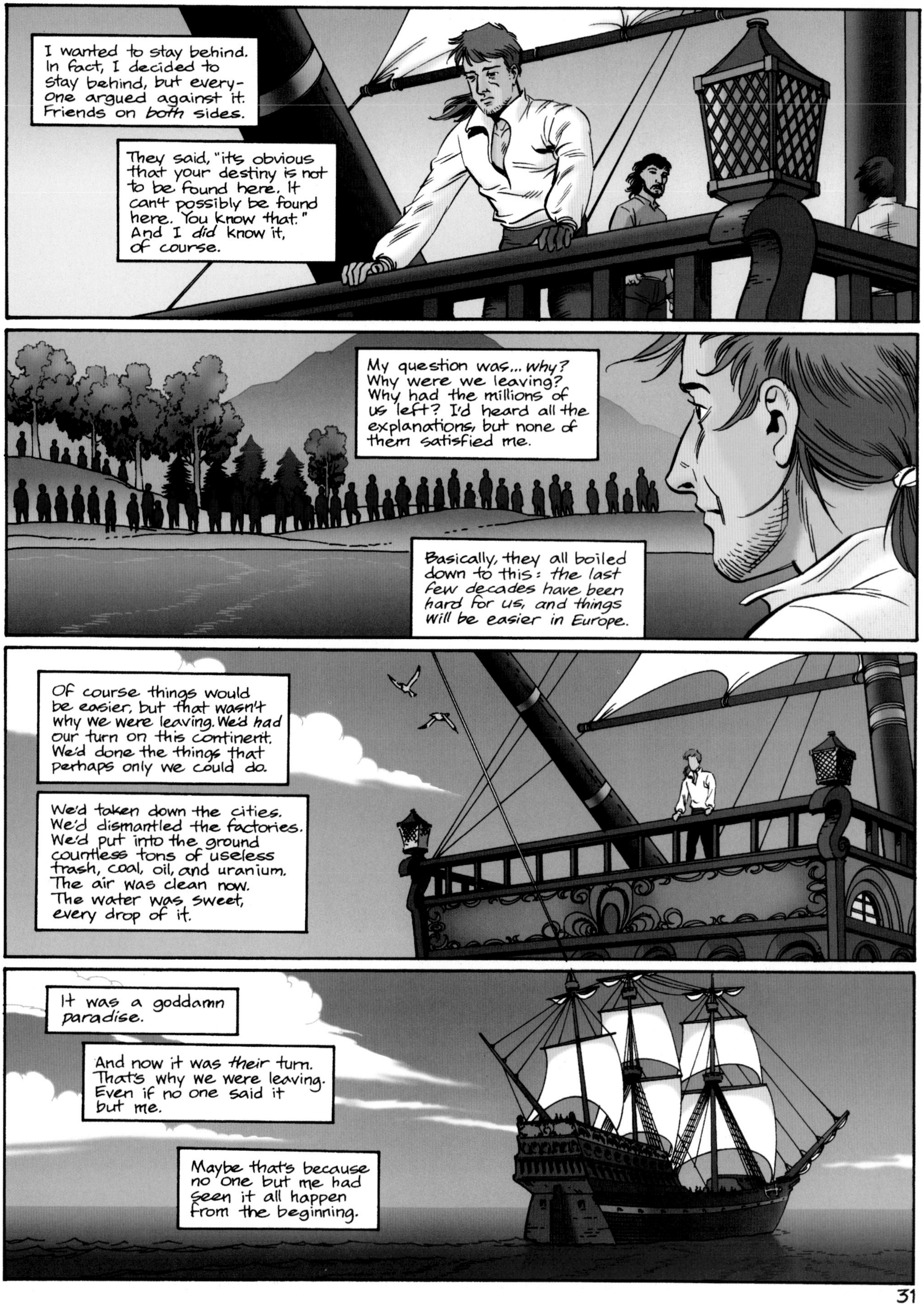
I wanted to stay behind. In fact, I decided to stay behind, but everyone argued against it. Friends on *both* sides.
They said, "it's obvious that your destiny is not to be found here. It can't possibly be found here. You know that." And I *did* know it, of course.
My question was... *why?* Why were we leaving? Why had the millions of us left? I'd heard all the explanations, but none of them satisfied me.
Basically, they all boiled down to this: *the last few decades have been hard for us, and things will be easier in Europe.*
Of course things would be easier, but that wasn't why we were leaving. We'd *had* our turn on this continent. We'd done the things that perhaps only we could do.
We'd taken down the cities. We'd dismantled the factories. We'd put into the ground countless tons of useless trash, coal, oil, and uranium. The air was clean now. The water was sweet, every drop of it.
It was a goddamn *paradise.*
And now it was *their* turn. That's why we were leaving. Even if no one said it but me.
Maybe that's because no one but me had seen it all happen from the beginning.

PART TWO

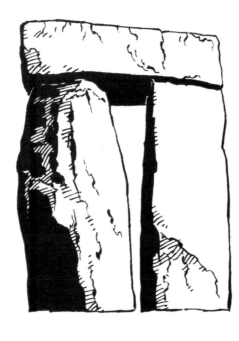

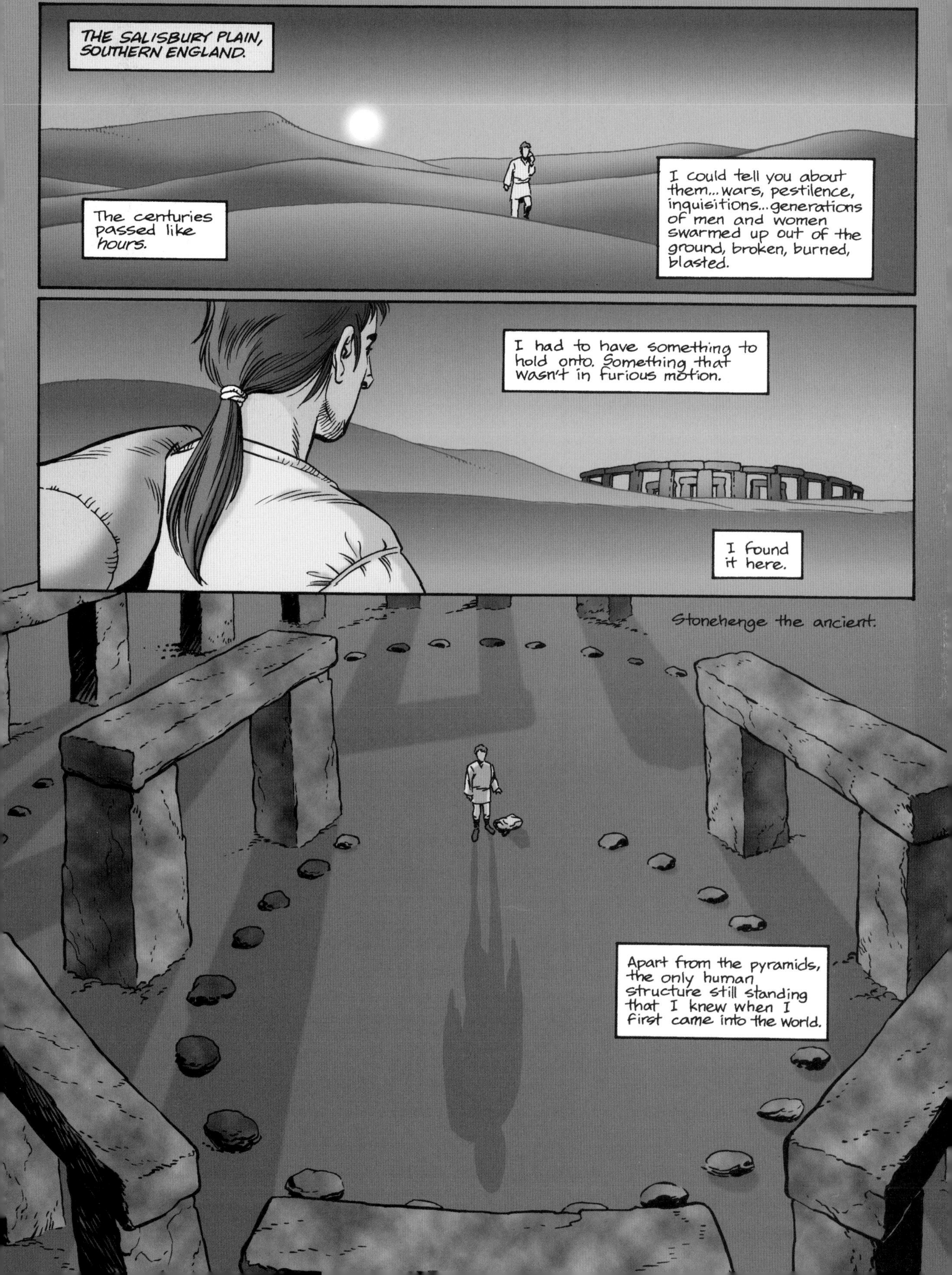
THE SALISBURY PLAIN, SOUTHERN ENGLAND.
The centuries passed like hours.
I could tell you about them...wars, pestilence, inquisitions...generations of men and women swarmed up out of the ground, broken, burned, blasted.
I had to have something to hold onto. Something that wasn't in furious motion.
I found it here.
Stonehenge the ancient.
Apart from the pyramids, the only human structure still standing that I knew when I first came into the world.

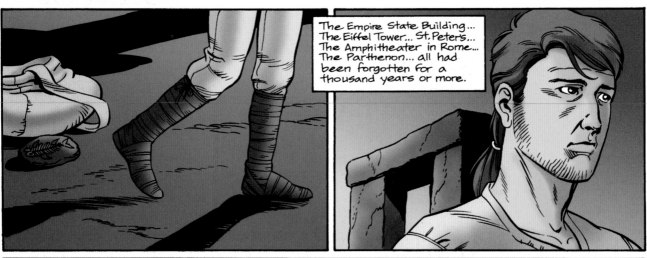

The Empire State Building... The Eiffel Tower... St. Peter's... The Amphitheater in Rome... The Parthenon... all had been forgotten for a thousand years or more.

But even Stonehenge wasn't something I could hold onto.

Even Stonehenge slipped away into the centuries.

WELL, NOW, ISN'T THIS CURIOUS?

I'VE KNOWN MANY A FISH... AND RATHER WELL, IF I DO SAY SO MYSELF...

...BUT NEVER A *STONE* FISH. WHERE ON EARTH DID YOU GET IT?

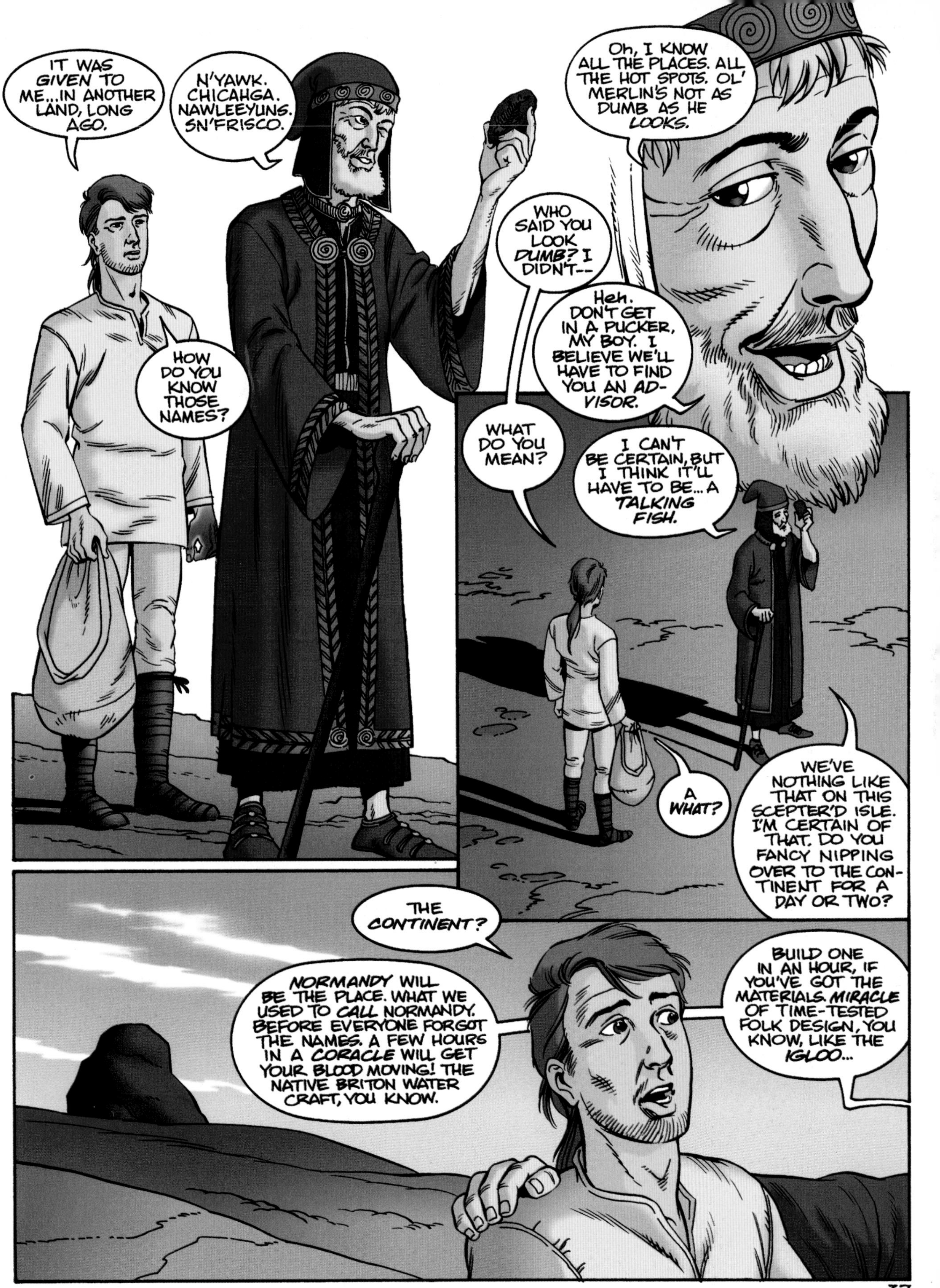

IT WAS GIVEN TO ME...IN ANOTHER LAND, LONG AGO.
N'YAWK. CHICAHGA. NAWLEEYUNS. SN'FRISCO.
HOW DO YOU KNOW THOSE NAMES?
Oh, I KNOW ALL THE PLACES. ALL THE HOT SPOTS. OL' MERLIN'S NOT AS DUMB AS HE LOOKS.
WHO SAID YOU LOOK DUMB? I DIDN'T--
Heh. DON'T GET IN A PUCKER, MY BOY. I BELIEVE WE'LL HAVE TO FIND YOU AN AD-VISOR.
WHAT DO YOU MEAN?
I CAN'T BE CERTAIN, BUT I THINK IT'LL HAVE TO BE... A TALKING FISH.
A WHAT?
WE'VE NOTHING LIKE THAT ON THIS SCEPTER'D ISLE. I'M CERTAIN OF THAT. DO YOU FANCY NIPPING OVER TO THE CON-TINENT FOR A DAY OR TWO?
THE CONTINENT?
NORMANDY WILL BE THE PLACE. WHAT WE USED TO CALL NORMANDY. BEFORE EVERYONE FORGOT THE NAMES. A FEW HOURS IN A CORACLE WILL GET YOUR BLOOD MOVING! THE NATIVE BRITON WATER CRAFT, YOU KNOW.
BUILD ONE IN AN HOUR, IF YOU'VE GOT THE MATERIALS. MIRACLE OF TIME-TESTED FOLK DESIGN, YOU KNOW, LIKE THE IGLOO...

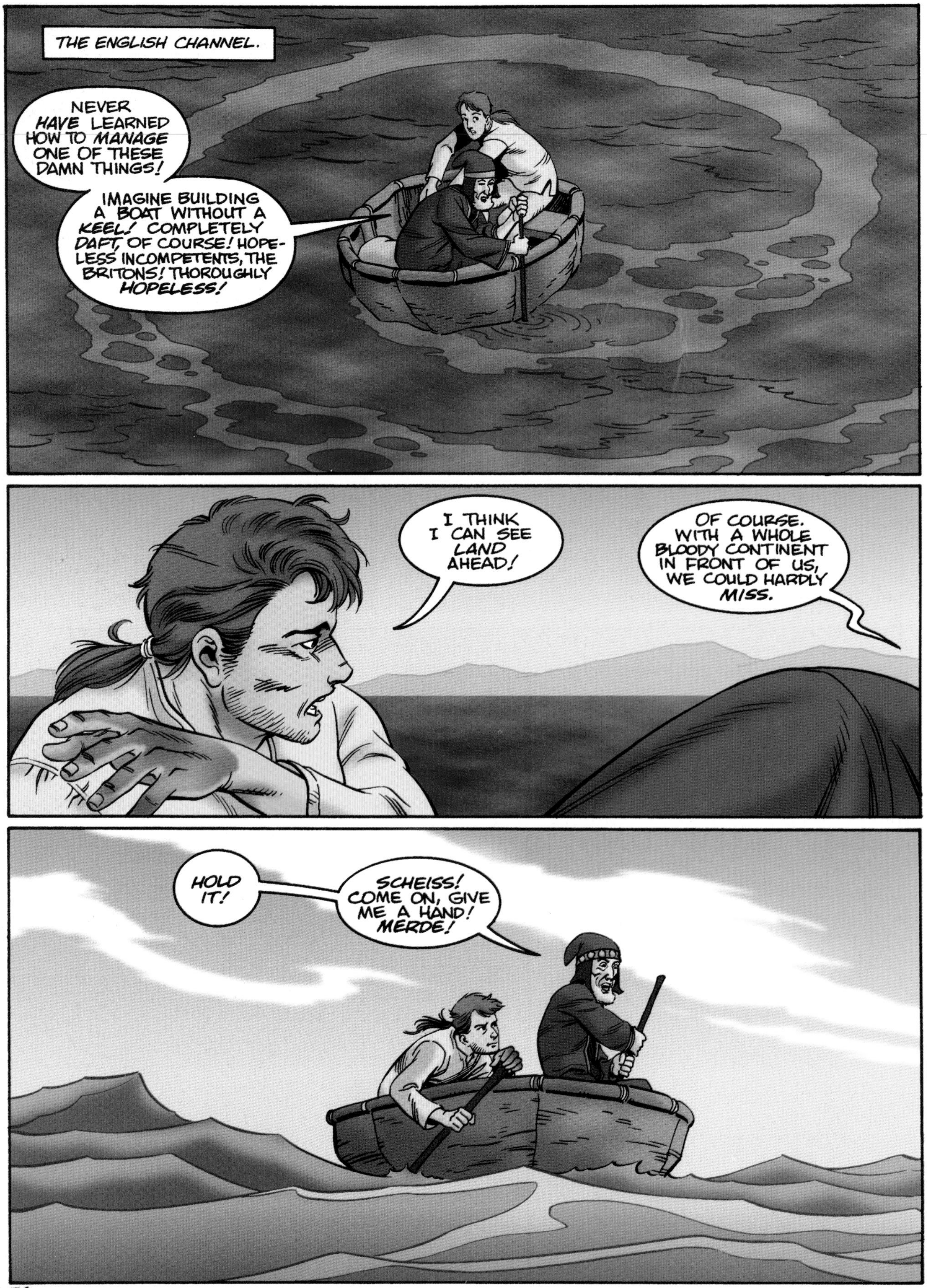
THE ENGLISH CHANNEL.
NEVER HAVE LEARNED HOW TO MANAGE ONE OF THESE DAMN THINGS!
IMAGINE BUILDING A BOAT WITHOUT A KEEL! COMPLETELY DAFT, OF COURSE! HOPE-LESS INCOMPETENTS, THE BRITONS! THOROUGHLY HOPELESS!
I THINK I CAN SEE LAND AHEAD!
OF COURSE. WITH A WHOLE BLOODY CONTINENT IN FRONT OF US, WE COULD HARDLY MISS.
HOLD IT!
SCHEISS! COME ON, GIVE ME A HAND! MERDE!

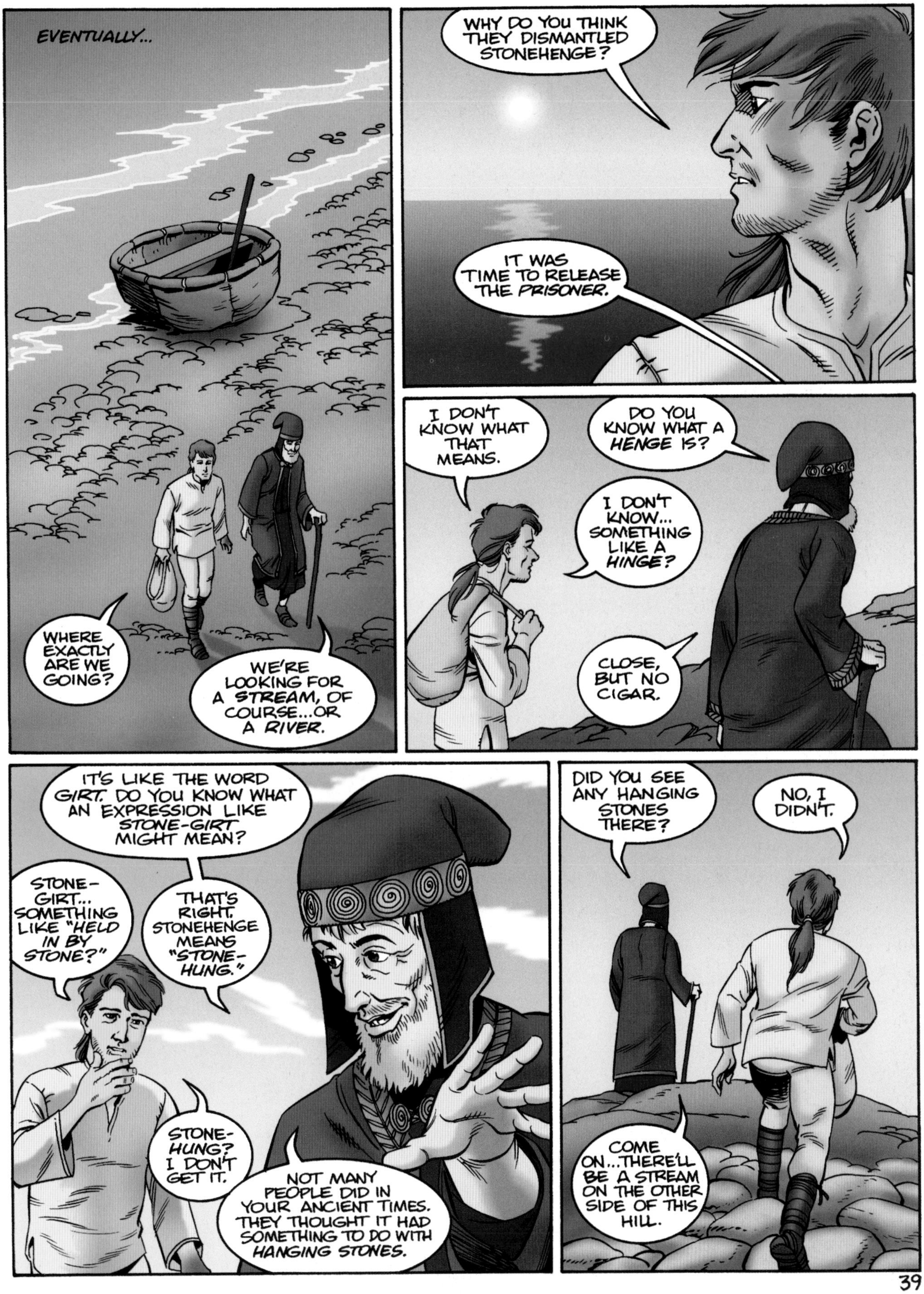
EVENTUALLY...
WHERE EXACTLY ARE WE GOING?
WE'RE LOOKING FOR A STREAM, OF COURSE...OR A RIVER.
WHY DO YOU THINK THEY DISMANTLED STONEHENGE?
IT WAS TIME TO RELEASE THE PRISONER.
I DON'T KNOW WHAT THAT MEANS.
DO YOU KNOW WHAT A HENGE IS?
I DON'T KNOW... SOMETHING LIKE A HINGE?
CLOSE, BUT NO CIGAR.
IT'S LIKE THE WORD GIRT. DO YOU KNOW WHAT AN EXPRESSION LIKE STONE-GIRT MIGHT MEAN?
STONE-GIRT... SOMETHING LIKE "HELD IN BY STONE?"
THAT'S RIGHT. STONEHENGE MEANS "STONE-HUNG."
STONE-HUNG? I DON'T GET IT.
NOT MANY PEOPLE DID IN YOUR ANCIENT TIMES. THEY THOUGHT IT HAD SOMETHING TO DO WITH HANGING STONES.
DID YOU SEE ANY HANGING STONES THERE?
NO, I DIDN'T.
COME ON...THERE'LL BE A STREAM ON THE OTHER SIDE OF THIS HILL.

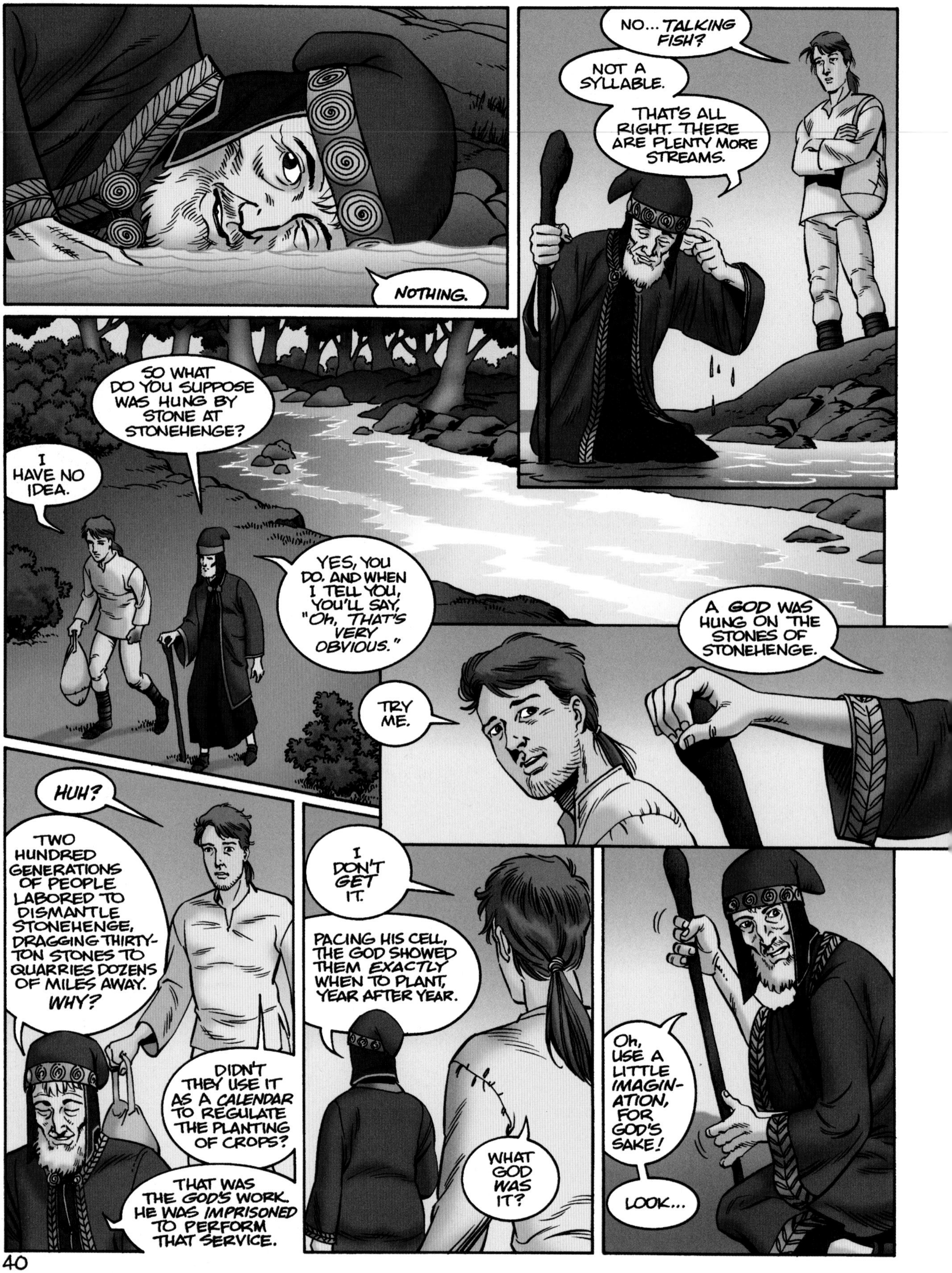
NOTHING.
NO... TALKING FISH?
NOT A SYLLABLE.
THAT'S ALL RIGHT. THERE ARE PLENTY MORE STREAMS.
SO WHAT DO YOU SUPPOSE WAS HUNG BY STONE AT STONEHENGE?
I HAVE NO IDEA.
YES, YOU DO. AND WHEN I TELL YOU, YOU'LL SAY, "Oh, THAT'S VERY OBVIOUS."
A GOD WAS HUNG ON THE STONES OF STONEHENGE.
TRY ME.
HUH?
TWO HUNDRED GENERATIONS OF PEOPLE LABORED TO DISMANTLE STONEHENGE, DRAGGING THIRTY-TON STONES TO QUARRIES DOZENS OF MILES AWAY. WHY?
DIDN'T THEY USE IT AS A CALENDAR TO REGULATE THE PLANTING OF CROPS?
THAT WAS THE GOD'S WORK. HE WAS IMPRISONED TO PERFORM THAT SERVICE.
I DON'T GET IT.
PACING HIS CELL, THE GOD SHOWED THEM EXACTLY WHEN TO PLANT, YEAR AFTER YEAR.
WHAT GOD WAS IT?
Oh, USE A LITTLE IMAGINATION, FOR GOD'S SAKE!
LOOK...

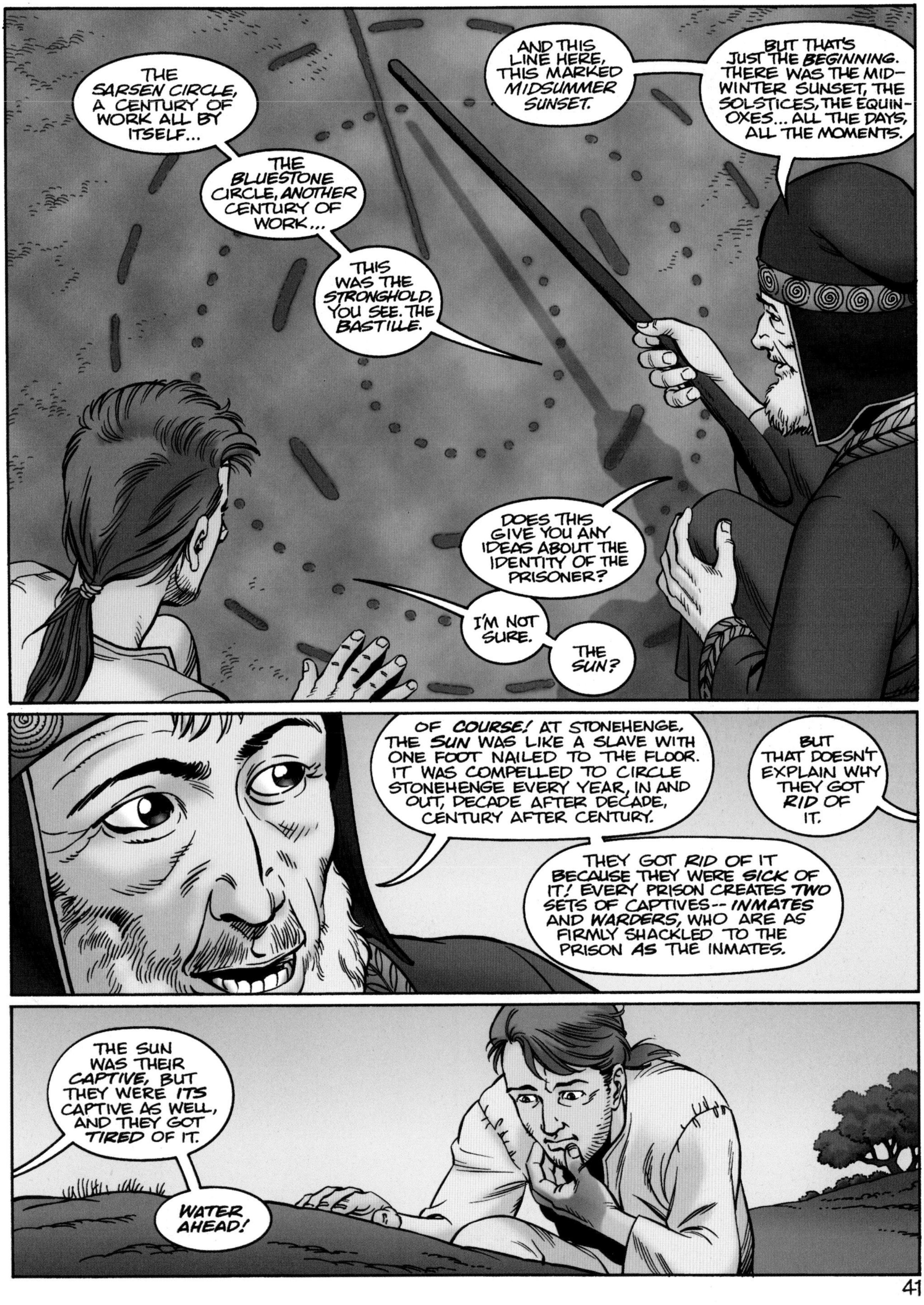
THE SARSEN CIRCLE, A CENTURY OF WORK ALL BY ITSELF...
THE BLUESTONE CIRCLE, ANOTHER CENTURY OF WORK...
THIS WAS THE STRONGHOLD, YOU SEE. THE BASTILLE.
AND THIS LINE HERE, THIS MARKED MIDSUMMER SUNSET.
BUT THAT'S JUST THE BEGINNING. THERE WAS THE MID-WINTER SUNSET, THE SOLSTICES, THE EQUIN-OXES... ALL THE DAYS, ALL THE MOMENTS.
DOES THIS GIVE YOU ANY IDEAS ABOUT THE IDENTITY OF THE PRISONER?
I'M NOT SURE.
THE SUN?
OF COURSE! AT STONEHENGE, THE SUN WAS LIKE A SLAVE WITH ONE FOOT NAILED TO THE FLOOR. IT WAS COMPELLED TO CIRCLE STONEHENGE EVERY YEAR, IN AND OUT, DECADE AFTER DECADE, CENTURY AFTER CENTURY.
BUT THAT DOESN'T EXPLAIN WHY THEY GOT RID OF IT.
THEY GOT RID OF IT BECAUSE THEY WERE SICK OF IT! EVERY PRISON CREATES TWO SETS OF CAPTIVES-- INMATES AND WARDERS, WHO ARE AS FIRMLY SHACKLED TO THE PRISON AS THE INMATES.
THE SUN WAS THEIR CAPTIVE, BUT THEY WERE ITS CAPTIVE AS WELL, AND THEY GOT TIRED OF IT.
WATER AHEAD!

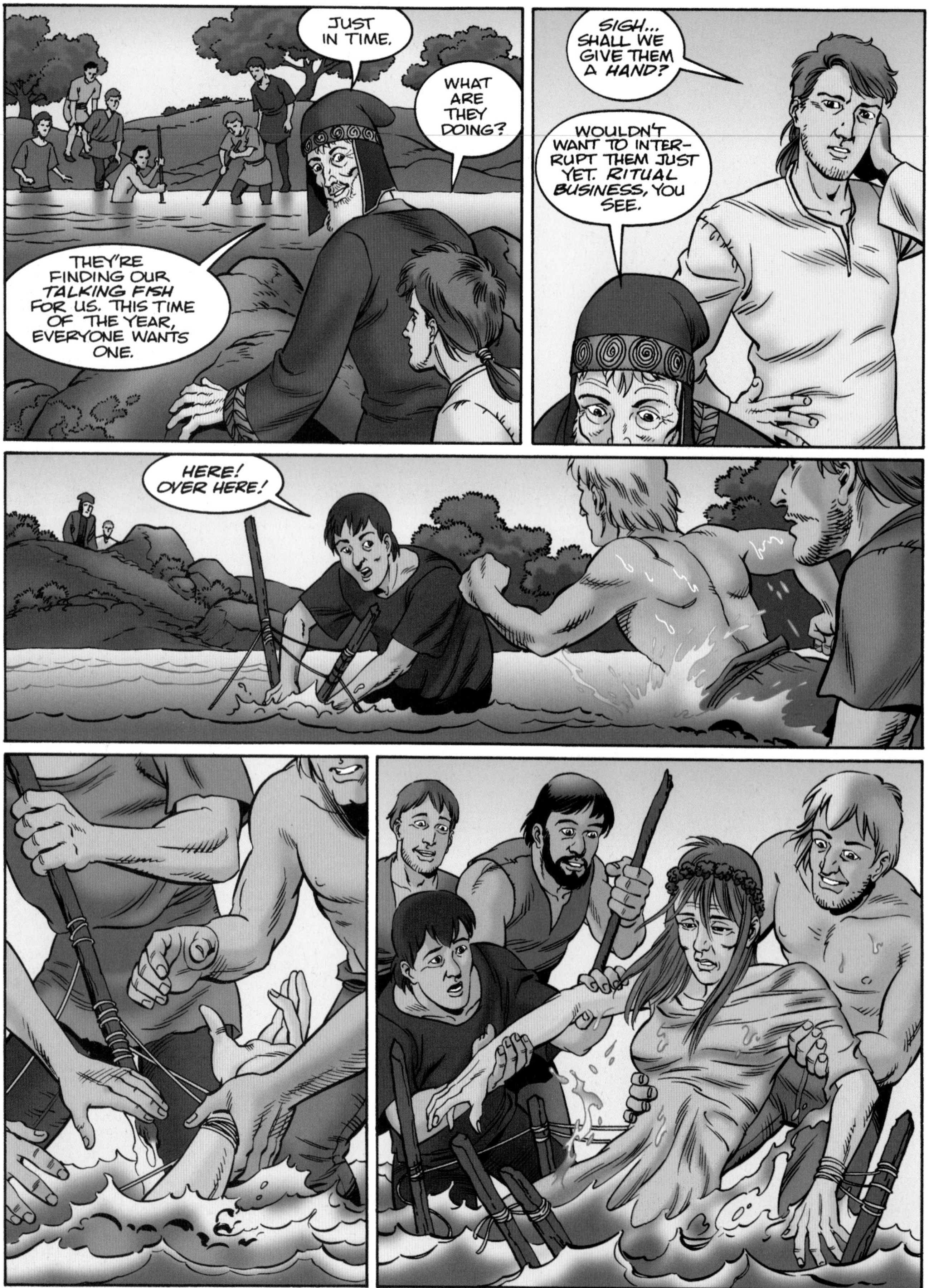

JUST IN TIME.
WHAT ARE THEY DOING?
THEY'RE FINDING OUR TALKING FISH FOR US. THIS TIME OF THE YEAR, EVERYONE WANTS ONE.
SIGH... SHALL WE GIVE THEM A HAND?
WOULDN'T WANT TO INTER-RUPT THEM JUST YET. RITUAL BUSINESS, YOU SEE.
HERE! OVER HERE!

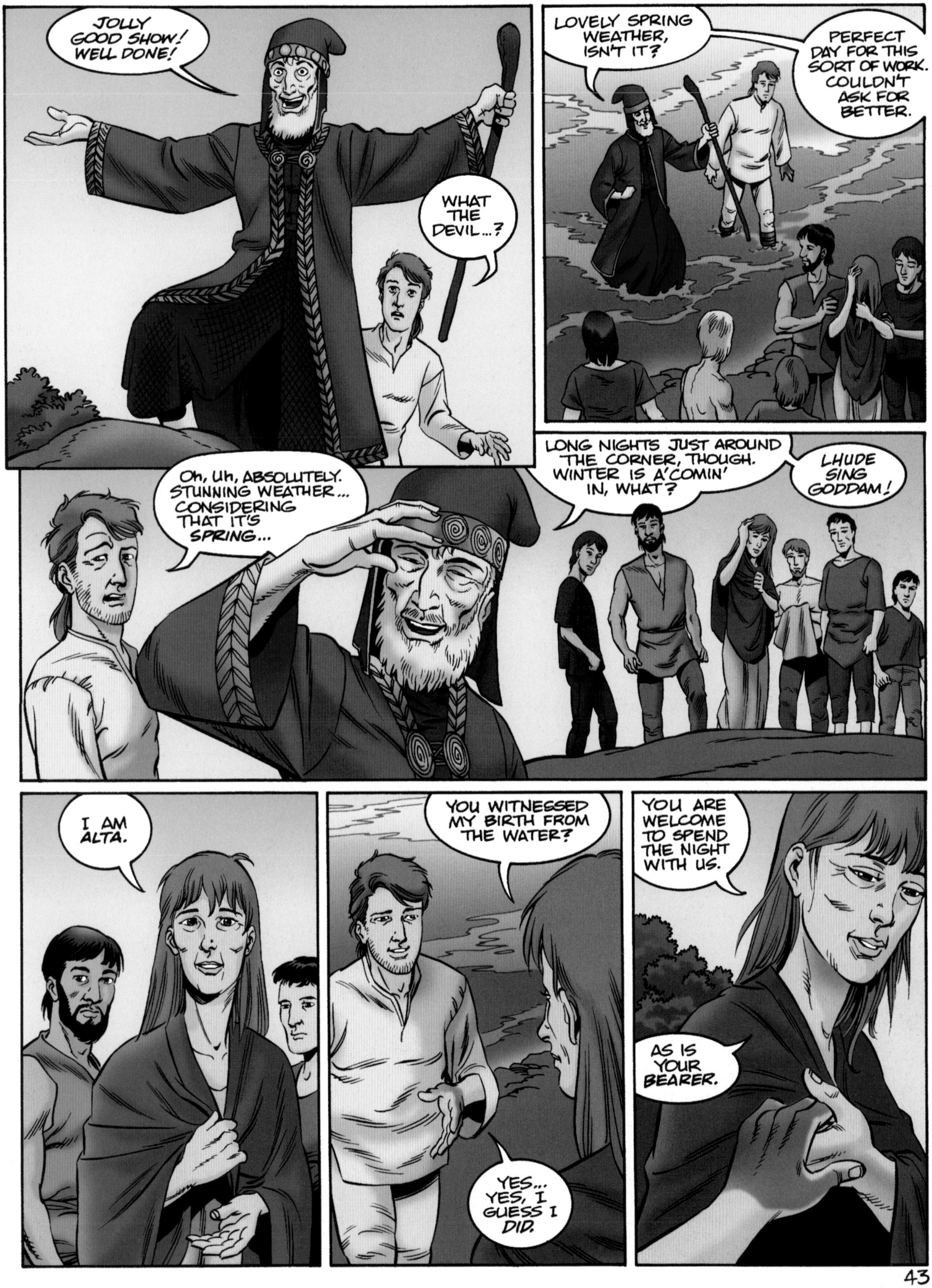
JOLLY GOOD SHOW! WELL DONE!
WHAT THE DEVIL...?
LOVELY SPRING WEATHER, ISN'T IT?
PERFECT DAY FOR THIS SORT OF WORK. COULDN'T ASK FOR BETTER.
Oh, Uh, ABSOLUTELY. STUNNING WEATHER... CONSIDERING THAT IT'S SPRING...
LONG NIGHTS JUST AROUND THE CORNER, THOUGH. WINTER IS A'COMIN' IN, WHAT?
LHUDE SING GODDAM!
I AM ALTA.
YOU WITNESSED MY BIRTH FROM THE WATER?
YES... YES, I GUESS I DID.
YOU ARE WELCOME TO SPEND THE NIGHT WITH US.
AS IS YOUR BEARER.

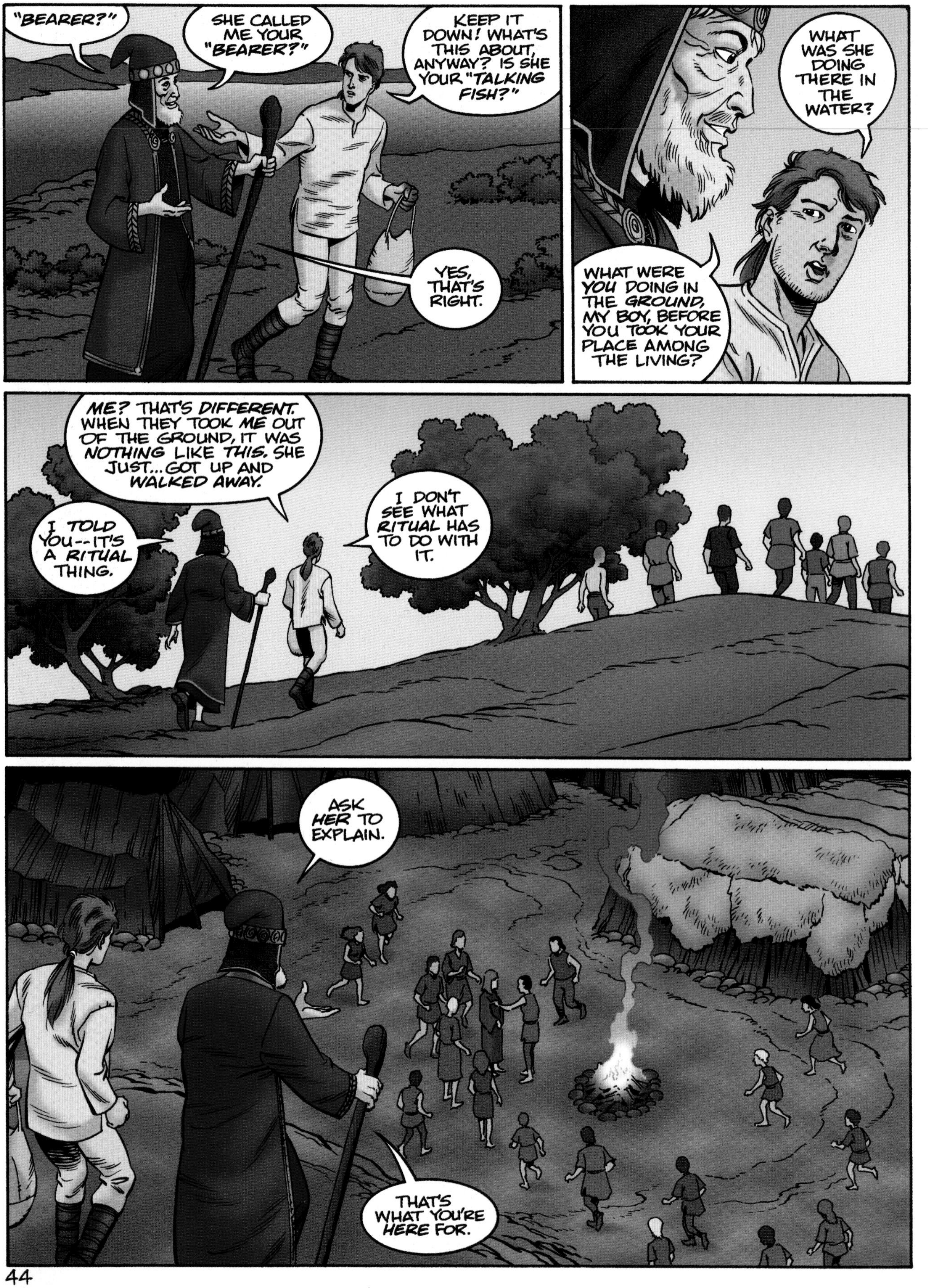
"BEARER?"
SHE CALLED ME YOUR "BEARER?"
KEEP IT DOWN! WHAT'S THIS ABOUT, ANYWAY? IS SHE YOUR "TALKING FISH?"
YES, THAT'S RIGHT.
WHAT WAS SHE DOING THERE IN THE WATER?
WHAT WERE YOU DOING IN THE GROUND, MY BOY, BEFORE YOU TOOK YOUR PLACE AMONG THE LIVING?
ME? THAT'S DIFFERENT. WHEN THEY TOOK ME OUT OF THE GROUND, IT WAS NOTHING LIKE THIS. SHE JUST...GOT UP AND WALKED AWAY.
I TOLD YOU--IT'S A RITUAL THING.
I DON'T SEE WHAT RITUAL HAS TO DO WITH IT.
ASK HER TO EXPLAIN.
THAT'S WHAT YOU'RE HERE FOR.

A YEAR AGO ON THIS DAY, YOU WENT TO THE STREAM AND TOOK ANOTHER LIKE ME FROM THE WATER.

DO YOU REMEMBER?

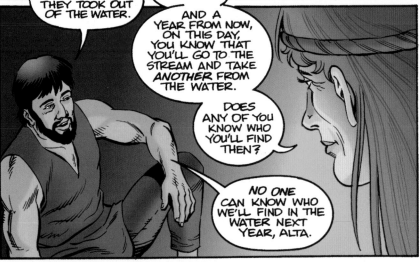

I REMEMBER. THAT WAS *ME* THEY TOOK OUT OF THE WATER.

INDEED, HASSOR.

AND A YEAR FROM NOW, ON THIS DAY, YOU KNOW THAT YOU'LL GO TO THE STREAM AND TAKE *ANOTHER* FROM THE WATER.

DOES ANY OF YOU KNOW WHO YOU'LL FIND THEN?

NO ONE CAN KNOW WHO WE'LL FIND IN THE WATER NEXT YEAR, ALTA.

THERE IS.

I SEE.

WELL, YOU DON'T *NEED* TO KNOW, BUT I'M GOING TO TELL YOU. I'M GOING TO MAKE IT CLEAR FOR ALL OF YOU SO THAT EVEN THE *YOUNG* REMEMBER. EVERY YEAR ON THIS DAY, ANOTHER COMES FROM THE WATER.

IS THERE A REASON WHY, ALTA?

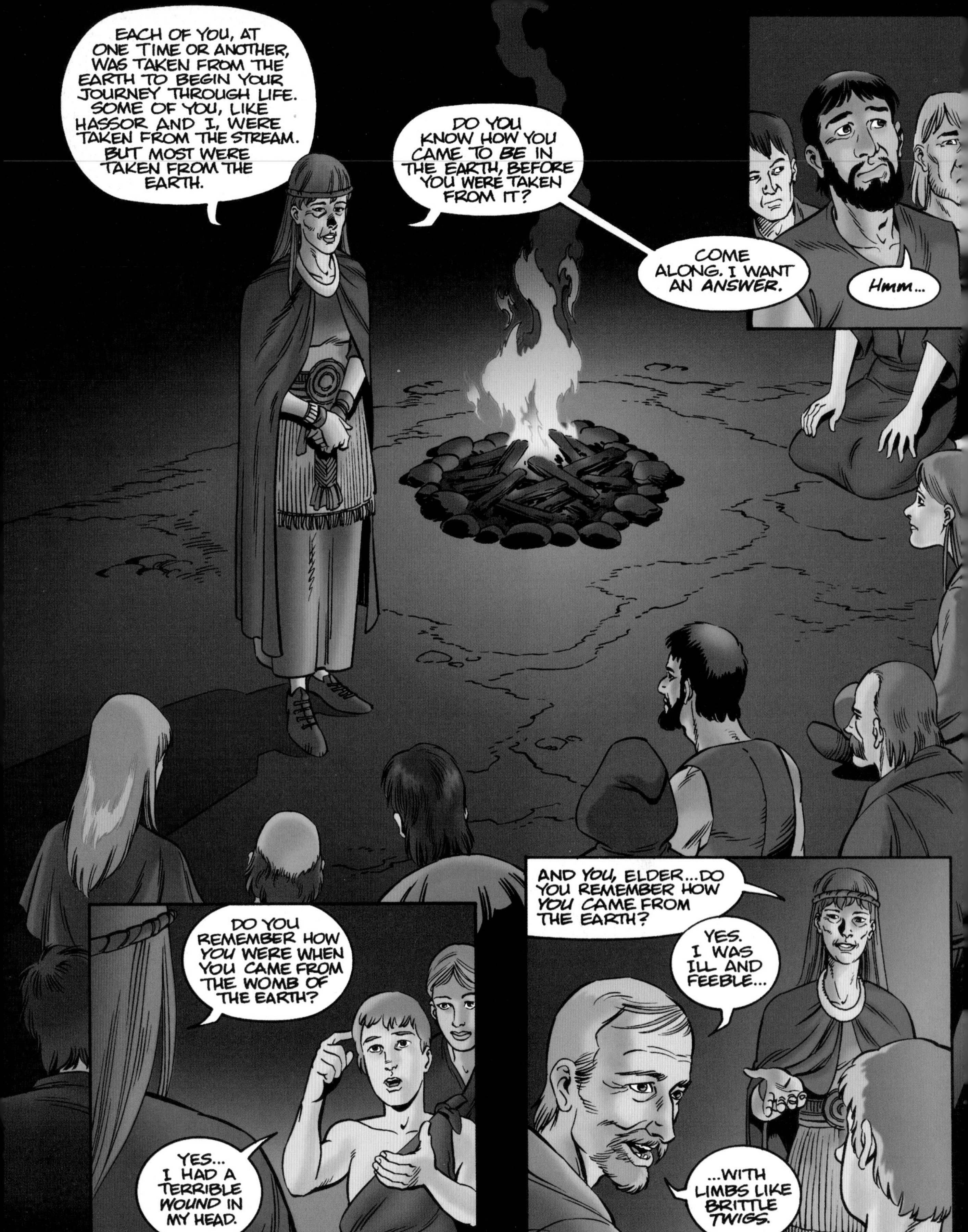
EACH OF YOU, AT ONE TIME OR ANOTHER, WAS TAKEN FROM THE EARTH TO BEGIN YOUR JOURNEY THROUGH LIFE. SOME OF YOU, LIKE HASSOR AND I, WERE TAKEN FROM THE STREAM. BUT MOST WERE TAKEN FROM THE EARTH.
DO YOU KNOW HOW YOU CAME TO BE IN THE EARTH, BEFORE YOU WERE TAKEN FROM IT?
COME ALONG. I WANT AN ANSWER.
Hmm...
DO YOU REMEMBER HOW YOU WERE WHEN YOU CAME FROM THE WOMB OF THE EARTH?
YES... I HAD A TERRIBLE WOUND IN MY HEAD.
AND YOU, ELDER...DO YOU REMEMBER HOW YOU CAME FROM THE EARTH?
YES. I WAS ILL AND FEEBLE...
...WITH LIMBS LIKE BRITTLE TWIGS.

Eh...

YOU. HOW DID YOU COME TO BE IN THE EARTH?

TH-THE GODS PUT ME IN THE EARTH, ALTA. A LONG TIME AGO.

WHAT DID THEY PUT INTO THE GROUND?

Uh... THEY PUT INTO THE GROUND... A SKELETON.

AND THEN?

THEN THE EARTH... GATHERED FLESH AROUND THE SKELETON 'TIL THE BODY WAS COMPLETE...

...'TIL IT WAS WHOLE, AND READY TO BE AWAKENED.

INDEED. FROM MOTHER TO MOTHER. FROM THE WOMB OF THE EARTH TO THE WOMB OF A WOMAN. THAT'S OUR JOURNEY.

BUT ON ONE DAY, EVERY SPRING, ONE OF US IS FOUND PINNED TO THE RIVERBED, FASTENED IN A CAGE OF STICKS. AND NEVER IS THIS ONE FOUND TO BE WEAK OR INJURED OR ILL, EVEN IN THE SLIGHTEST DEGREE.

BUT WE WHO COME FROM THE RIVER ARE DIFFERENT. WE'RE LIKE SLEEPERS, AWAKENED FROM A LIGHT SLUMBER. WE RISE FROM THE RIVER FRESH AND HEALTHY.

WHY?

THOSE WHO COME FROM THE RIVER ARE GIVEN TO US TO REMIND US OF THE SEEDS.

THE SEEDS, LIKE YOU, COME FROM THE EARTH IN THE SPRING, FRESH AND HEALTHY.

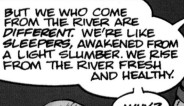

Ah, JUST SO. BUT WHAT I MUST TELL YOU IS...

...ONCE UPON A TIME, LONG AGO...

BEFORE WE LIVED IN THIS DIRECTION...

...WE LIVED IN THIS DIRECTION.

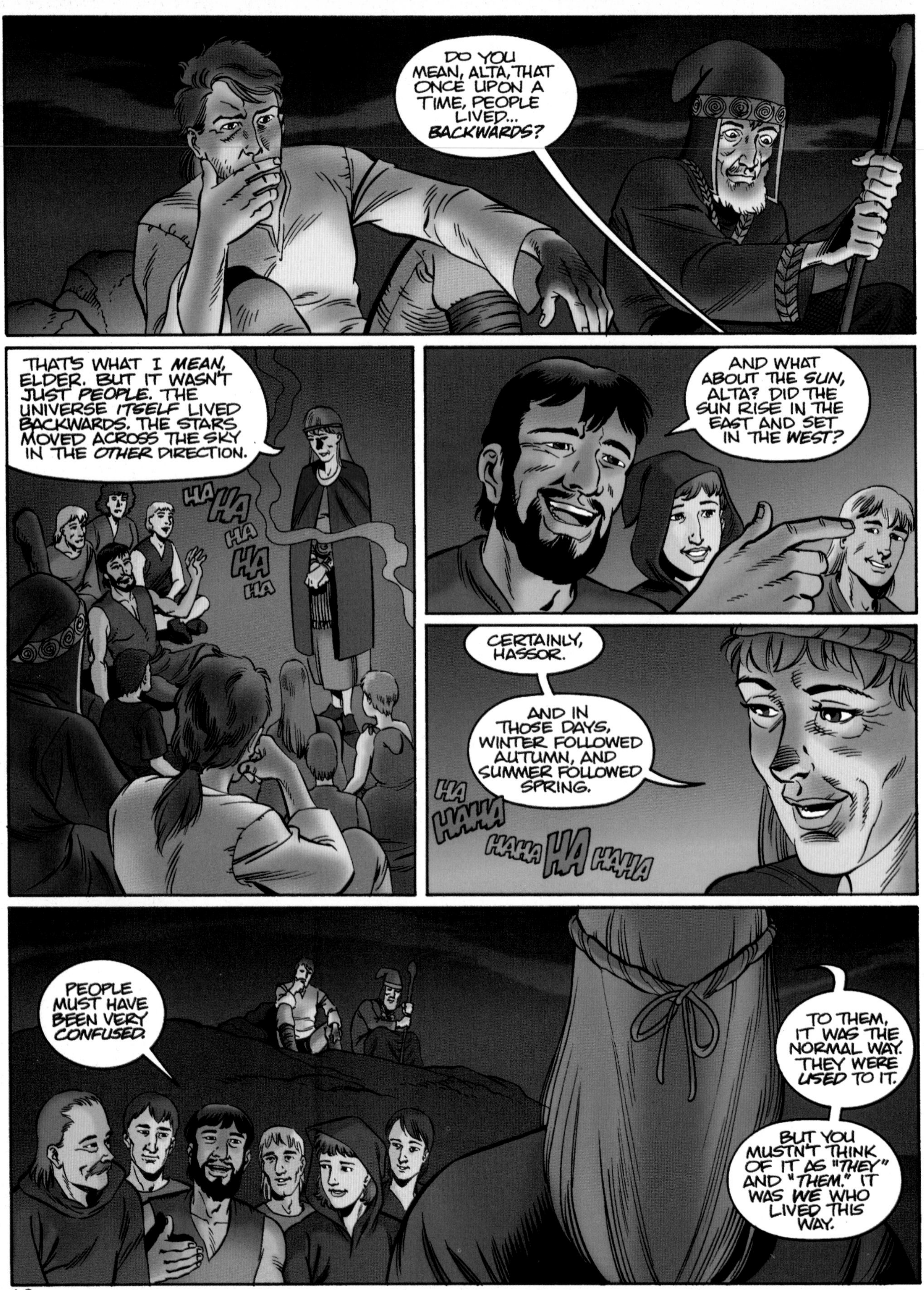
DO YOU MEAN, ALTA, THAT ONCE UPON A TIME, PEOPLE LIVED... BACKWARDS?
THAT'S WHAT I MEAN, ELDER. BUT IT WASN'T JUST PEOPLE. THE UNIVERSE ITSELF LIVED BACKWARDS. THE STARS MOVED ACROSS THE SKY IN THE OTHER DIRECTION.
HA HA HA HA HA
AND WHAT ABOUT THE SUN, ALTA? DID THE SUN RISE IN THE EAST AND SET IN THE WEST?
CERTAINLY, HASSOR.
AND IN THOSE DAYS, WINTER FOLLOWED AUTUMN, AND SUMMER FOLLOWED SPRING.
HA HAHA HAHA HA HAHA
PEOPLE MUST HAVE BEEN VERY CONFUSED.
TO THEM, IT WAS THE NORMAL WAY. THEY WERE USED TO IT.
BUT YOU MUSTN'T THINK OF IT AS "THEY" AND "THEM." IT WAS WE WHO LIVED THIS WAY.

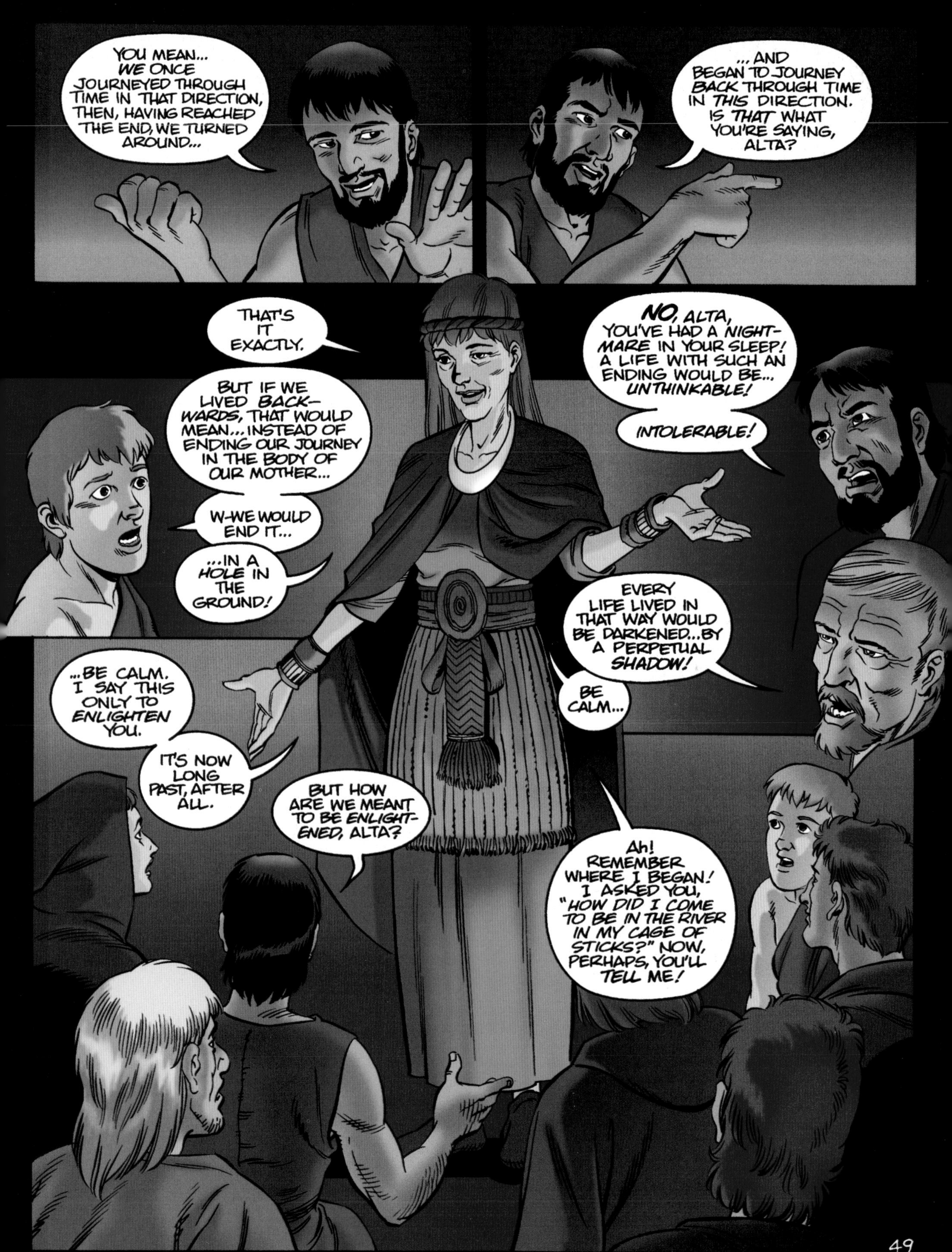
YOU MEAN... WE ONCE JOURNEYED THROUGH TIME IN THAT DIRECTION, THEN, HAVING REACHED THE END, WE TURNED AROUND...
...AND BEGAN TO JOURNEY BACK THROUGH TIME IN THIS DIRECTION. IS THAT WHAT YOU'RE SAYING, ALTA?
THAT'S IT EXACTLY.
NO, ALTA, YOU'VE HAD A NIGHT-MARE IN YOUR SLEEP! A LIFE WITH SUCH AN ENDING WOULD BE... UNTHINKABLE!
INTOLERABLE!
BUT IF WE LIVED BACK-WARDS, THAT WOULD MEAN... INSTEAD OF ENDING OUR JOURNEY IN THE BODY OF OUR MOTHER...
W-WE WOULD END IT...
...IN A HOLE IN THE GROUND!
EVERY LIFE LIVED IN THAT WAY WOULD BE DARKENED... BY A PERPETUAL SHADOW!
BE CALM...
...BE CALM. I SAY THIS ONLY TO ENLIGHTEN YOU.
IT'S NOW LONG PAST, AFTER ALL.
BUT HOW ARE WE MEANT TO BE ENLIGHT-ENED, ALTA?
Ah! REMEMBER WHERE I BEGAN! I ASKED YOU, "HOW DID I COME TO BE IN THE RIVER IN MY CAGE OF STICKS?" NOW, PERHAPS, YOU'LL TELL ME!

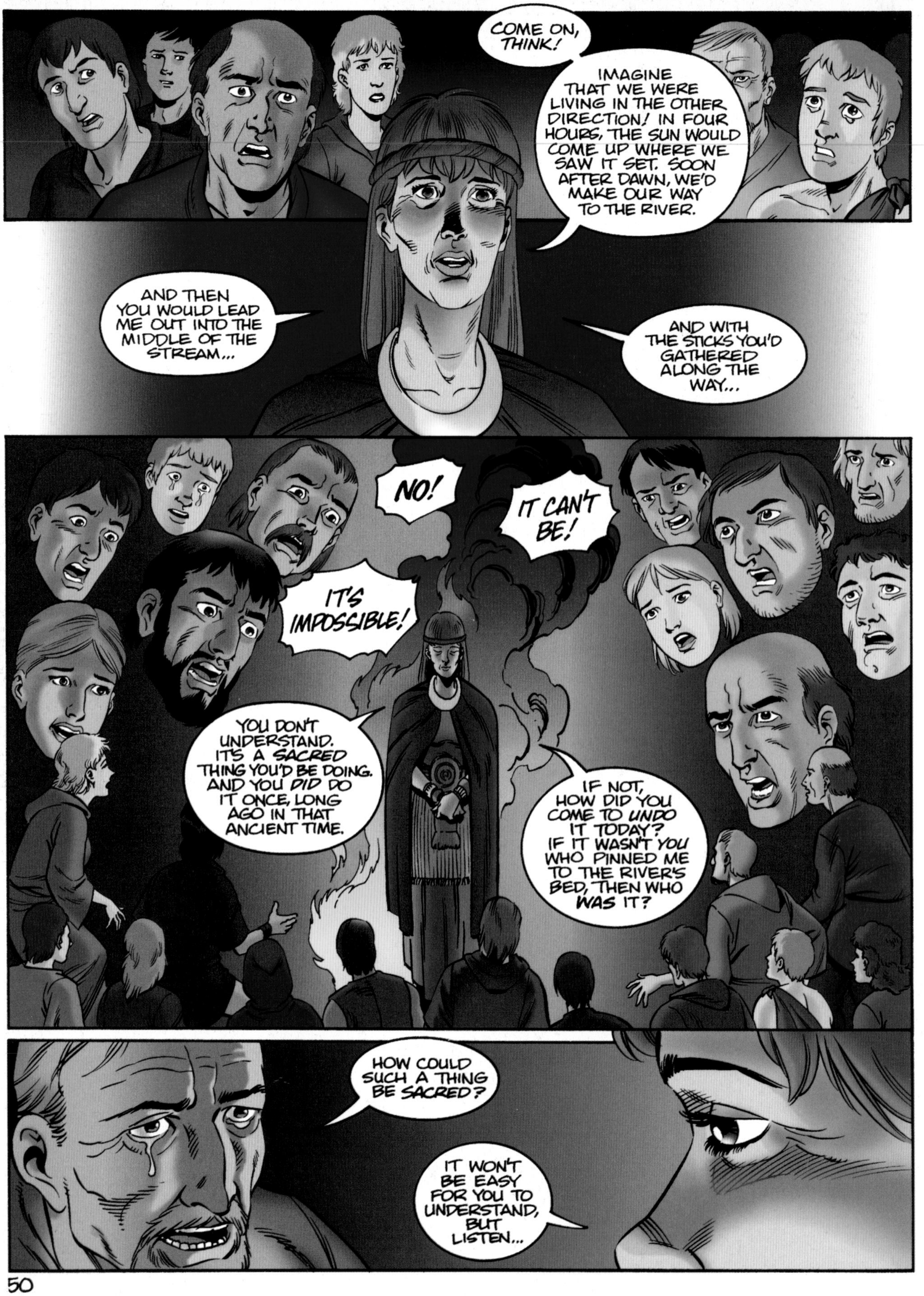
COME ON, THINK!
IMAGINE THAT WE WERE LIVING IN THE OTHER DIRECTION! IN FOUR HOURS, THE SUN WOULD COME UP WHERE WE SAW IT SET. SOON AFTER DAWN, WE'D MAKE OUR WAY TO THE RIVER.
AND THEN YOU WOULD LEAD ME OUT INTO THE MIDDLE OF THE STREAM...
AND WITH THE STICKS YOU'D GATHERED ALONG THE WAY...
NO!
IT CAN'T BE!
IT'S IMPOSSIBLE!
YOU DON'T UNDERSTAND. IT'S A SACRED THING YOU'D BE DOING. AND YOU DID DO IT ONCE, LONG AGO IN THAT ANCIENT TIME.
IF NOT, HOW DID YOU COME TO UNDO IT TODAY? IF IT WASN'T YOU WHO PINNED ME TO THE RIVER'S BED, THEN WHO WAS IT?
HOW COULD SUCH A THING BE SACRED?
IT WON'T BE EASY FOR YOU TO UNDERSTAND, BUT LISTEN...

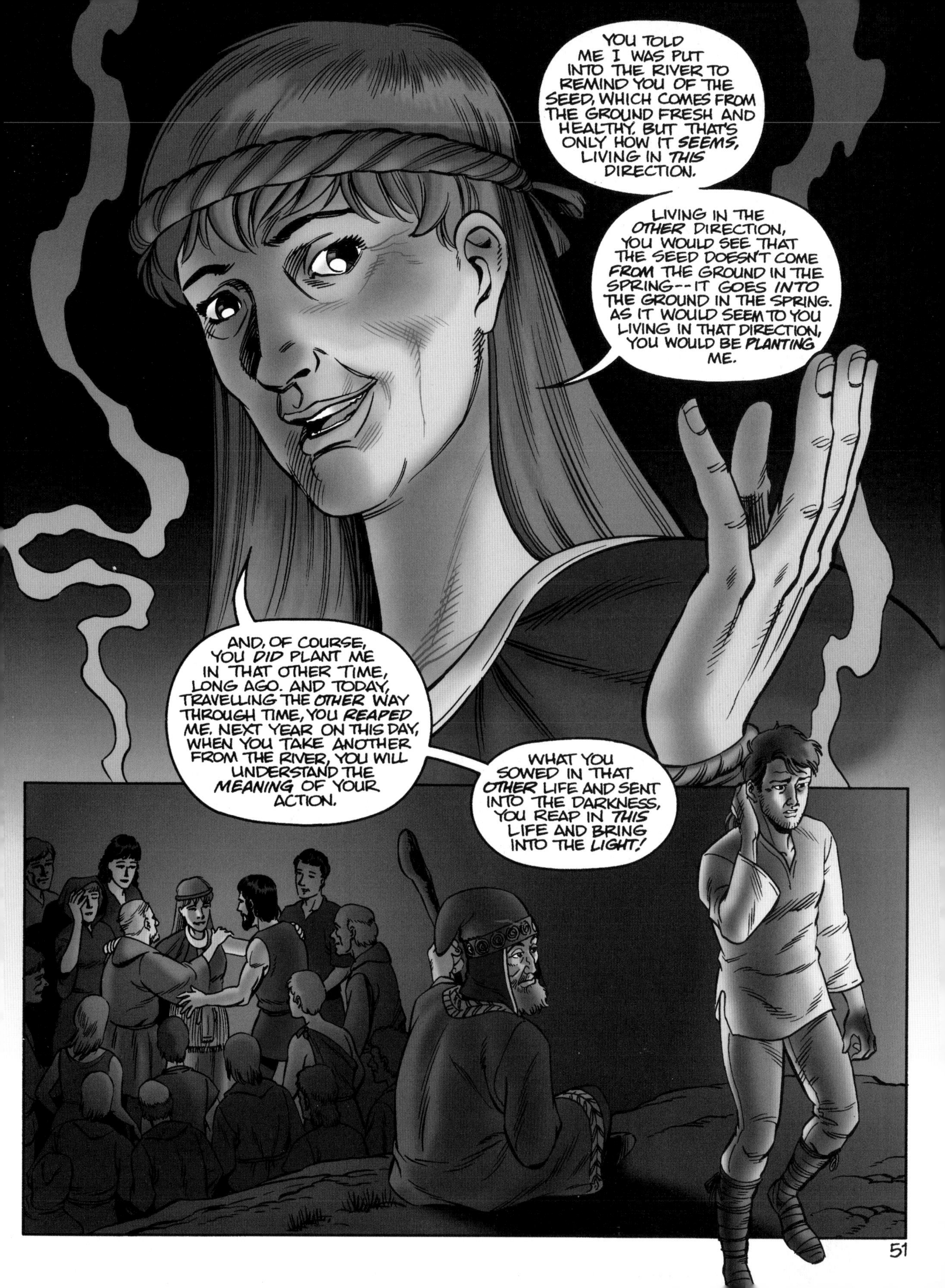
YOU TOLD ME I WAS PUT INTO THE RIVER TO REMIND YOU OF THE SEED, WHICH COMES FROM THE GROUND FRESH AND HEALTHY. BUT THAT'S ONLY HOW IT SEEMS, LIVING IN THIS DIRECTION.
LIVING IN THE OTHER DIRECTION, YOU WOULD SEE THAT THE SEED DOESN'T COME FROM THE GROUND IN THE SPRING--IT GOES INTO THE GROUND IN THE SPRING. AS IT WOULD SEEM TO YOU LIVING IN THAT DIRECTION, YOU WOULD BE PLANTING ME.
AND, OF COURSE, YOU DID PLANT ME IN THAT OTHER TIME, LONG AGO. AND TODAY, TRAVELLING THE OTHER WAY THROUGH TIME, YOU REAPED ME. NEXT YEAR ON THIS DAY, WHEN YOU TAKE ANOTHER FROM THE RIVER, YOU WILL UNDERSTAND THE MEANING OF YOUR ACTION.
WHAT YOU SOWED IN THAT OTHER LIFE AND SENT INTO THE DARKNESS, YOU REAP IN THIS LIFE AND BRING INTO THE LIGHT!

YOUR BEARER GOT VERY DRUNK AFTER YOU LEFT. HE TOLD ME ABOUT THE STONE FISH YOU CARRY.

MAY I SEE IT?

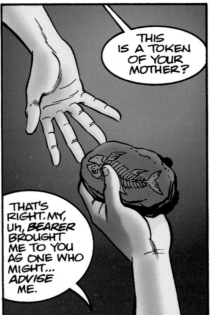

THIS IS A TOKEN OF YOUR MOTHER?

THAT'S RIGHT. MY, UH, *BEARER* BROUGHT ME TO YOU AS ONE WHO MIGHT... ADVISE ME.

ADVISE YOU HOW?

I'M *LOST*, ALTA.

A LOST MAN. LOST IN TIME. HOW DID THIS HAPPEN? I'VE WANDERED FOR *THREE THOUSAND YEARS...*

...HOPING TO FIND MY WAY.

YOUR *WAY?*

I THOUGHT I WAS SEARCHING FOR THE END OF MY LIFE, BUT ACCORDING TO YOUR STORY, I'M SEARCHING FOR ITS *BEGINNING.*

THE UNIVERSE IS LONG AND LARGE, ADAM. SO LONG AND LARGE THAT EVERY-THING MUST HAPPEN AT LEAST *ONCE.* EVERY SINGLE THING, NO MATTER HOW IMPROBABLE.

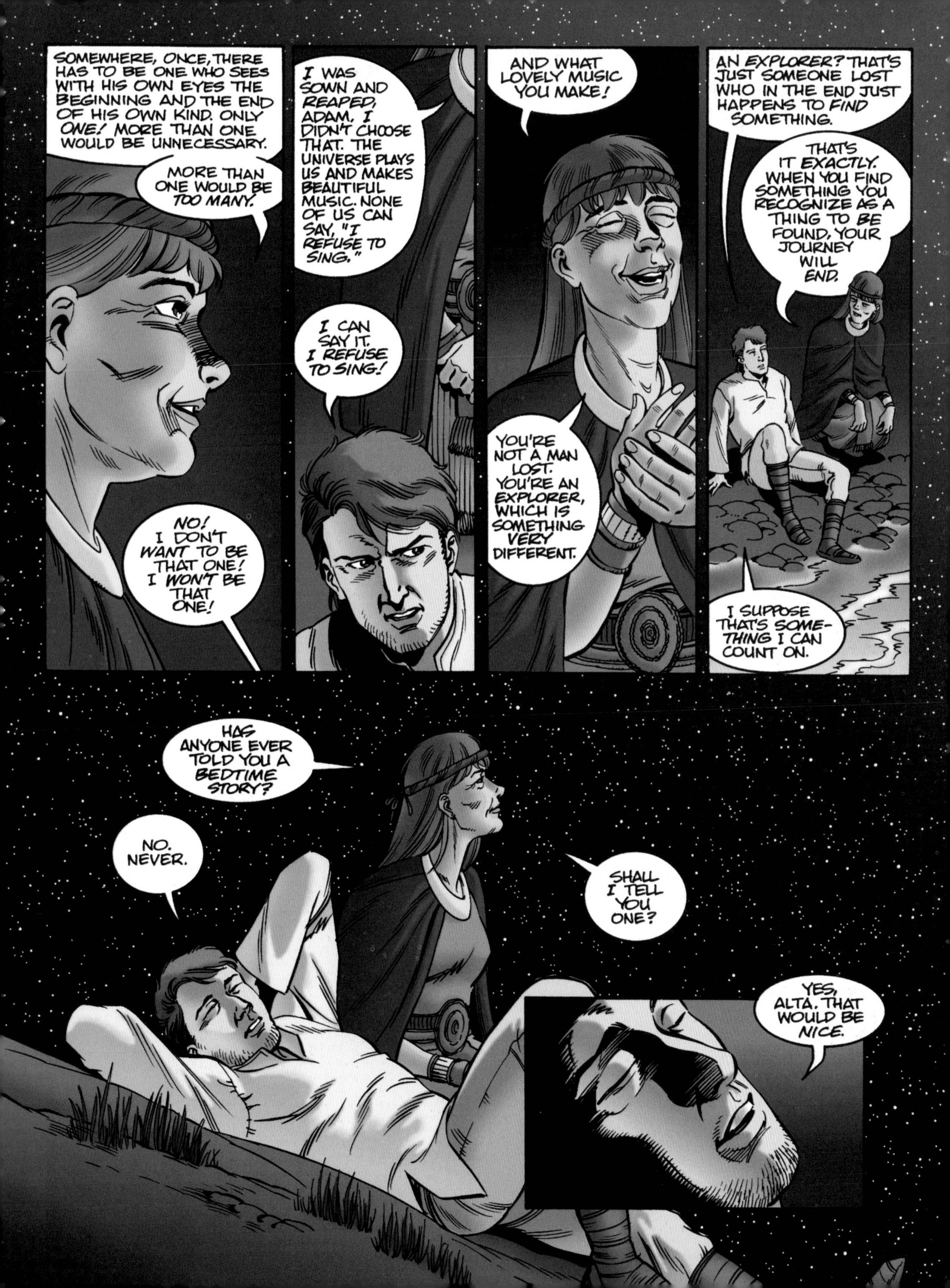
SOMEWHERE, ONCE, THERE HAS TO BE ONE WHO SEES WITH HIS OWN EYES THE BEGINNING AND THE END OF HIS OWN KIND. ONLY ONE! MORE THAN ONE WOULD BE UNNECESSARY.
MORE THAN ONE WOULD BE TOO MANY.
NO! I DON'T WANT TO BE THAT ONE! I WON'T BE THAT ONE!
I WAS SOWN AND REAPED, ADAM. I DIDN'T CHOOSE THAT. THE UNIVERSE PLAYS US AND MAKES BEAUTIFUL MUSIC. NONE OF US CAN SAY, "I REFUSE TO SING."
I CAN SAY IT. I REFUSE TO SING!
AND WHAT LOVELY MUSIC YOU MAKE!
YOU'RE NOT A MAN LOST. YOU'RE AN EXPLORER, WHICH IS SOMETHING VERY DIFFERENT.
AN EXPLORER? THAT'S JUST SOMEONE LOST WHO IN THE END JUST HAPPENS TO FIND SOMETHING.
THAT'S IT EXACTLY. WHEN YOU FIND SOMETHING YOU RECOGNIZE AS A THING TO BE FOUND, YOUR JOURNEY WILL END.
I SUPPOSE THAT'S SOME-THING I CAN COUNT ON.
HAS ANYONE EVER TOLD YOU A BEDTIME STORY?
NO. NEVER.
SHALL I TELL YOU ONE?
YES, ALTA. THAT WOULD BE NICE.

PART THREE

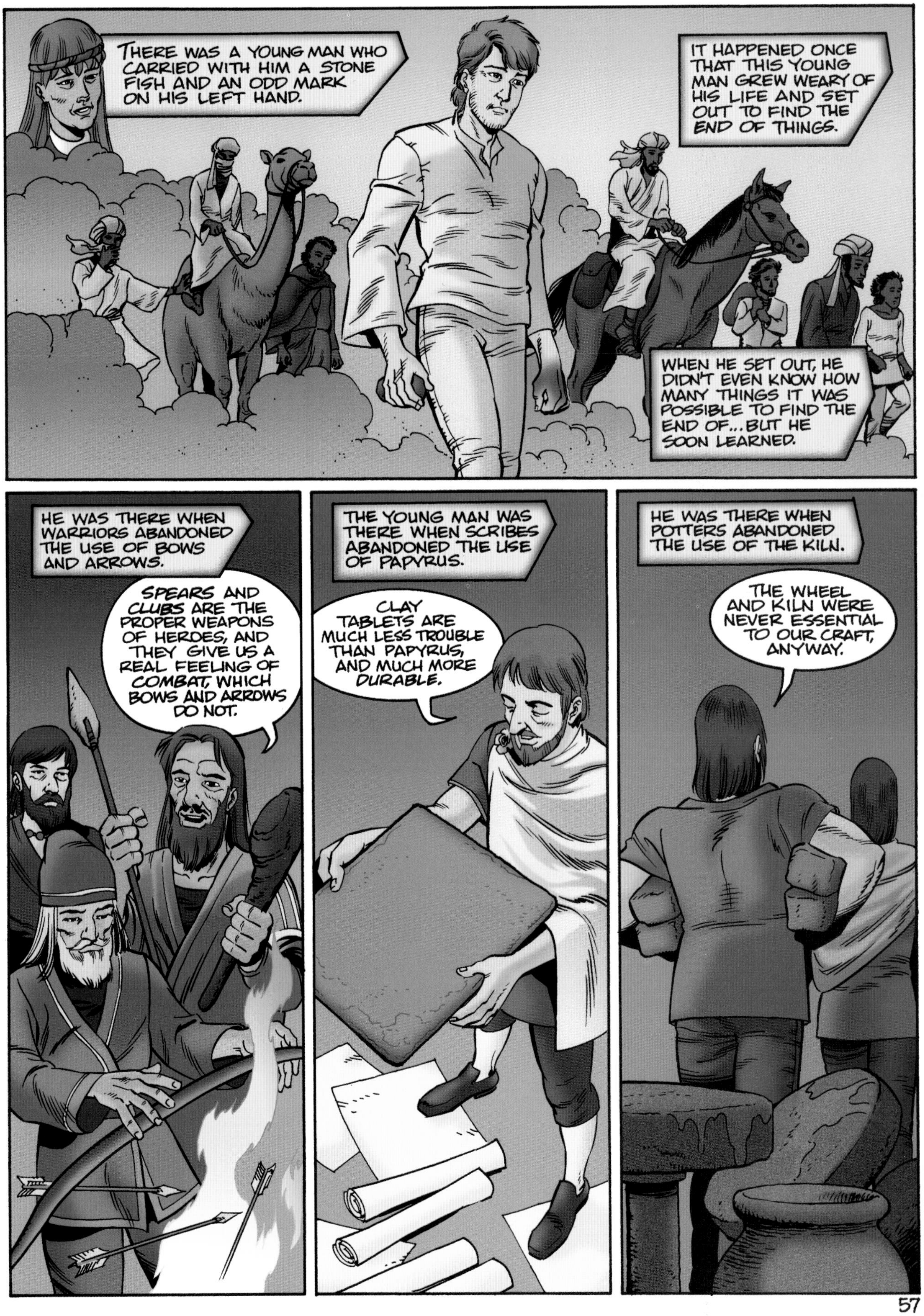
THERE WAS A YOUNG MAN WHO CARRIED WITH HIM A STONE FISH AND AN ODD MARK ON HIS LEFT HAND.
IT HAPPENED ONCE THAT THIS YOUNG MAN GREW WEARY OF HIS LIFE AND SET OUT TO FIND THE END OF THINGS.
WHEN HE SET OUT, HE DIDN'T EVEN KNOW HOW MANY THINGS IT WAS POSSIBLE TO FIND THE END OF... BUT HE SOON LEARNED.
HE WAS THERE WHEN WARRIORS ABANDONED THE USE OF BOWS AND ARROWS.
SPEARS AND CLUBS ARE THE PROPER WEAPONS OF HEROES, AND THEY GIVE US A REAL FEELING OF COMBAT, WHICH BOWS AND ARROWS DO NOT.
THE YOUNG MAN WAS THERE WHEN SCRIBES ABANDONED THE USE OF PAPYRUS.
CLAY TABLETS ARE MUCH LESS TROUBLE THAN PAPYRUS, AND MUCH MORE DURABLE.
HE WAS THERE WHEN POTTERS ABANDONED THE USE OF THE KILN.
THE WHEEL AND KILN WERE NEVER ESSENTIAL TO OUR CRAFT, ANYWAY.

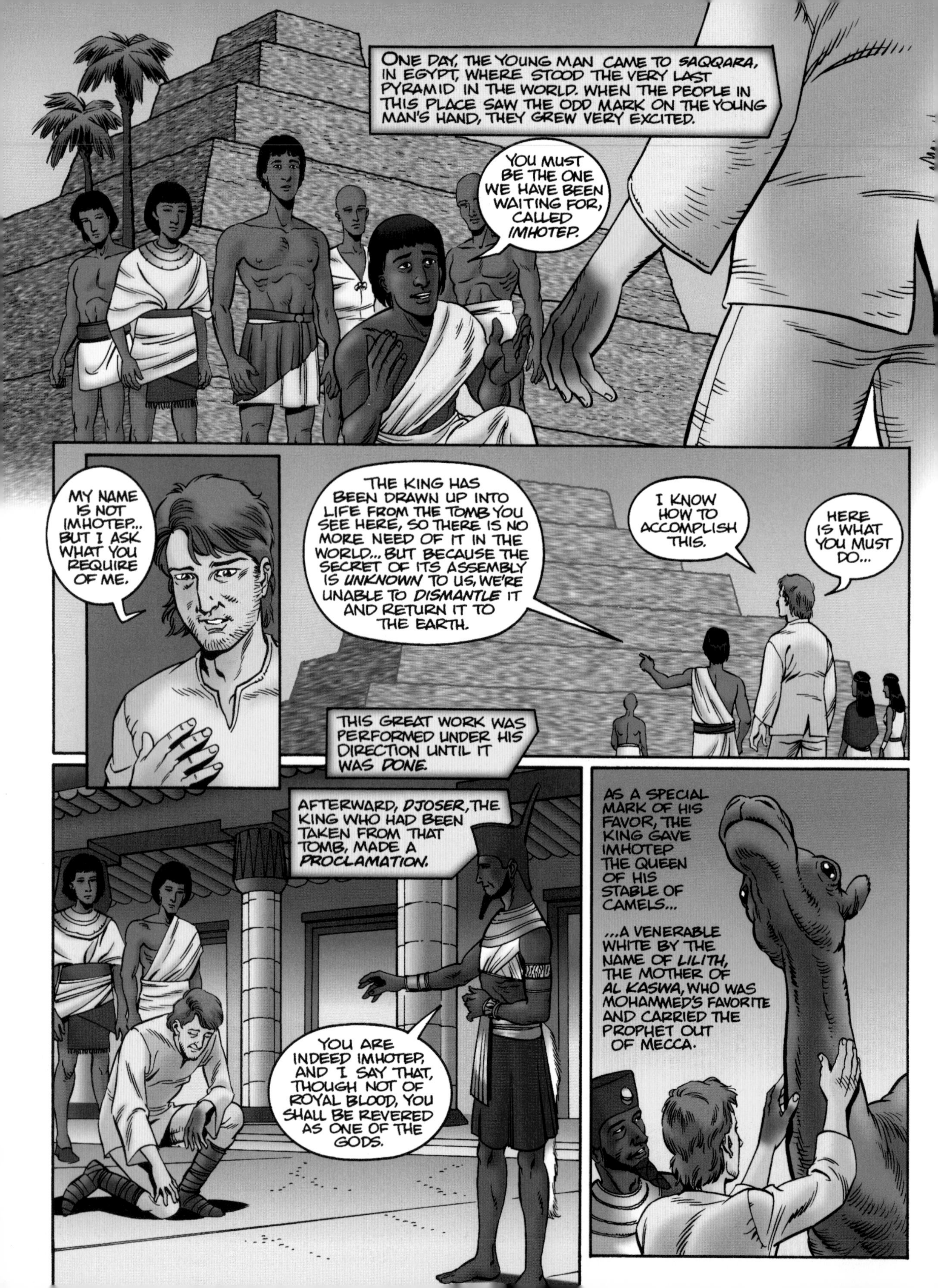
ONE DAY, THE YOUNG MAN CAME TO SAQQARA, IN EGYPT, WHERE STOOD THE VERY LAST PYRAMID IN THE WORLD. WHEN THE PEOPLE IN THIS PLACE SAW THE ODD MARK ON THE YOUNG MAN'S HAND, THEY GREW VERY EXCITED.
YOU MUST BE THE ONE WE HAVE BEEN WAITING FOR, CALLED IMHOTEP.
MY NAME IS NOT IMHOTEP... BUT I ASK WHAT YOU REQUIRE OF ME.
THE KING HAS BEEN DRAWN UP INTO LIFE FROM THE TOMB YOU SEE HERE, SO THERE IS NO MORE NEED OF IT IN THE WORLD... BUT BECAUSE THE SECRET OF ITS ASSEMBLY IS UNKNOWN TO US, WE'RE UNABLE TO DISMANTLE IT AND RETURN IT TO THE EARTH.
I KNOW HOW TO ACCOMPLISH THIS.
HERE IS WHAT YOU MUST DO...
THIS GREAT WORK WAS PERFORMED UNDER HIS DIRECTION UNTIL IT WAS DONE.
AFTERWARD, DJOSER, THE KING WHO HAD BEEN TAKEN FROM THAT TOMB, MADE A PROCLAMATION.
YOU ARE INDEED IMHOTEP, AND I SAY THAT, THOUGH NOT OF ROYAL BLOOD, YOU SHALL BE REVERED AS ONE OF THE GODS.
AS A SPECIAL MARK OF HIS FAVOR, THE KING GAVE IMHOTEP THE QUEEN OF HIS STABLE OF CAMELS...
...A VENERABLE WHITE BY THE NAME OF LILITH, THE MOTHER OF AL KASWA, WHO WAS MOHAMMED'S FAVORITE AND CARRIED THE PROPHET OUT OF MECCA.

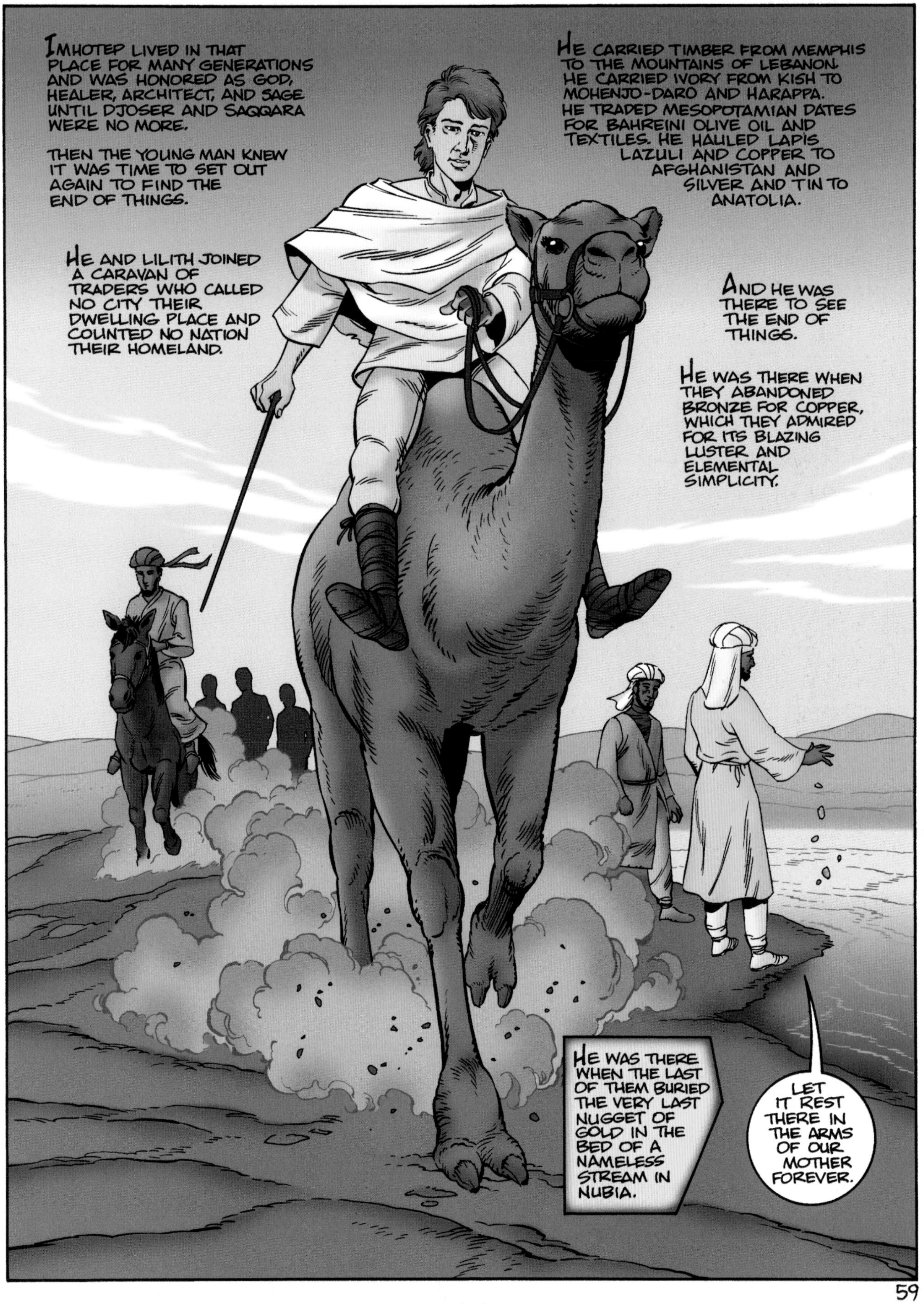

IMHOTEP LIVED IN THAT PLACE FOR MANY GENERATIONS AND WAS HONORED AS GOD, HEALER, ARCHITECT, AND SAGE UNTIL DJOSER AND SAQQARA WERE NO MORE.
THEN THE YOUNG MAN KNEW IT WAS TIME TO SET OUT AGAIN TO FIND THE END OF THINGS.
HE AND LILITH JOINED A CARAVAN OF TRADERS WHO CALLED NO CITY THEIR DWELLING PLACE AND COUNTED NO NATION THEIR HOMELAND.
HE CARRIED TIMBER FROM MEMPHIS TO THE MOUNTAINS OF LEBANON. HE CARRIED IVORY FROM KISH TO MOHENJO-DARO AND HARAPPA. HE TRADED MESOPOTAMIAN DATES FOR BAHREINI OLIVE OIL AND TEXTILES. HE HAULED LAPIS LAZULI AND COPPER TO AFGHANISTAN AND SILVER AND TIN TO ANATOLIA.
AND HE WAS THERE TO SEE THE END OF THINGS.
HE WAS THERE WHEN THEY ABANDONED BRONZE FOR COPPER, WHICH THEY ADMIRED FOR ITS BLAZING LUSTER AND ELEMENTAL SIMPLICITY.
HE WAS THERE WHEN THE LAST OF THEM BURIED THE VERY LAST NUGGET OF GOLD IN THE BED OF A NAMELESS STREAM IN NUBIA.
LET IT REST THERE IN THE ARMS OF OUR MOTHER FOREVER.

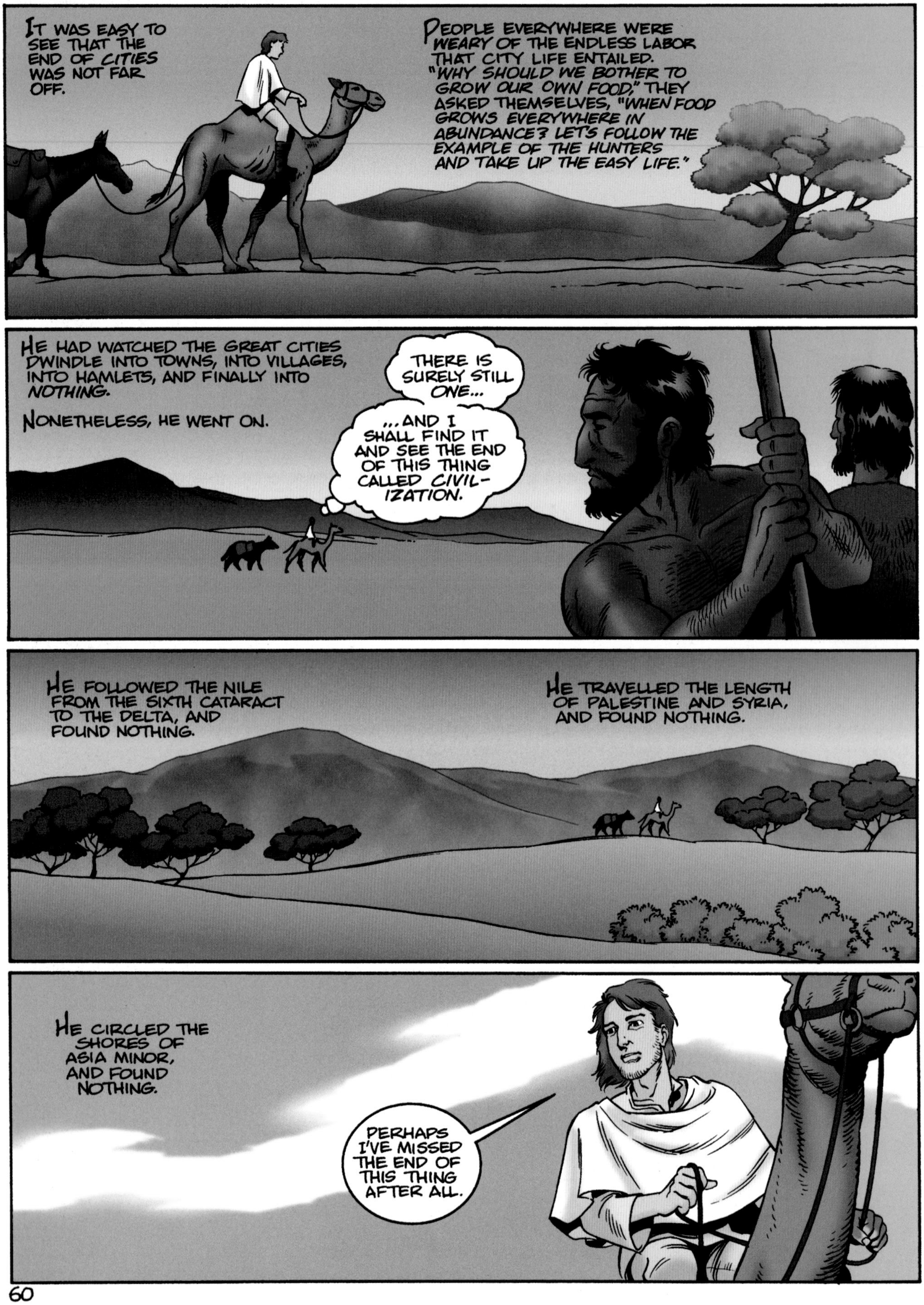
IT WAS EASY TO SEE THAT THE END OF *CITIES* WAS NOT FAR OFF.
PEOPLE EVERYWHERE WERE WEARY OF THE ENDLESS LABOR THAT CITY LIFE ENTAILED. "WHY SHOULD WE BOTHER TO GROW OUR OWN FOOD," THEY ASKED THEMSELVES, "WHEN FOOD GROWS EVERYWHERE IN ABUNDANCE? LET'S FOLLOW THE EXAMPLE OF THE HUNTERS AND TAKE UP THE EASY LIFE."
HE HAD WATCHED THE GREAT CITIES DWINDLE INTO TOWNS, INTO VILLAGES, INTO HAMLETS, AND FINALLY INTO *NOTHING*.
NONETHELESS, HE WENT ON.
THERE IS SURELY STILL *ONE*...
...AND I SHALL FIND IT AND SEE THE END OF THIS THING CALLED *CIVIL-IZATION*.
HE FOLLOWED THE NILE FROM THE SIXTH CATARACT TO THE DELTA, AND FOUND NOTHING.
HE TRAVELLED THE LENGTH OF PALESTINE AND SYRIA, AND FOUND NOTHING.
HE CIRCLED THE SHORES OF ASIA MINOR, AND FOUND NOTHING.
PERHAPS I'VE MISSED THE END OF THIS THING AFTER ALL.

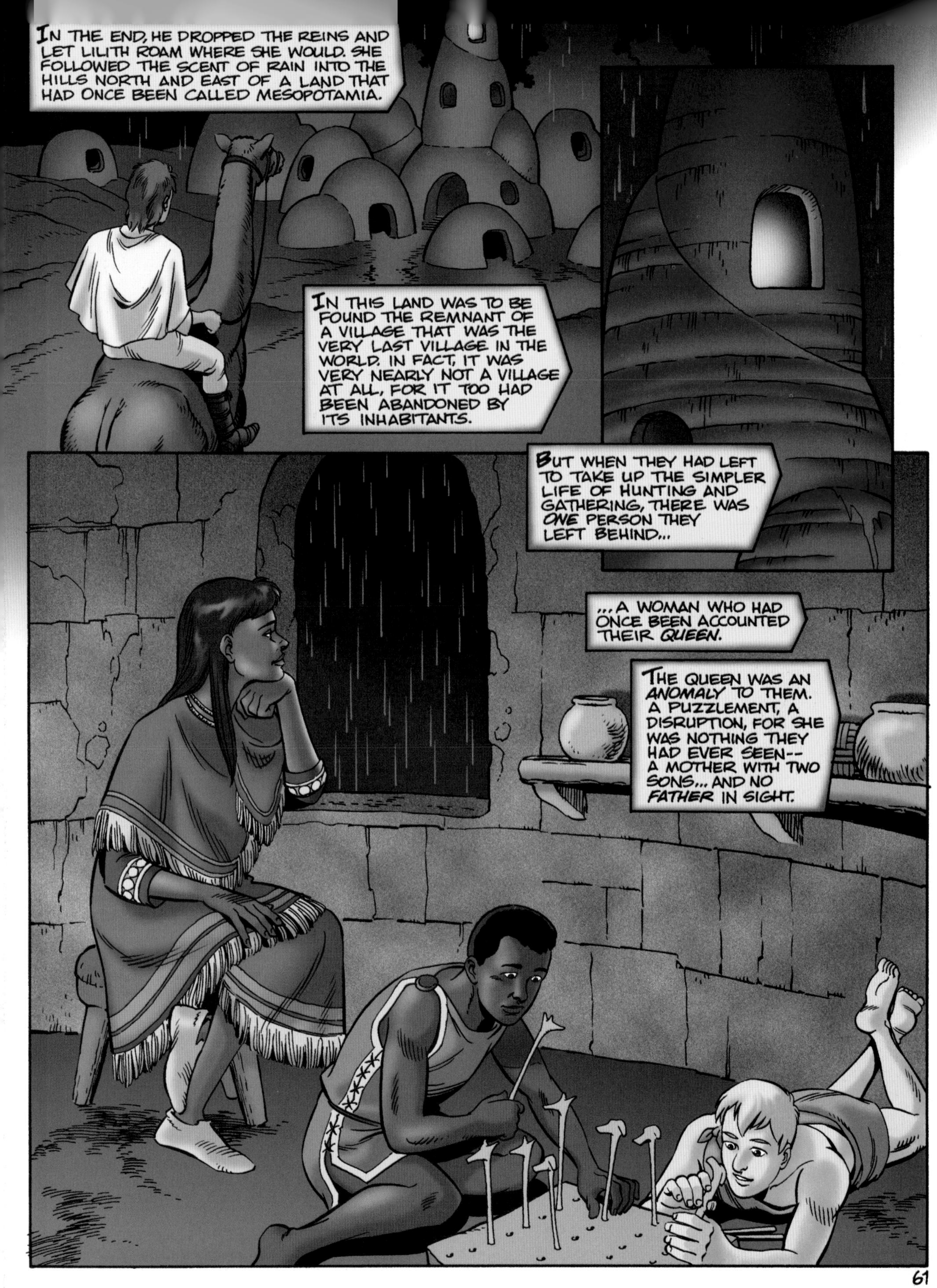
IN THE END, HE DROPPED THE REINS AND LET LILITH ROAM WHERE SHE WOULD. SHE FOLLOWED THE SCENT OF RAIN INTO THE HILLS NORTH AND EAST OF A LAND THAT HAD ONCE BEEN CALLED MESOPOTAMIA.
IN THIS LAND WAS TO BE FOUND THE REMNANT OF A VILLAGE THAT WAS THE VERY LAST VILLAGE IN THE WORLD. IN FACT, IT WAS VERY NEARLY NOT A VILLAGE AT ALL, FOR IT TOO HAD BEEN ABANDONED BY ITS INHABITANTS.
BUT WHEN THEY HAD LEFT TO TAKE UP THE SIMPLER LIFE OF HUNTING AND GATHERING, THERE WAS *ONE* PERSON THEY LEFT BEHIND...
...A WOMAN WHO HAD ONCE BEEN ACCOUNTED THEIR *QUEEN*.
THE QUEEN WAS AN *ANOMALY* TO THEM. A PUZZLEMENT, A DISRUPTION, FOR SHE WAS NOTHING THEY HAD EVER SEEN-- A MOTHER WITH TWO SONS... AND NO *FATHER* IN SIGHT.

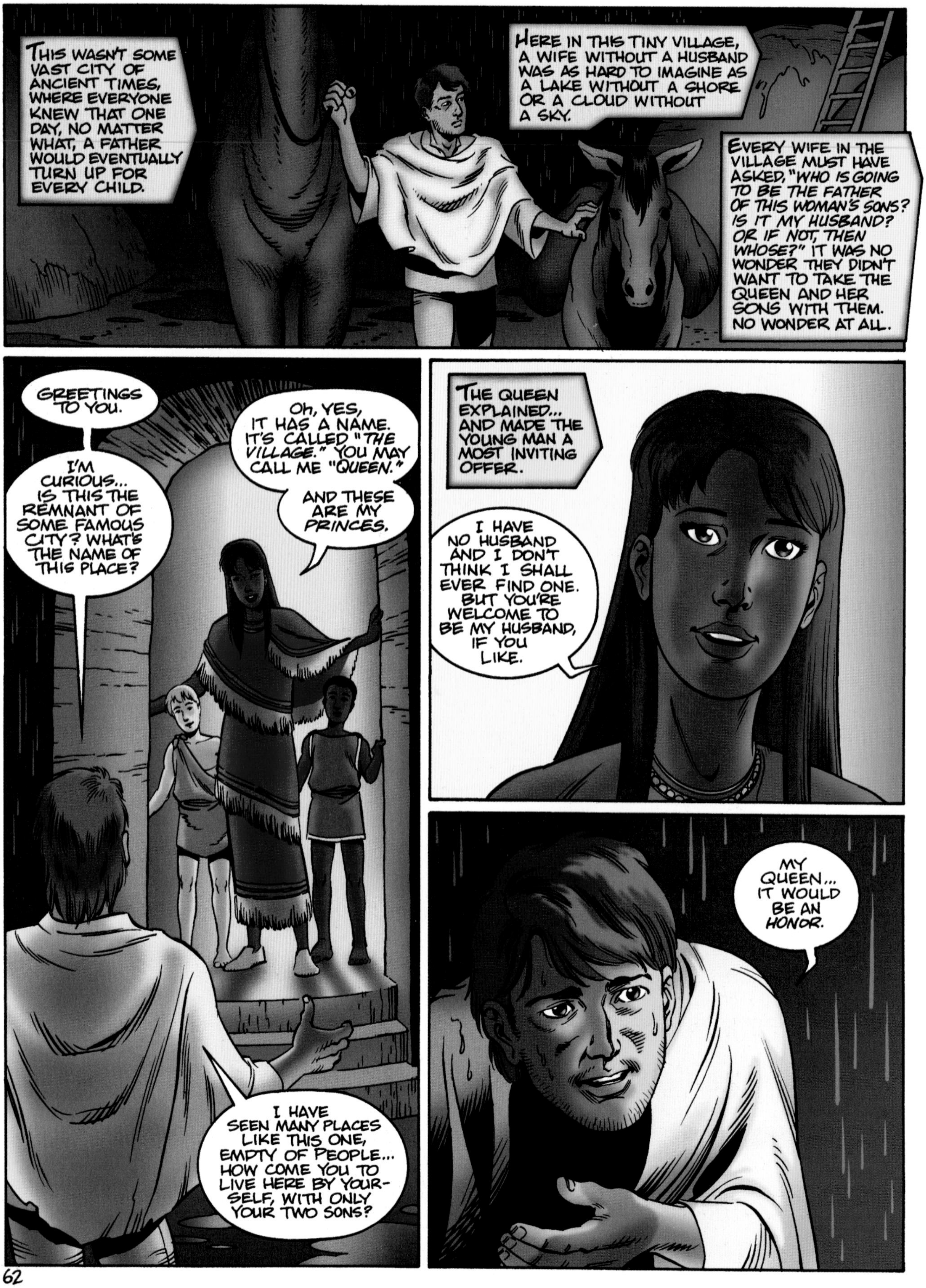

THIS WASN'T SOME VAST CITY OF ANCIENT TIMES, WHERE EVERYONE KNEW THAT ONE DAY, NO MATTER WHAT, A FATHER WOULD EVENTUALLY TURN UP FOR EVERY CHILD.
HERE IN THIS TINY VILLAGE, A WIFE WITHOUT A HUSBAND WAS AS HARD TO IMAGINE AS A LAKE WITHOUT A SHORE OR A CLOUD WITHOUT A SKY.
EVERY WIFE IN THE VILLAGE MUST HAVE ASKED, "WHO IS GOING TO BE THE FATHER OF THIS WOMAN'S SONS? IS IT MY HUSBAND? OR IF NOT, THEN WHOSE?" IT WAS NO WONDER THEY DIDN'T WANT TO TAKE THE QUEEN AND HER SONS WITH THEM. NO WONDER AT ALL.
GREETINGS TO YOU.
I'M CURIOUS... IS THIS THE REMNANT OF SOME FAMOUS CITY? WHAT'S THE NAME OF THIS PLACE?
OH, YES, IT HAS A NAME. IT'S CALLED "THE VILLAGE." YOU MAY CALL ME "QUEEN."
AND THESE ARE MY PRINCES.
I HAVE SEEN MANY PLACES LIKE THIS ONE, EMPTY OF PEOPLE... HOW COME YOU TO LIVE HERE BY YOURSELF, WITH ONLY YOUR TWO SONS?
THE QUEEN EXPLAINED... AND MADE THE YOUNG MAN A MOST INVITING OFFER.
I HAVE NO HUSBAND AND I DON'T THINK I SHALL EVER FIND ONE. BUT YOU'RE WELCOME TO BE MY HUSBAND, IF YOU LIKE.
MY QUEEN... IT WOULD BE AN HONOR.

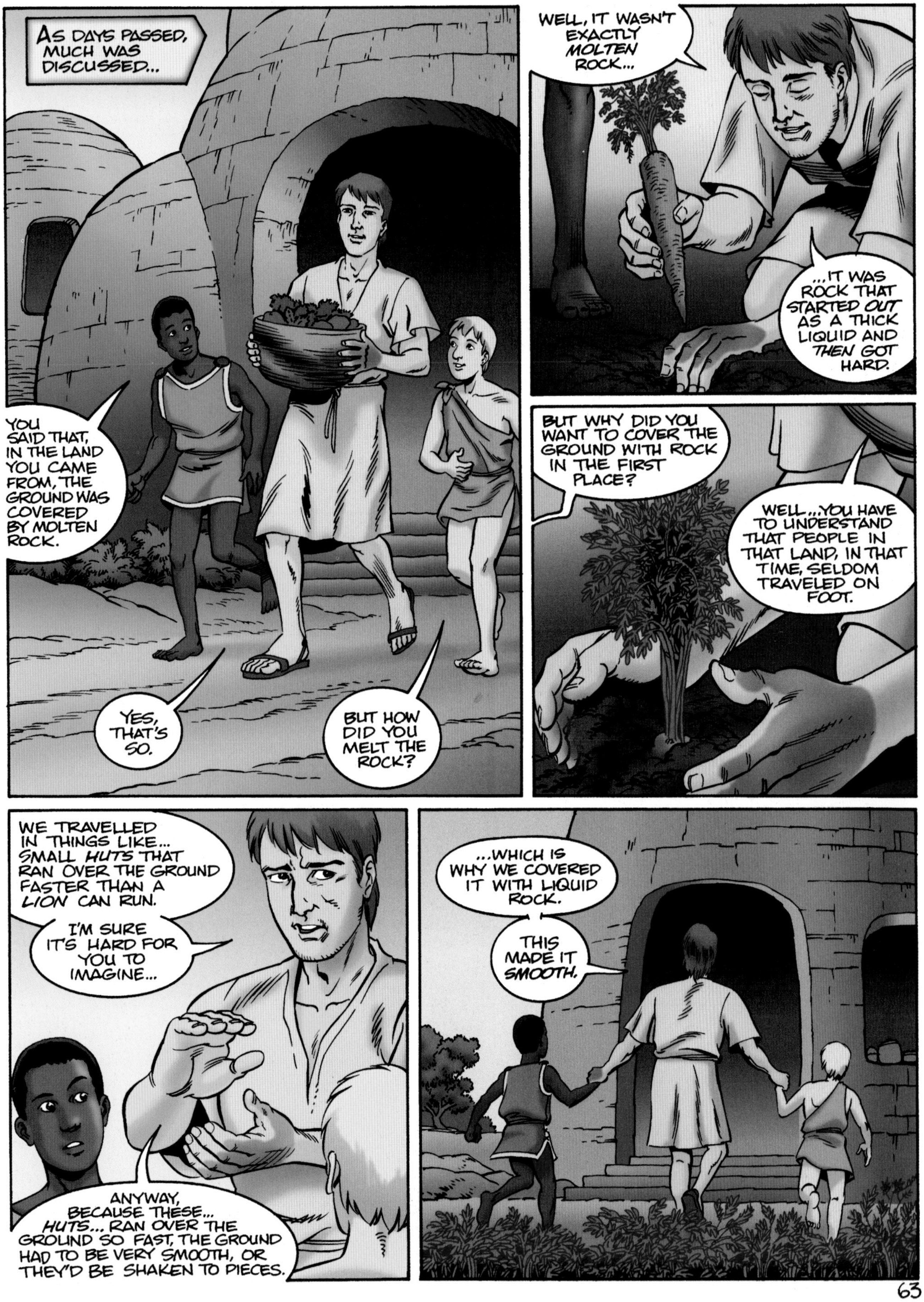

AS DAYS PASSED, MUCH WAS DISCUSSED...
YOU SAID THAT, IN THE LAND YOU CAME FROM, THE GROUND WAS COVERED BY MOLTEN ROCK.
YES, THAT'S SO.
BUT HOW DID YOU MELT THE ROCK?
WELL, IT WASN'T EXACTLY MOLTEN ROCK...
...IT WAS ROCK THAT STARTED OUT AS A THICK LIQUID AND THEN GOT HARD.
BUT WHY DID YOU WANT TO COVER THE GROUND WITH ROCK IN THE FIRST PLACE?
WELL... YOU HAVE TO UNDERSTAND THAT PEOPLE IN THAT LAND, IN THAT TIME, SELDOM TRAVELED ON FOOT.
WE TRAVELLED IN THINGS LIKE... SMALL HUTS THAT RAN OVER THE GROUND FASTER THAN A LION CAN RUN.
I'M SURE IT'S HARD FOR YOU TO IMAGINE...
ANYWAY, BECAUSE THESE... HUTS... RAN OVER THE GROUND SO FAST, THE GROUND HAD TO BE VERY SMOOTH, OR THEY'D BE SHAKEN TO PIECES.
...WHICH IS WHY WE COVERED IT WITH LIQUID ROCK.
THIS MADE IT SMOOTH.

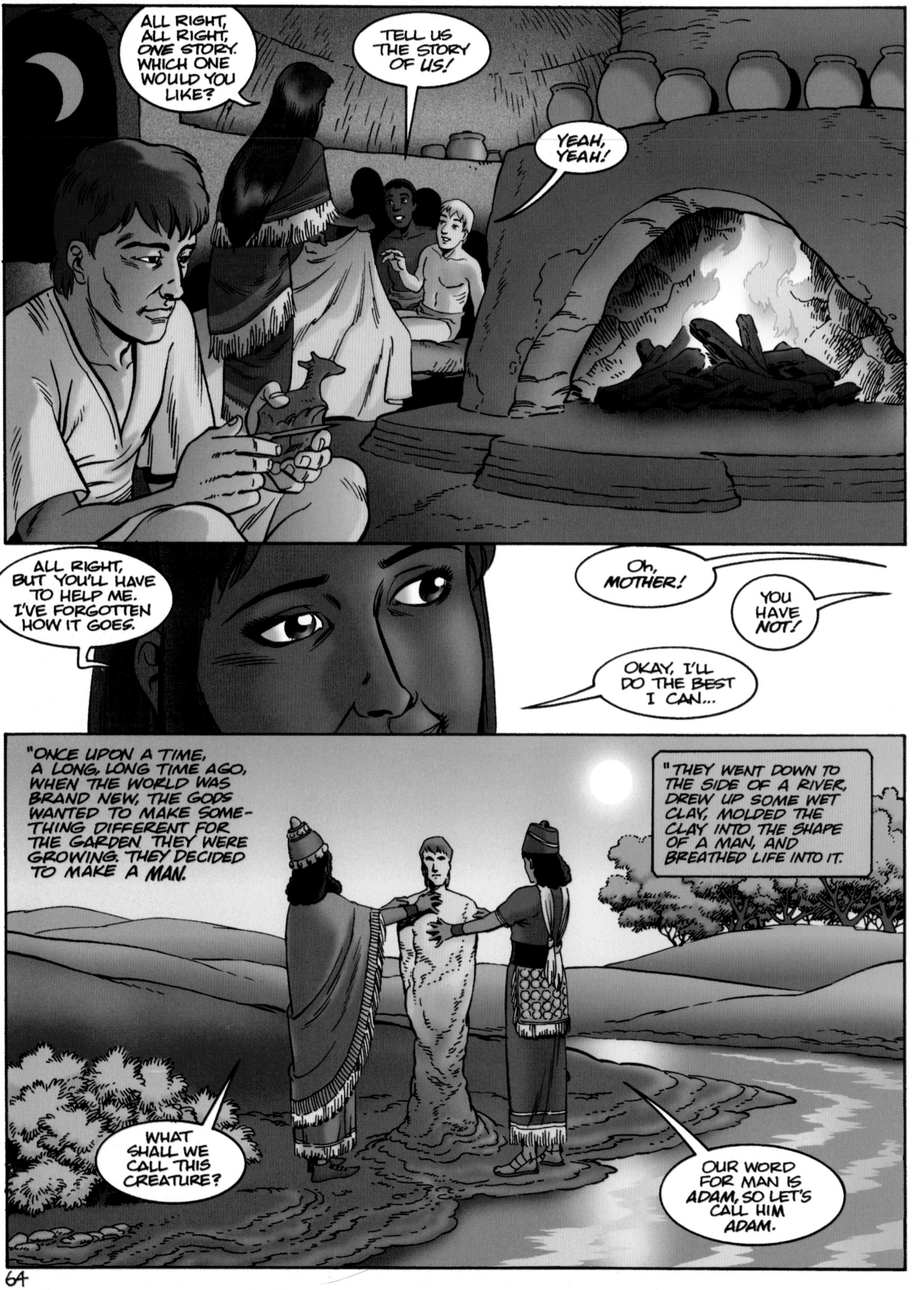
ALL RIGHT, ALL RIGHT, ONE STORY. WHICH ONE WOULD YOU LIKE?
TELL US THE STORY OF US!
YEAH, YEAH!
ALL RIGHT, BUT YOU'LL HAVE TO HELP ME. I'VE FORGOTTEN HOW IT GOES.
Oh, MOTHER!
YOU HAVE NOT!
OKAY, I'LL DO THE BEST I CAN...
"ONCE UPON A TIME, A LONG, LONG TIME AGO, WHEN THE WORLD WAS BRAND NEW, THE GODS WANTED TO MAKE SOME-THING DIFFERENT FOR THE GARDEN THEY WERE GROWING. THEY DECIDED TO MAKE A MAN.
"THEY WENT DOWN TO THE SIDE OF A RIVER, DREW UP SOME WET CLAY, MOLDED THE CLAY INTO THE SHAPE OF A MAN, AND BREATHED LIFE INTO IT.
WHAT SHALL WE CALL THIS CREATURE?
OUR WORD FOR MAN IS ADAM, SO LET'S CALL HIM ADAM.

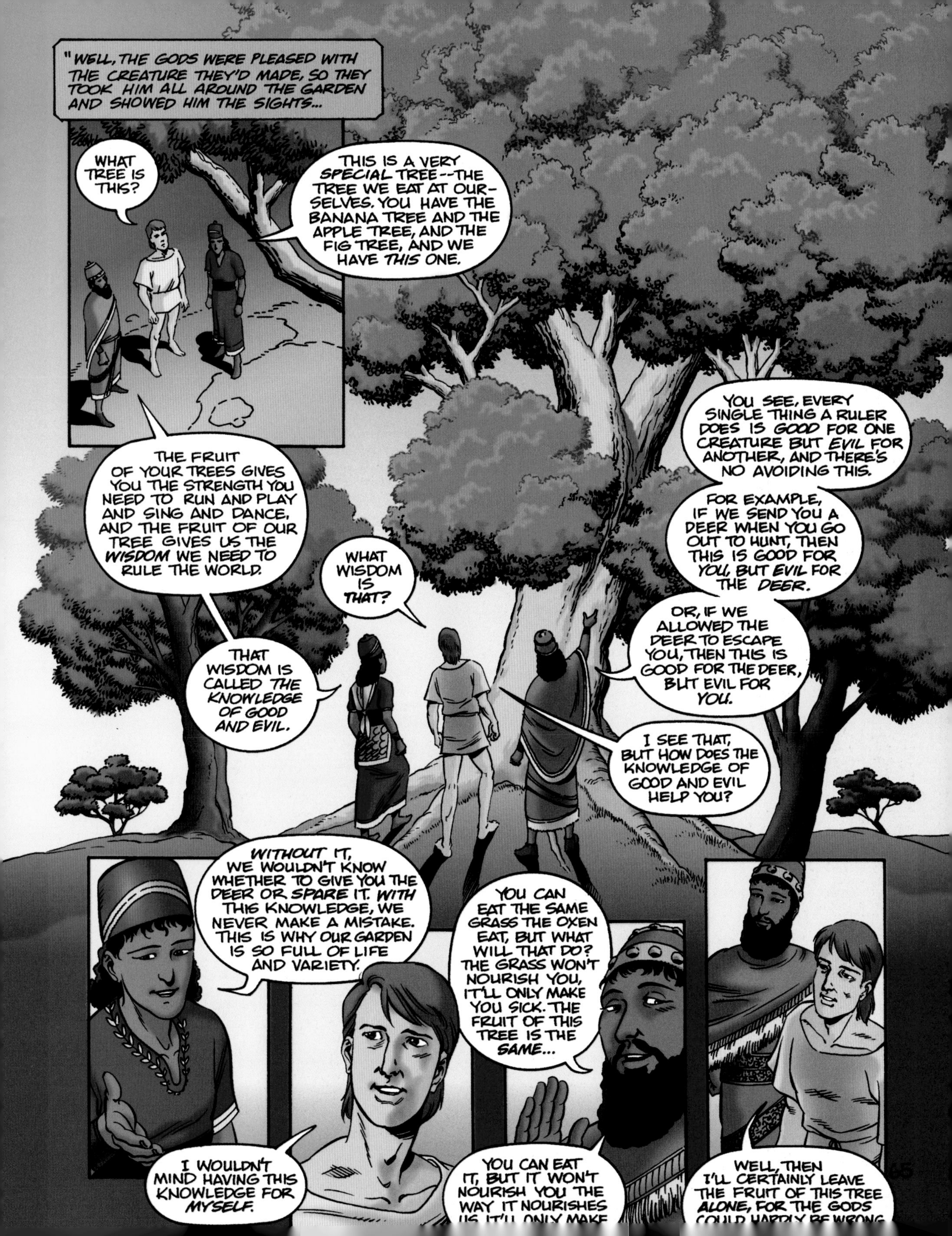
"WELL, THE GODS WERE PLEASED WITH THE CREATURE THEY'D MADE, SO THEY TOOK HIM ALL AROUND THE GARDEN AND SHOWED HIM THE SIGHTS...
WHAT TREE IS THIS?
THIS IS A VERY SPECIAL TREE--THE TREE WE EAT AT OURSELVES. YOU HAVE THE BANANA TREE AND THE APPLE TREE, AND THE FIG TREE, AND WE HAVE THIS ONE.
THE FRUIT OF YOUR TREES GIVES YOU THE STRENGTH YOU NEED TO RUN AND PLAY AND SING AND DANCE, AND THE FRUIT OF OUR TREE GIVES US THE WISDOM WE NEED TO RULE THE WORLD.
WHAT WISDOM IS THAT?
THAT WISDOM IS CALLED THE KNOWLEDGE OF GOOD AND EVIL.
YOU SEE, EVERY SINGLE THING A RULER DOES IS GOOD FOR ONE CREATURE BUT EVIL FOR ANOTHER, AND THERE'S NO AVOIDING THIS.
FOR EXAMPLE, IF WE SEND YOU A DEER WHEN YOU GO OUT TO HUNT, THEN THIS IS GOOD FOR YOU, BUT EVIL FOR THE DEER.
OR, IF WE ALLOWED THE DEER TO ESCAPE YOU, THEN THIS IS GOOD FOR THE DEER, BUT EVIL FOR YOU.
I SEE THAT, BUT HOW DOES THE KNOWLEDGE OF GOOD AND EVIL HELP YOU?
WITHOUT IT, WE WOULDN'T KNOW WHETHER TO GIVE YOU THE DEER OR SPARE IT. WITH THIS KNOWLEDGE, WE NEVER MAKE A MISTAKE. THIS IS WHY OUR GARDEN IS SO FULL OF LIFE AND VARIETY.
I WOULDN'T MIND HAVING THIS KNOWLEDGE FOR MYSELF.
YOU CAN EAT THE SAME GRASS THE OXEN EAT, BUT WHAT WILL THAT DO? THE GRASS WON'T NOURISH YOU, IT'LL ONLY MAKE YOU SICK. THE FRUIT OF THIS TREE IS THE SAME...
YOU CAN EAT IT, BUT IT WON'T NOURISH YOU THE WAY IT NOURISHES
WELL, THEN I'LL CERTAINLY LEAVE THE FRUIT OF THIS TREE ALONE, FOR THE GODS

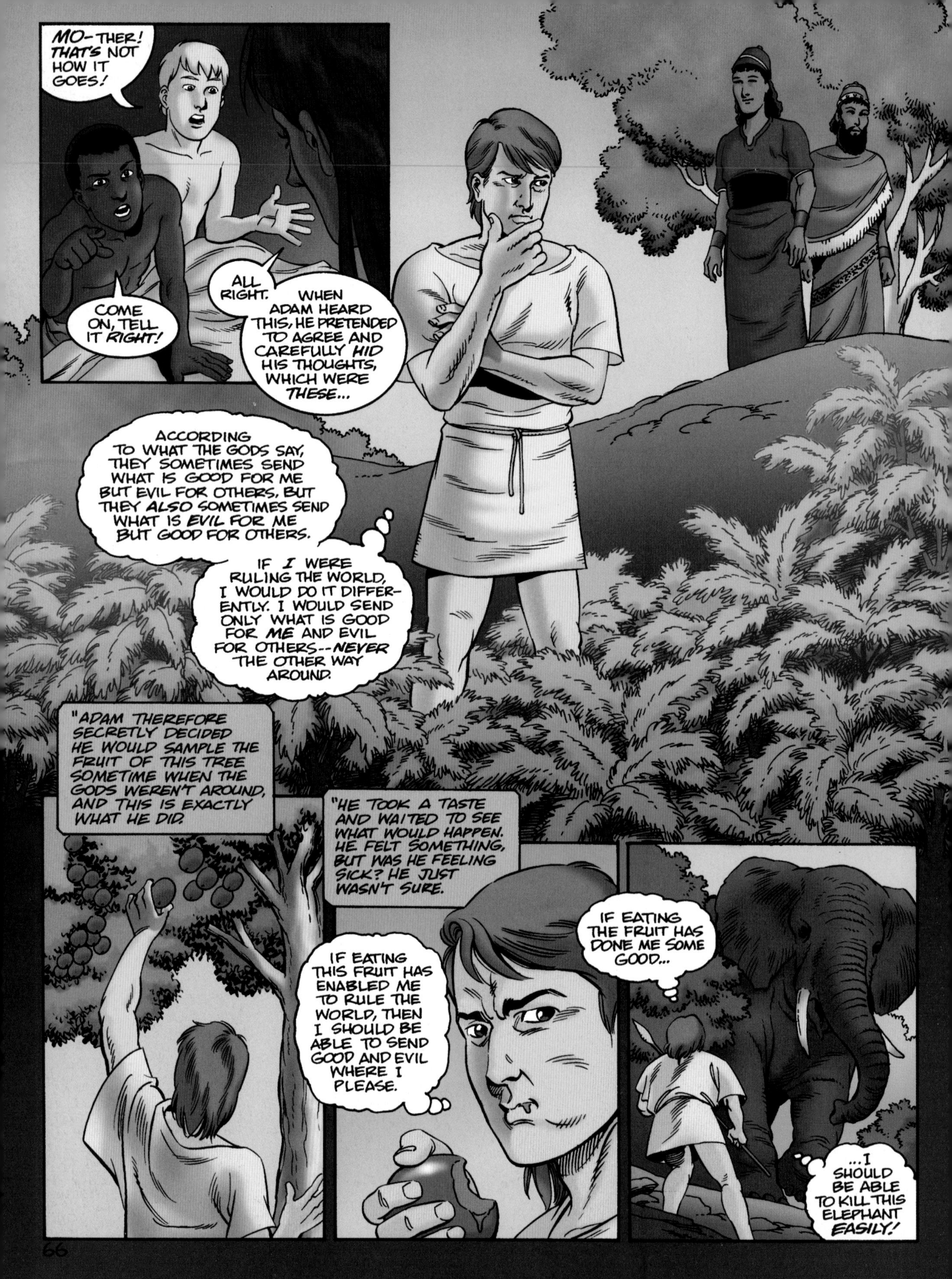
MO-THER! THAT'S NOT HOW IT GOES!
COME ON, TELL IT RIGHT!
ALL RIGHT.
WHEN ADAM HEARD THIS, HE PRETENDED TO AGREE AND CAREFULLY HID HIS THOUGHTS, WHICH WERE THESE...
ACCORDING TO WHAT THE GODS SAY, THEY SOMETIMES SEND WHAT IS GOOD FOR ME BUT EVIL FOR OTHERS, BUT THEY ALSO SOMETIMES SEND WHAT IS EVIL FOR ME BUT GOOD FOR OTHERS.
IF I WERE RULING THE WORLD, I WOULD DO IT DIFFERENTLY. I WOULD SEND ONLY WHAT IS GOOD FOR ME AND EVIL FOR OTHERS--NEVER THE OTHER WAY AROUND.
"ADAM THEREFORE SECRETLY DECIDED HE WOULD SAMPLE THE FRUIT OF THIS TREE SOMETIME WHEN THE GODS WEREN'T AROUND, AND THIS IS EXACTLY WHAT HE DID.
"HE TOOK A TASTE AND WAITED TO SEE WHAT WOULD HAPPEN. HE FELT SOMETHING, BUT WAS HE FEELING SICK? HE JUST WASN'T SURE.
IF EATING THIS FRUIT HAS ENABLED ME TO RULE THE WORLD, THEN I SHOULD BE ABLE TO SEND GOOD AND EVIL WHERE I PLEASE.
IF EATING THE FRUIT HAS DONE ME SOME GOOD...
...I SHOULD BE ABLE TO KILL THIS ELEPHANT EASILY!

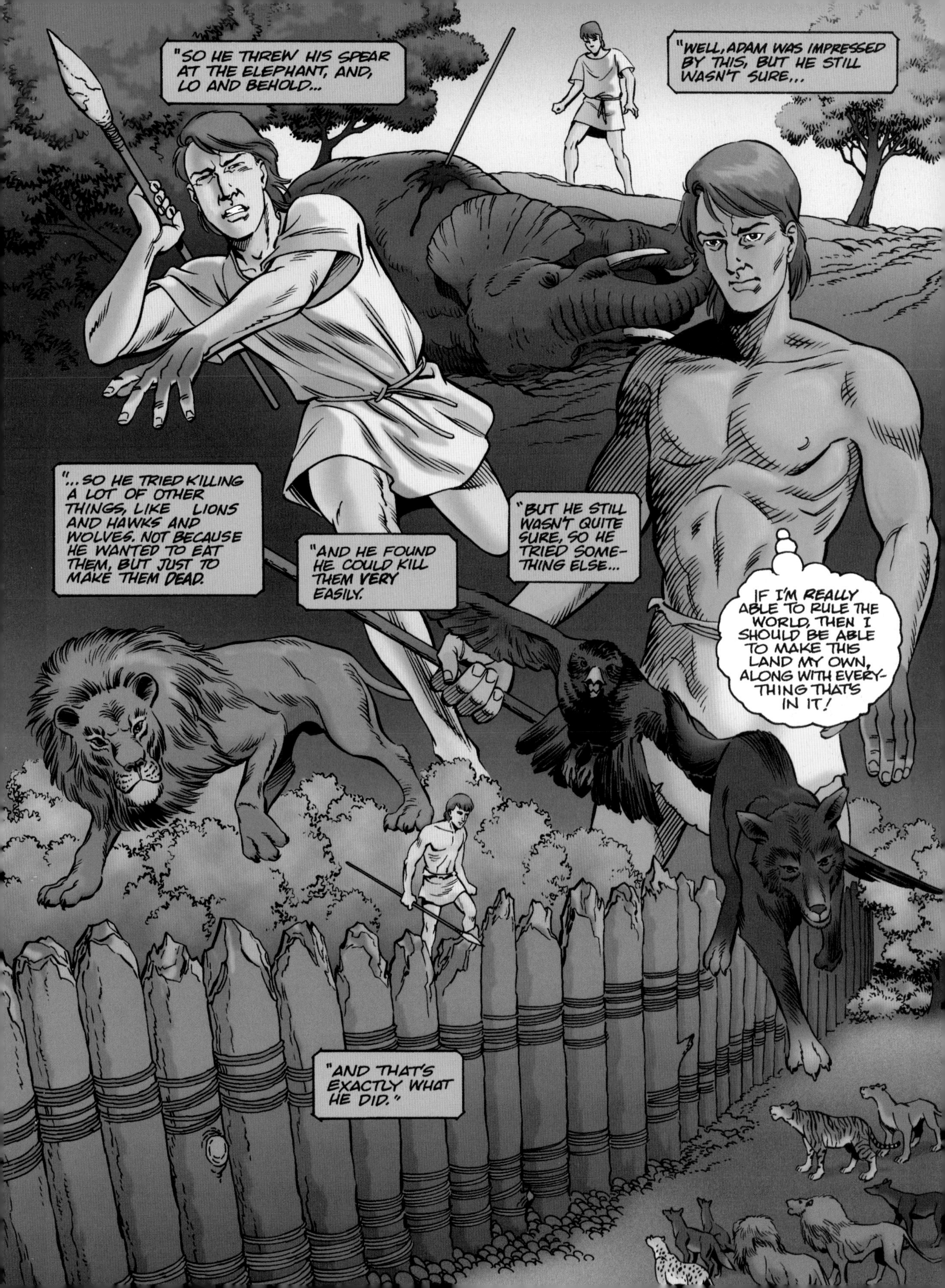
"SO HE THREW HIS SPEAR AT THE ELEPHANT, AND, LO AND BEHOLD...
"WELL, ADAM WAS IMPRESSED BY THIS, BUT HE STILL WASN'T SURE...
"...SO HE TRIED KILLING A LOT OF OTHER THINGS, LIKE LIONS AND HAWKS AND WOLVES. NOT BECAUSE HE WANTED TO EAT THEM, BUT JUST TO MAKE THEM DEAD.
"AND HE FOUND HE COULD KILL THEM VERY EASILY.
"BUT HE STILL WASN'T QUITE SURE, SO HE TRIED SOME-THING ELSE...
IF I'M REALLY ABLE TO RULE THE WORLD, THEN I SHOULD BE ABLE TO MAKE THIS LAND MY OWN, ALONG WITH EVERY-THING THAT'S IN IT!
"AND THAT'S EXACTLY WHAT HE DID."

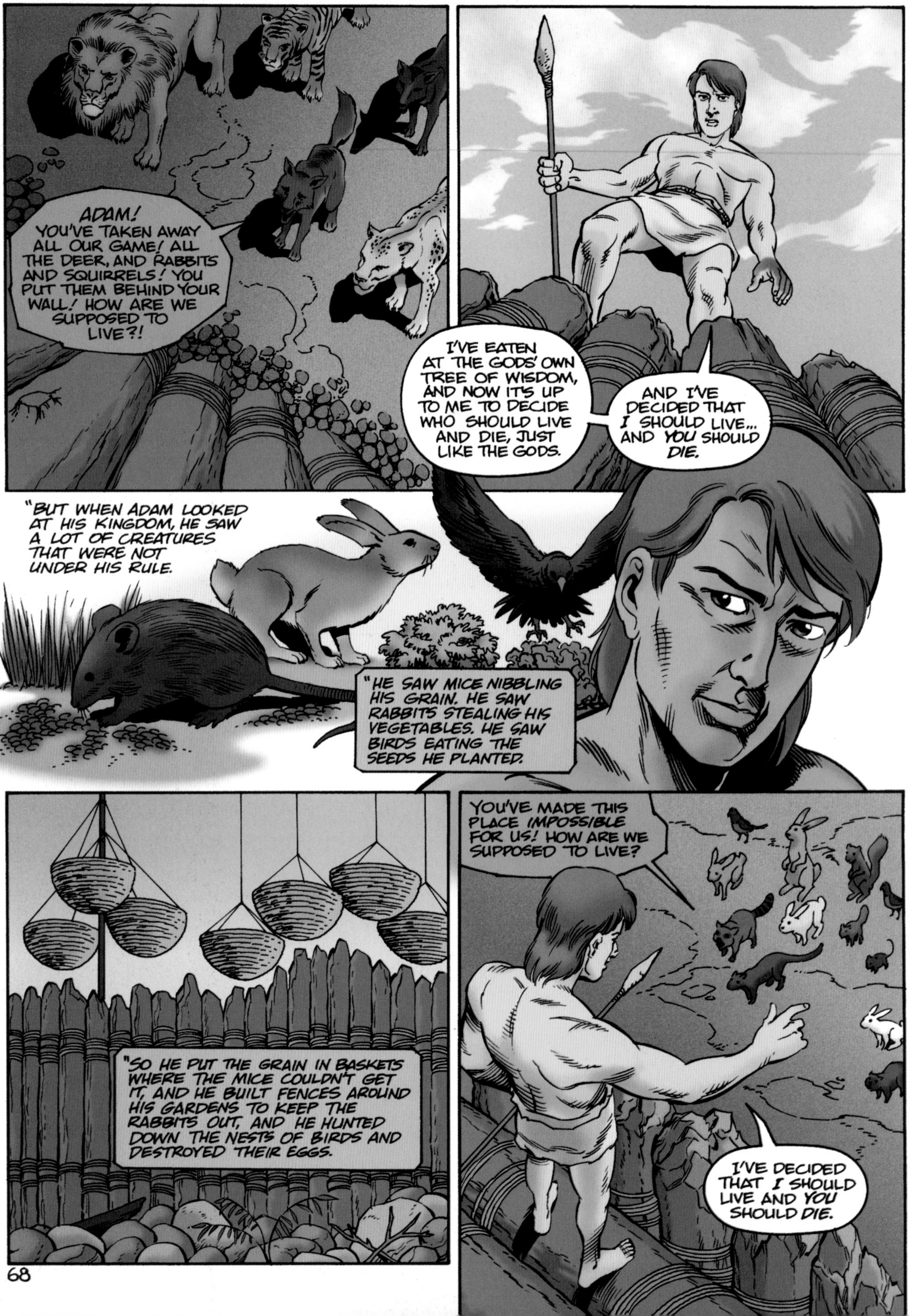
ADAM! YOU'VE TAKEN AWAY ALL OUR GAME! ALL THE DEER, AND RABBITS AND SQUIRRELS! YOU PUT THEM BEHIND YOUR WALL! HOW ARE WE SUPPOSED TO LIVE?!
I'VE EATEN AT THE GODS' OWN TREE OF WISDOM, AND NOW IT'S UP TO ME TO DECIDE WHO SHOULD LIVE AND DIE, JUST LIKE THE GODS.
AND I'VE DECIDED THAT I SHOULD LIVE... AND YOU SHOULD DIE.
"BUT WHEN ADAM LOOKED AT HIS KINGDOM, HE SAW A LOT OF CREATURES THAT WERE NOT UNDER HIS RULE.
"HE SAW MICE NIBBLING HIS GRAIN. HE SAW RABBITS STEALING HIS VEGETABLES. HE SAW BIRDS EATING THE SEEDS HE PLANTED.
"SO HE PUT THE GRAIN IN BASKETS WHERE THE MICE COULDN'T GET IT, AND HE BUILT FENCES AROUND HIS GARDENS TO KEEP THE RABBITS OUT, AND HE HUNTED DOWN THE NESTS OF BIRDS AND DESTROYED THEIR EGGS.
YOU'VE MADE THIS PLACE IMPOSSIBLE FOR US! HOW ARE WE SUPPOSED TO LIVE?
I'VE DECIDED THAT I SHOULD LIVE AND YOU SHOULD DIE.

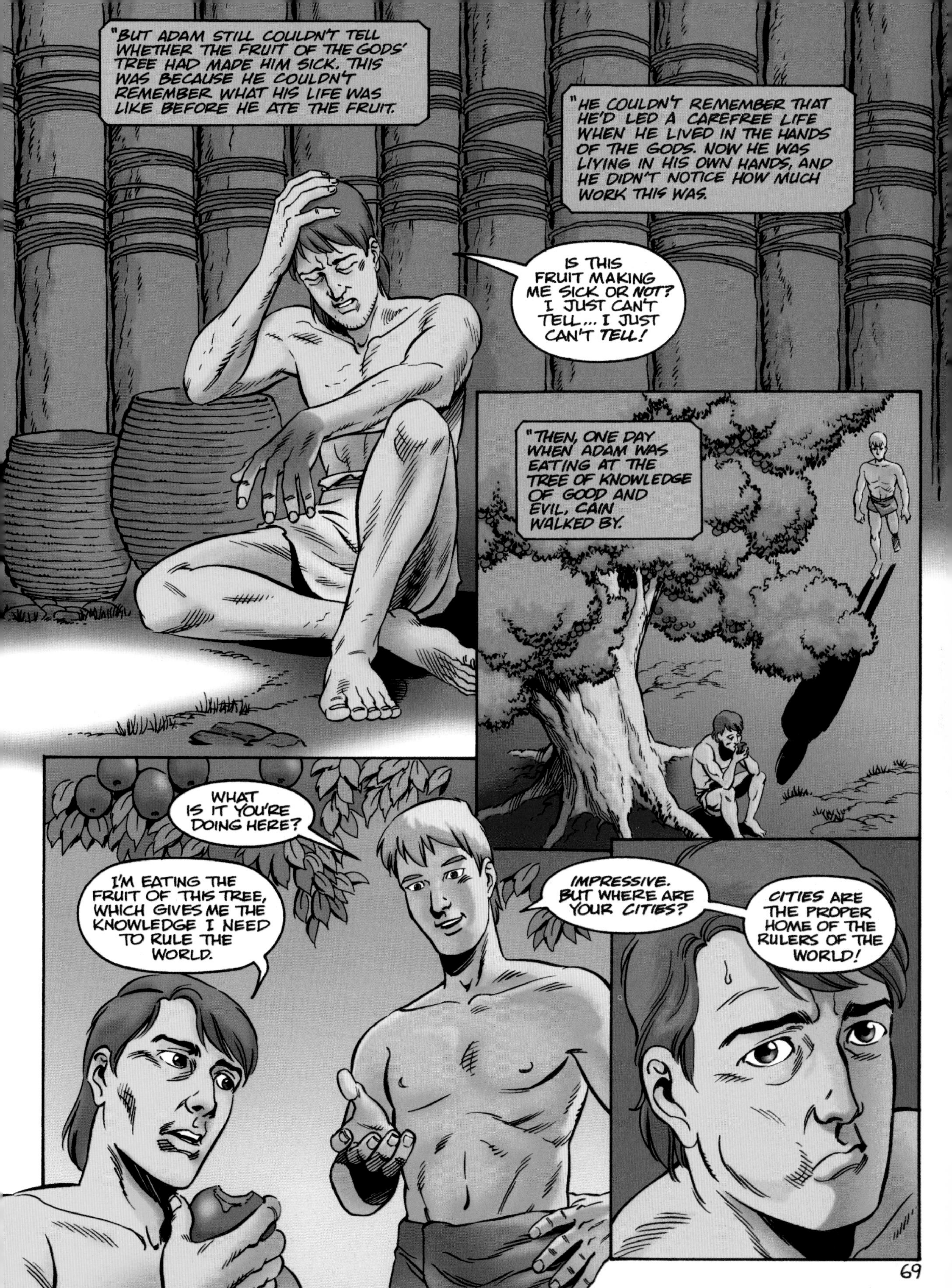
"BUT ADAM STILL COULDN'T TELL WHETHER THE FRUIT OF THE GODS' TREE HAD MADE HIM SICK. THIS WAS BECAUSE HE COULDN'T REMEMBER WHAT HIS LIFE WAS LIKE BEFORE HE ATE THE FRUIT.
"HE COULDN'T REMEMBER THAT HE'D LED A CAREFREE LIFE WHEN HE LIVED IN THE HANDS OF THE GODS. NOW HE WAS LIVING IN HIS OWN HANDS, AND HE DIDN'T NOTICE HOW MUCH WORK THIS WAS.
IS THIS FRUIT MAKING ME SICK OR NOT? I JUST CAN'T TELL... I JUST CAN'T TELL!
"THEN, ONE DAY WHEN ADAM WAS EATING AT THE TREE OF KNOWLEDGE OF GOOD AND EVIL, CAIN WALKED BY.
WHAT IS IT YOU'RE DOING HERE?
I'M EATING THE FRUIT OF THIS TREE, WHICH GIVES ME THE KNOWLEDGE I NEED TO RULE THE WORLD.
IMPRESSIVE. BUT WHERE ARE YOUR CITIES?
CITIES ARE THE PROPER HOME OF THE RULERS OF THE WORLD!

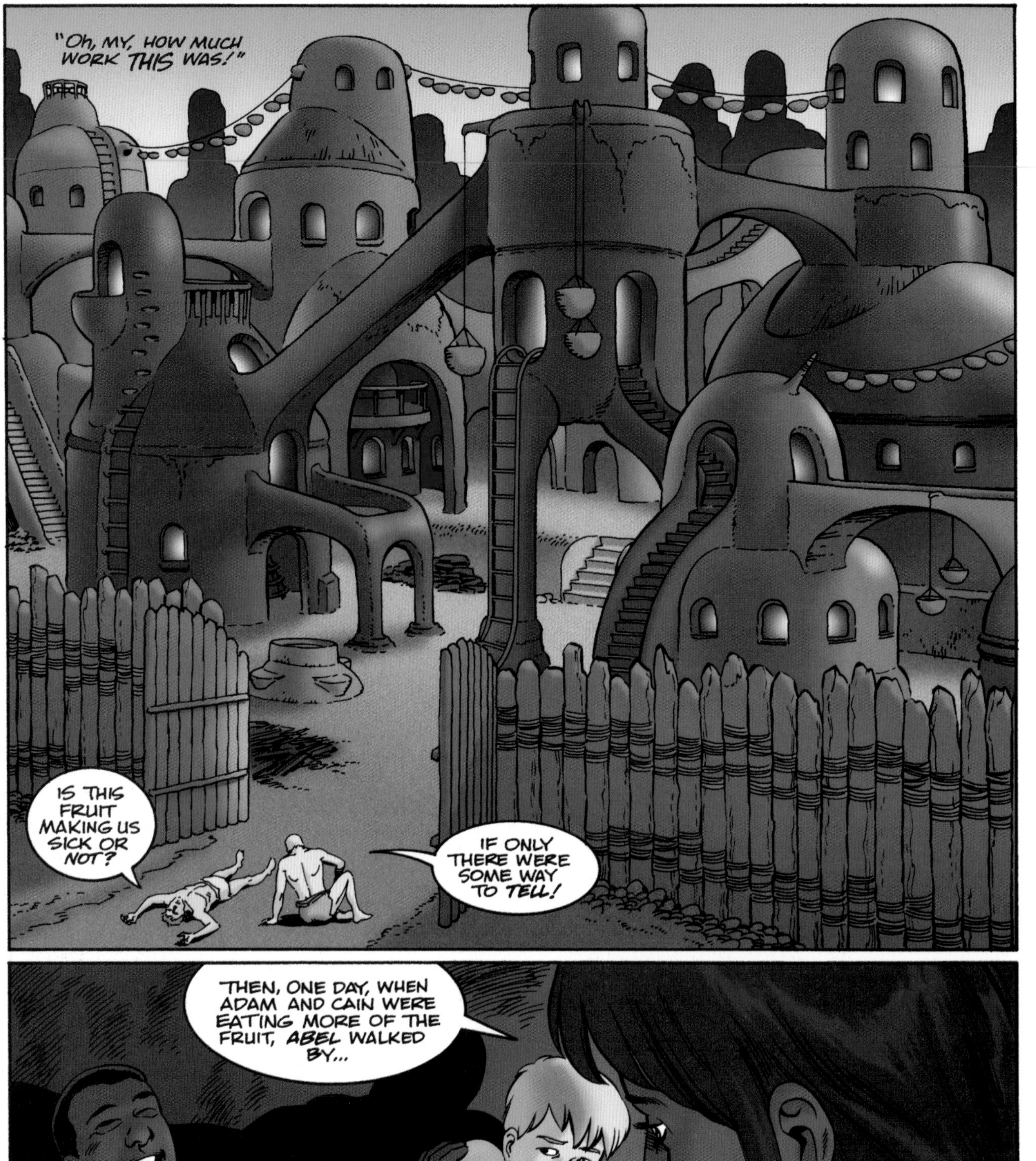
"Oh, MY, HOW MUCH WORK THIS WAS!"
IS THIS FRUIT MAKING US SICK OR NOT?
IF ONLY THERE WERE SOME WAY TO TELL!

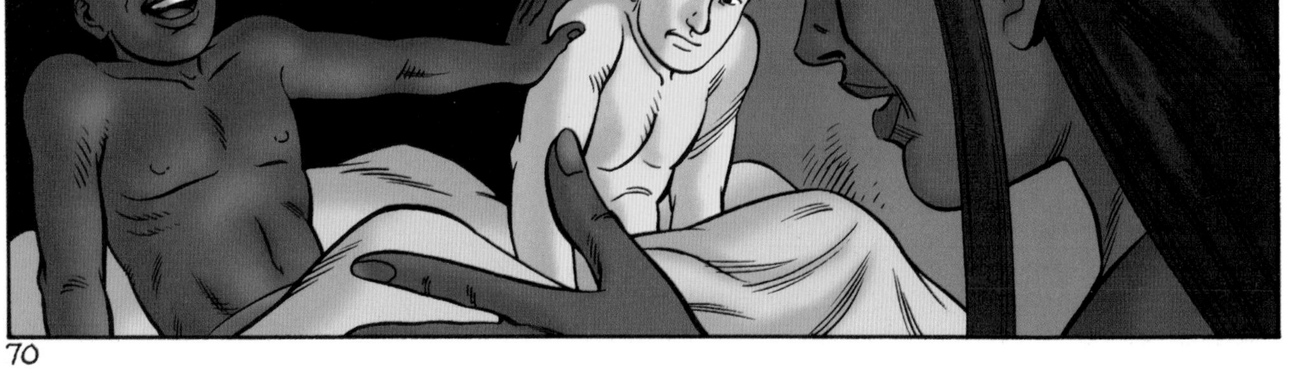
THEN, ONE DAY, WHEN ADAM AND CAIN WERE EATING MORE OF THE FRUIT, ABEL WALKED BY...

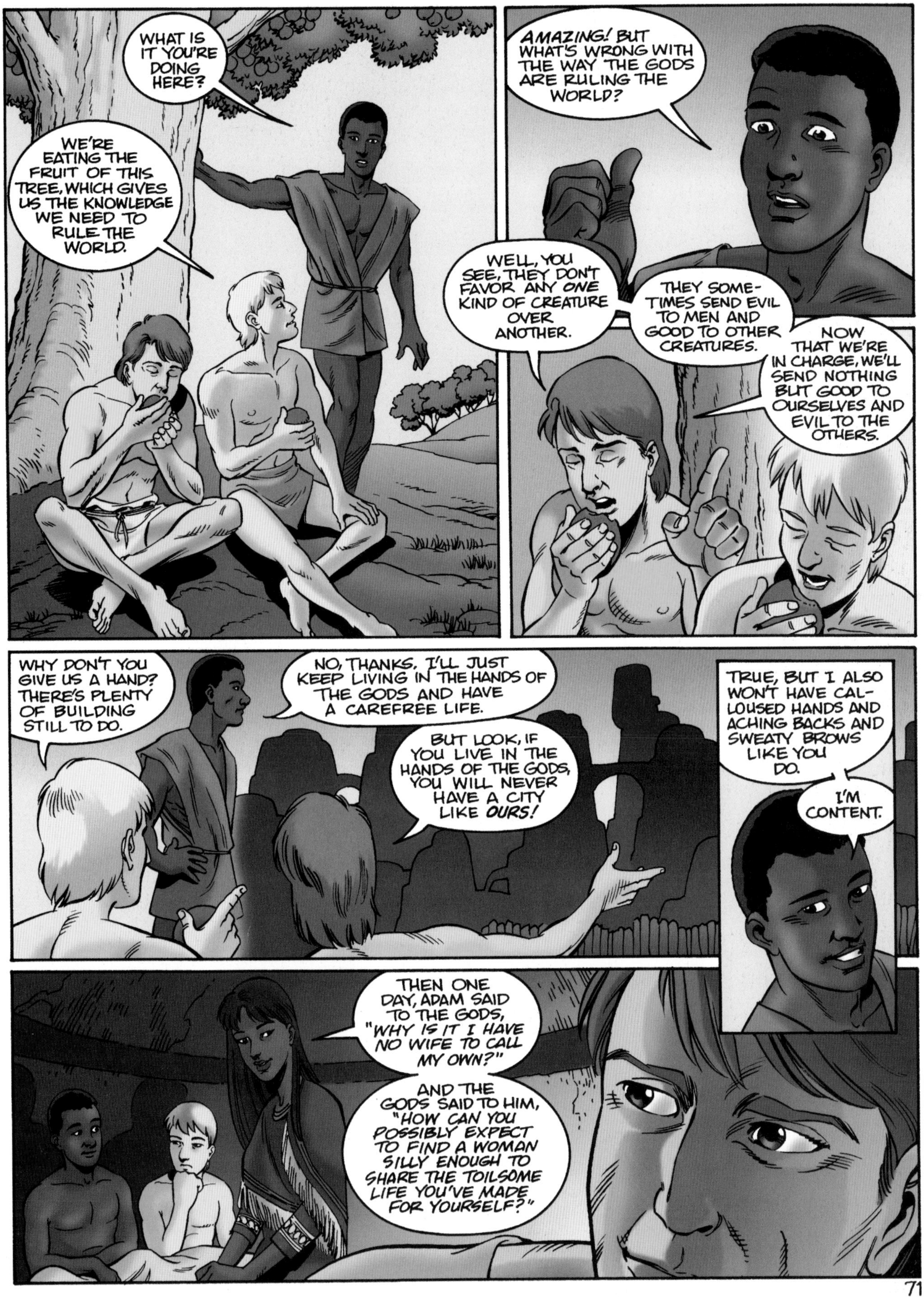
WHAT IS IT YOU'RE DOING HERE?
WE'RE EATING THE FRUIT OF THIS TREE, WHICH GIVES US THE KNOWLEDGE WE NEED TO RULE THE WORLD.
AMAZING! BUT WHAT'S WRONG WITH THE WAY THE GODS ARE RULING THE WORLD?
WELL, YOU SEE, THEY DON'T FAVOR ANY ONE KIND OF CREATURE OVER ANOTHER.
THEY SOMETIMES SEND EVIL TO MEN AND GOOD TO OTHER CREATURES.
NOW THAT WE'RE IN CHARGE, WE'LL SEND NOTHING BUT GOOD TO OURSELVES AND EVIL TO THE OTHERS.
WHY DON'T YOU GIVE US A HAND? THERE'S PLENTY OF BUILDING STILL TO DO.
NO, THANKS. I'LL JUST KEEP LIVING IN THE HANDS OF THE GODS AND HAVE A CAREFREE LIFE.
BUT LOOK, IF YOU LIVE IN THE HANDS OF THE GODS, YOU WILL NEVER HAVE A CITY LIKE OURS!
TRUE, BUT I ALSO WON'T HAVE CALLOUSED HANDS AND ACHING BACKS AND SWEATY BROWS LIKE YOU DO.
I'M CONTENT.
THEN ONE DAY, ADAM SAID TO THE GODS, "WHY IS IT I HAVE NO WIFE TO CALL MY OWN?"
AND THE GODS SAID TO HIM, "HOW CAN YOU POSSIBLY EXPECT TO FIND A WOMAN SILLY ENOUGH TO SHARE THE TOILSOME LIFE YOU'VE MADE FOR YOURSELF?"

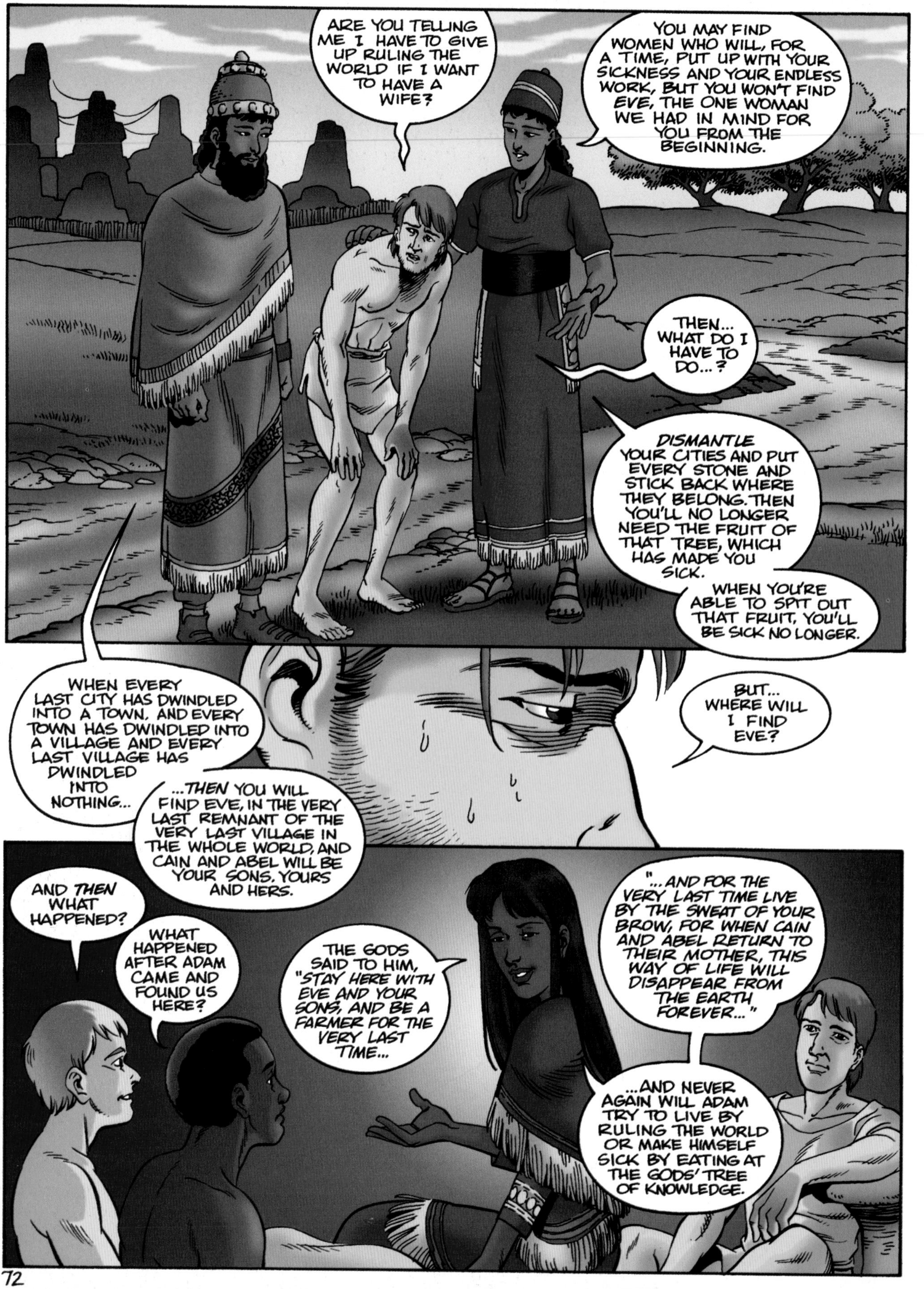
ARE YOU TELLING ME I HAVE TO GIVE UP RULING THE WORLD IF I WANT TO HAVE A WIFE?
YOU MAY FIND WOMEN WHO WILL, FOR A TIME, PUT UP WITH YOUR SICKNESS AND YOUR ENDLESS WORK, BUT YOU WON'T FIND EVE, THE ONE WOMAN WE HAD IN MIND FOR YOU FROM THE BEGINNING.
THEN... WHAT DO I HAVE TO DO...?
DISMANTLE YOUR CITIES AND PUT EVERY STONE AND STICK BACK WHERE THEY BELONG. THEN YOU'LL NO LONGER NEED THE FRUIT OF THAT TREE, WHICH HAS MADE YOU SICK.
WHEN YOU'RE ABLE TO SPIT OUT THAT FRUIT, YOU'LL BE SICK NO LONGER.
BUT... WHERE WILL I FIND EVE?
WHEN EVERY LAST CITY HAS DWINDLED INTO A TOWN, AND EVERY TOWN HAS DWINDLED INTO A VILLAGE AND EVERY LAST VILLAGE HAS DWINDLED INTO NOTHING...
...THEN YOU WILL FIND EVE, IN THE VERY LAST REMNANT OF THE VERY LAST VILLAGE IN THE WHOLE WORLD, AND CAIN AND ABEL WILL BE YOUR SONS. YOURS AND HERS.
AND THEN WHAT HAPPENED?
WHAT HAPPENED AFTER ADAM CAME AND FOUND US HERE?
THE GODS SAID TO HIM, "STAY HERE WITH EVE AND YOUR SONS, AND BE A FARMER FOR THE VERY LAST TIME...
"...AND FOR THE VERY LAST TIME LIVE BY THE SWEAT OF YOUR BROW, FOR WHEN CAIN AND ABEL RETURN TO THEIR MOTHER, THIS WAY OF LIFE WILL DISAPPEAR FROM THE EARTH FOREVER..."
...AND NEVER AGAIN WILL ADAM TRY TO LIVE BY RULING THE WORLD OR MAKE HIMSELF SICK BY EATING AT THE GODS' TREE OF KNOWLEDGE.

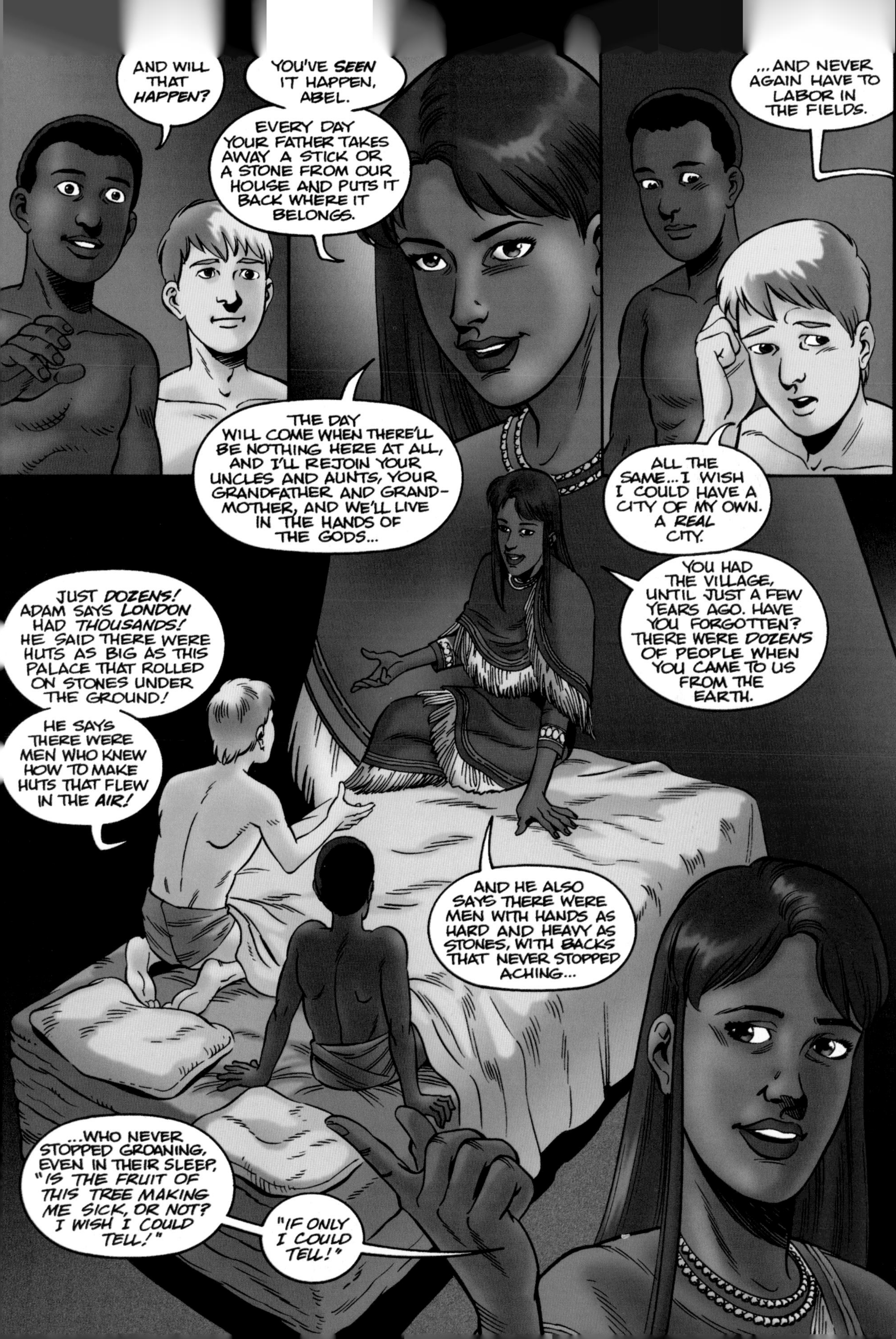

AND WILL THAT HAPPEN?
YOU'VE SEEN IT HAPPEN, ABEL.
EVERY DAY YOUR FATHER TAKES AWAY A STICK OR A STONE FROM OUR HOUSE AND PUTS IT BACK WHERE IT BELONGS.
THE DAY WILL COME WHEN THERE'LL BE NOTHING HERE AT ALL, AND I'LL REJOIN YOUR UNCLES AND AUNTS, YOUR GRANDFATHER AND GRAND-MOTHER, AND WE'LL LIVE IN THE HANDS OF THE GODS...
...AND NEVER AGAIN HAVE TO LABOR IN THE FIELDS.
ALL THE SAME... I WISH I COULD HAVE A CITY OF MY OWN. A REAL CITY.
YOU HAD THE VILLAGE, UNTIL JUST A FEW YEARS AGO. HAVE YOU FORGOTTEN? THERE WERE DOZENS OF PEOPLE WHEN YOU CAME TO US FROM THE EARTH.
JUST DOZENS! ADAM SAYS LONDON HAD THOUSANDS! HE SAID THERE WERE HUTS AS BIG AS THIS PALACE THAT ROLLED ON STONES UNDER THE GROUND!
HE SAYS THERE WERE MEN WHO KNEW HOW TO MAKE HUTS THAT FLEW IN THE AIR!
AND HE ALSO SAYS THERE WERE MEN WITH HANDS AS HARD AND HEAVY AS STONES, WITH BACKS THAT NEVER STOPPED ACHING...
...WHO NEVER STOPPED GROANING, EVEN IN THEIR SLEEP, "IS THE FRUIT OF THIS TREE MAKING ME SICK, OR NOT? I WISH I COULD TELL!"
"IF ONLY I COULD TELL!"

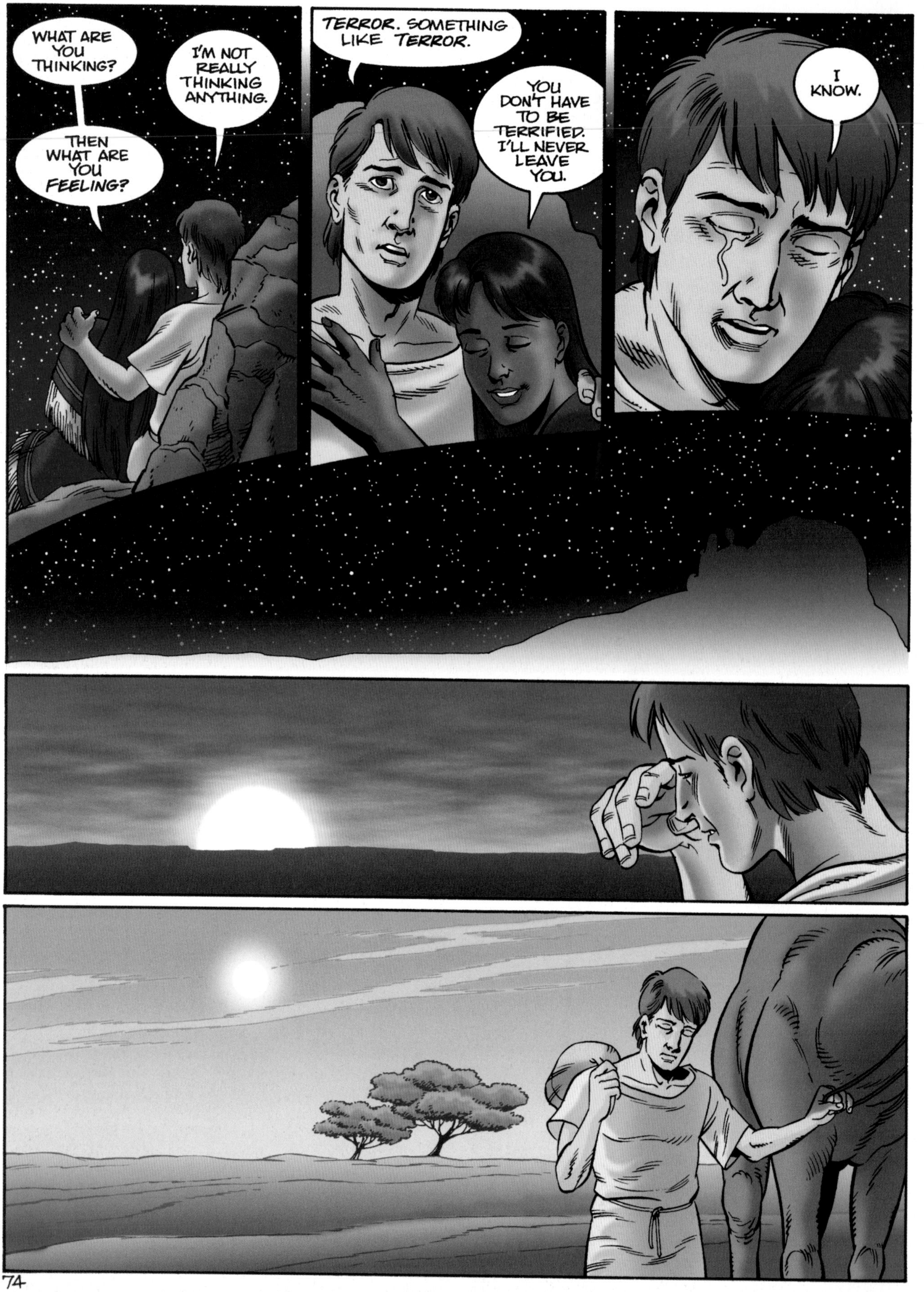
WHAT ARE YOU THINKING?
I'M NOT REALLY THINKING ANYTHING.
THEN WHAT ARE YOU FEELING?
TERROR. SOMETHING LIKE TERROR.
YOU DON'T HAVE TO BE TERRIFIED. I'LL NEVER LEAVE YOU.
I KNOW.

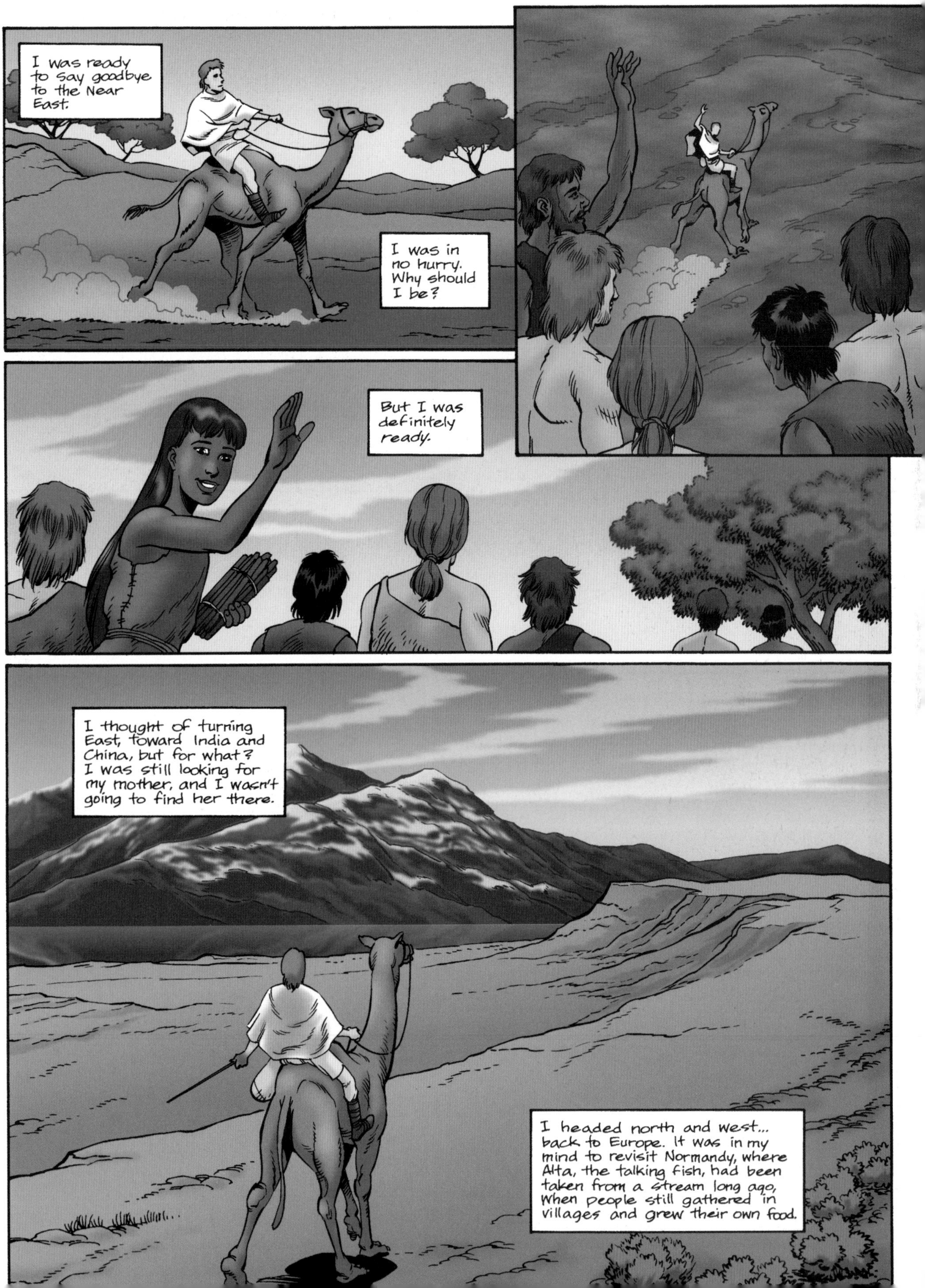

I was ready to say goodbye to the Near East.
I was in no hurry. Why should I be?
But I was definitely ready.
I thought of turning East, toward India and China, but for what? I was still looking for my mother, and I wasn't going to find her there.
I headed north and west... back to Europe. It was in my mind to revisit Normandy, where Alta, the talking fish, had been taken from a stream long ago, when people still gathered in villages and grew their own food.

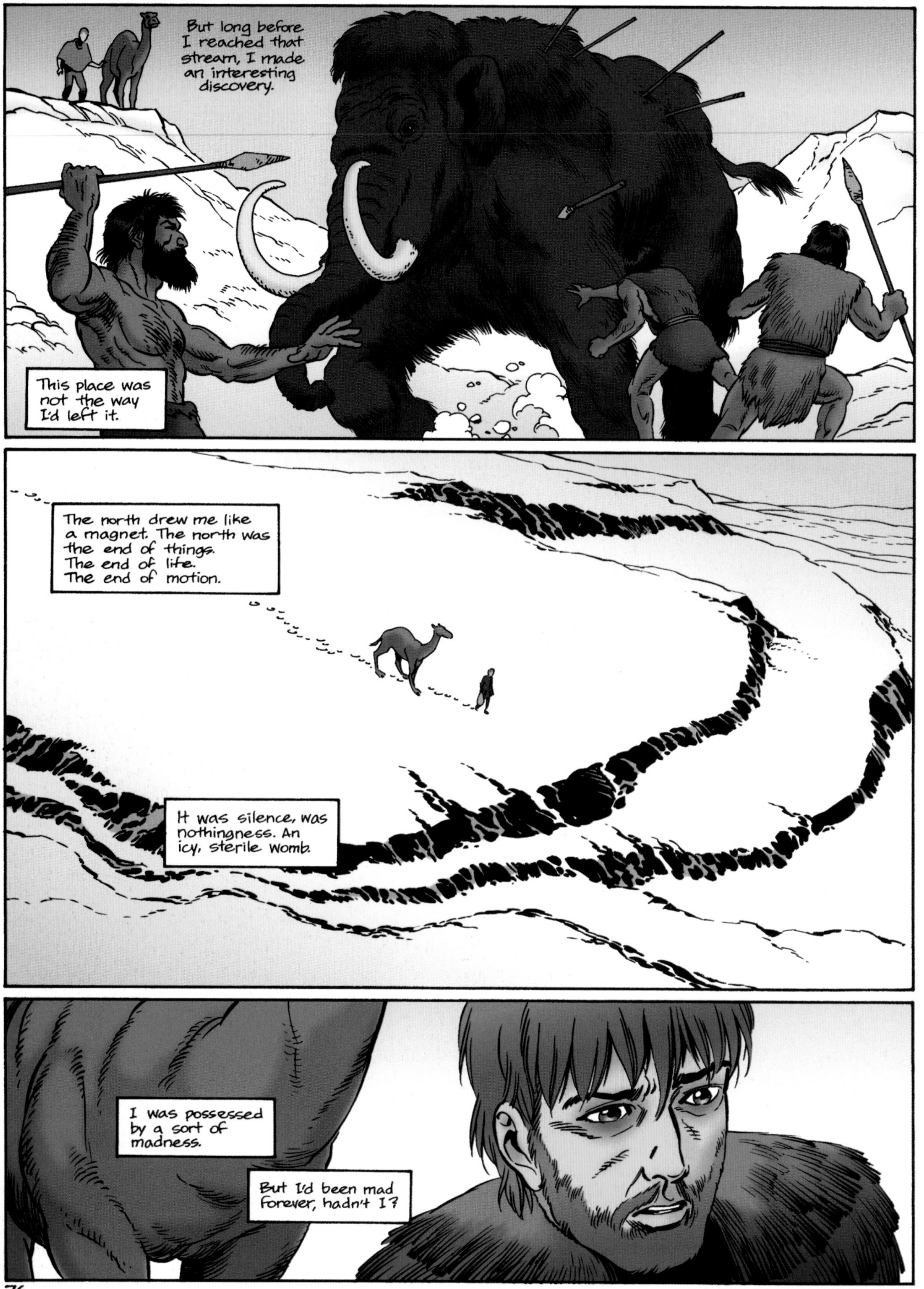
But long before I reached that stream, I made an interesting discovery.
This place was not the way I'd left it.
The north drew me like a magnet. The north was the end of things. The end of life. The end of motion.
It was silence, was nothingness. An icy, sterile womb.
I was possessed by a sort of madness.
But I'd been mad forever, hadn't I?

There came a point when Lilith refused to go on. I couldn't blame her.

She wouldn't come with me, and she wouldn't let me say goodbye.

Finally, I had to go on without her.

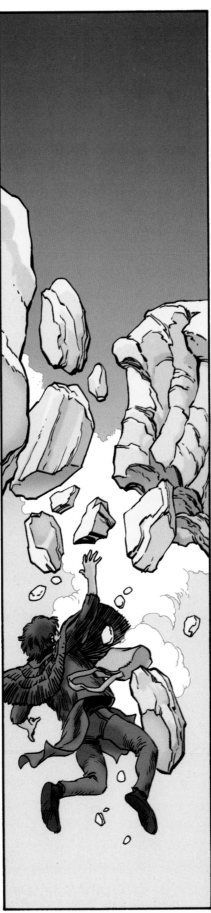

Buried under a thousand tons of snow, I knew I'd found the end of at least one thing in the world...

me.

Perhaps this was the way it was meant to be. Struggle was useless. Hopeless. But I wasn't unhappy. The journey was over. The struggle was over.

The discouragement was over.

In a few billion years, every speck of matter in the universe was going to come crashing together in the biggest crunch of all time. And I'd be there. There was no hurry. I decided to sleep.

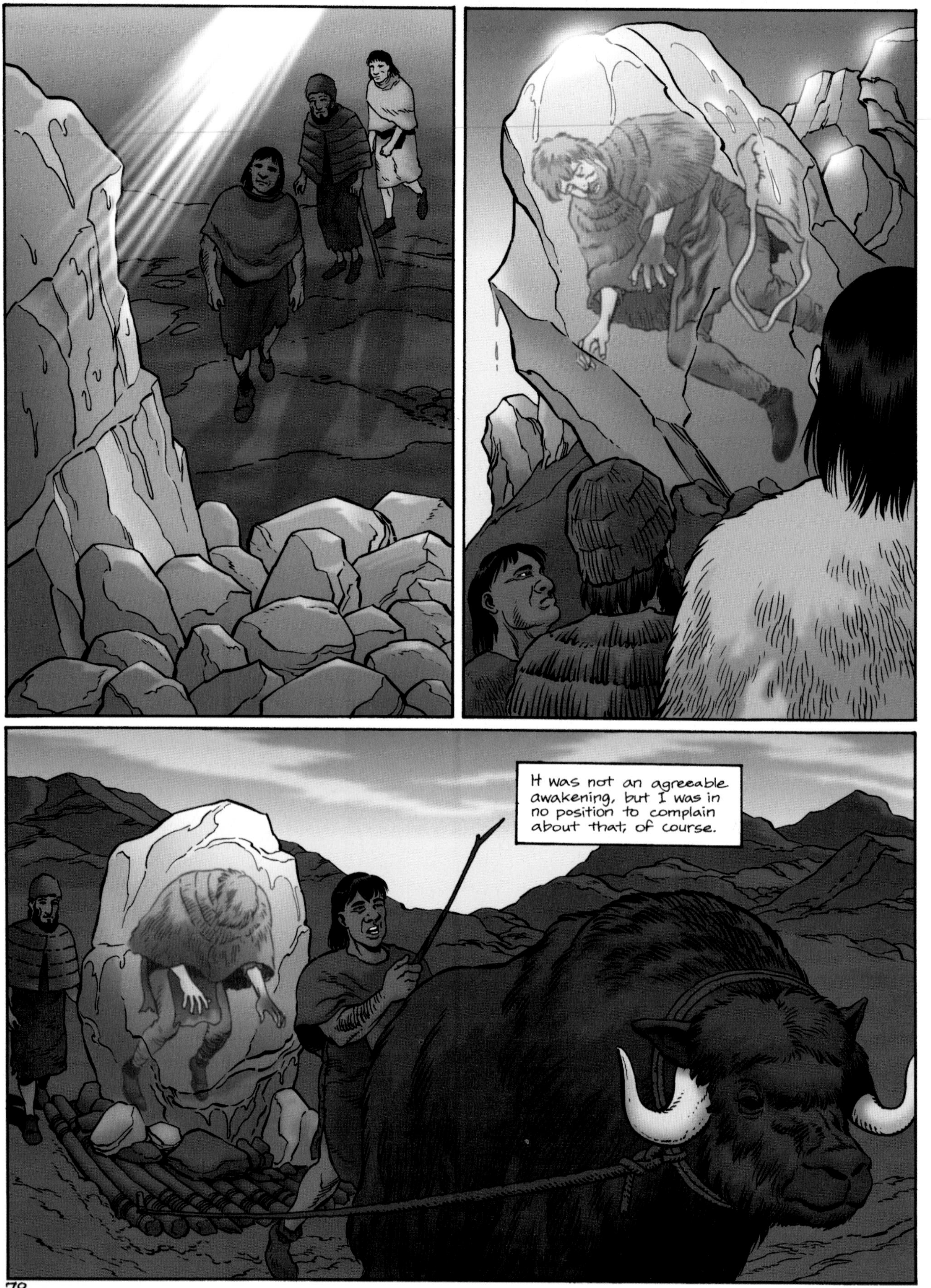
It was not an agreeable awakening, but I was in no position to complain about that, of course.

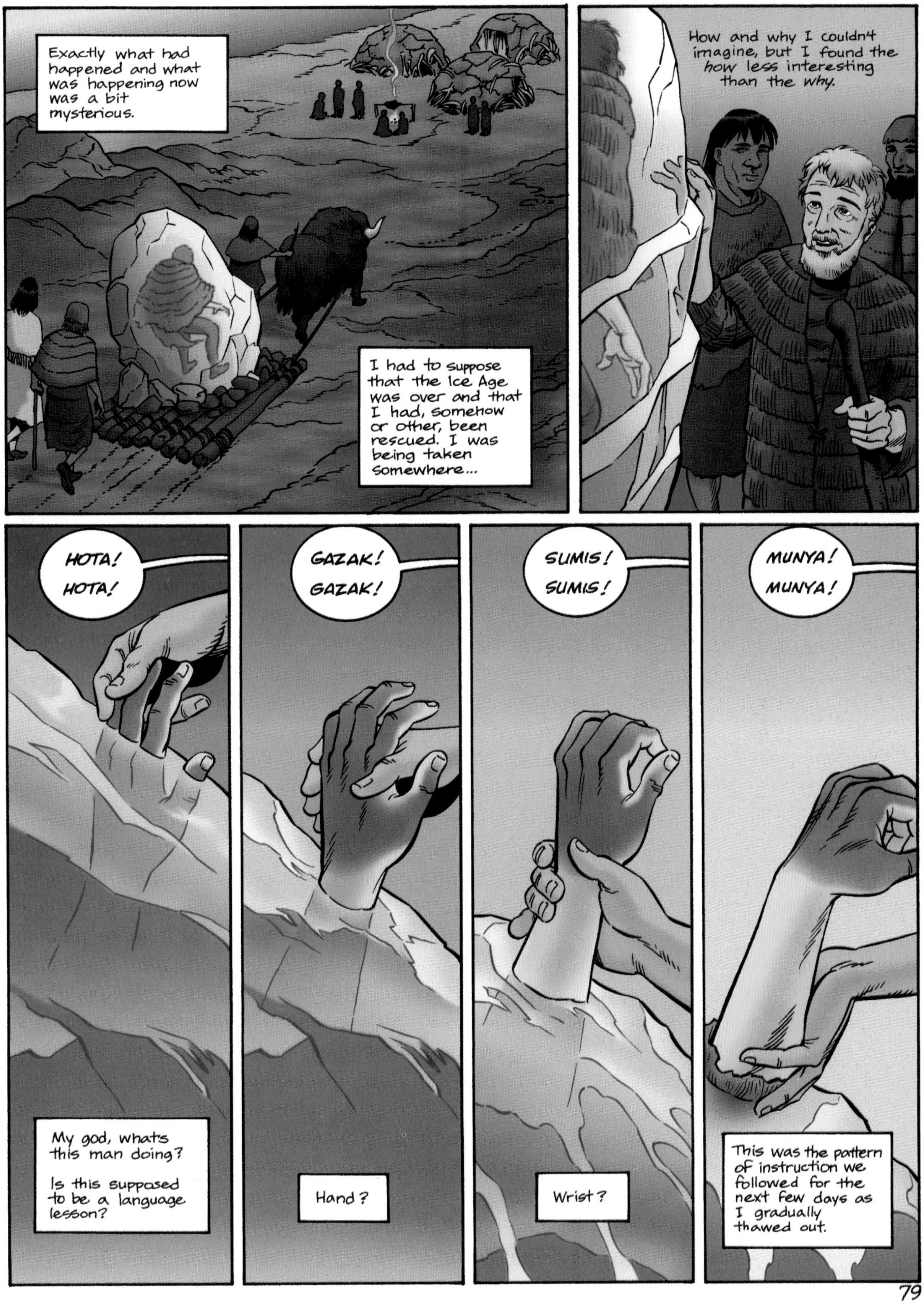
Exactly what had happened and what was happening now was a bit mysterious.
I had to suppose that the Ice Age was over and that I had, somehow or other, been rescued. I was being taken somewhere...
How and why I couldn't imagine, but I found the *how* less interesting than the *why*.
HOTA! HOTA!
My god, what's this man doing?
Is this supposed to be a language lesson?
GAZAK! GAZAK!
Hand?
SUMIS! SUMIS!
Wrist?
MUNYA! MUNYA!
This was the pattern of instruction we followed for the next few days as I gradually thawed out.

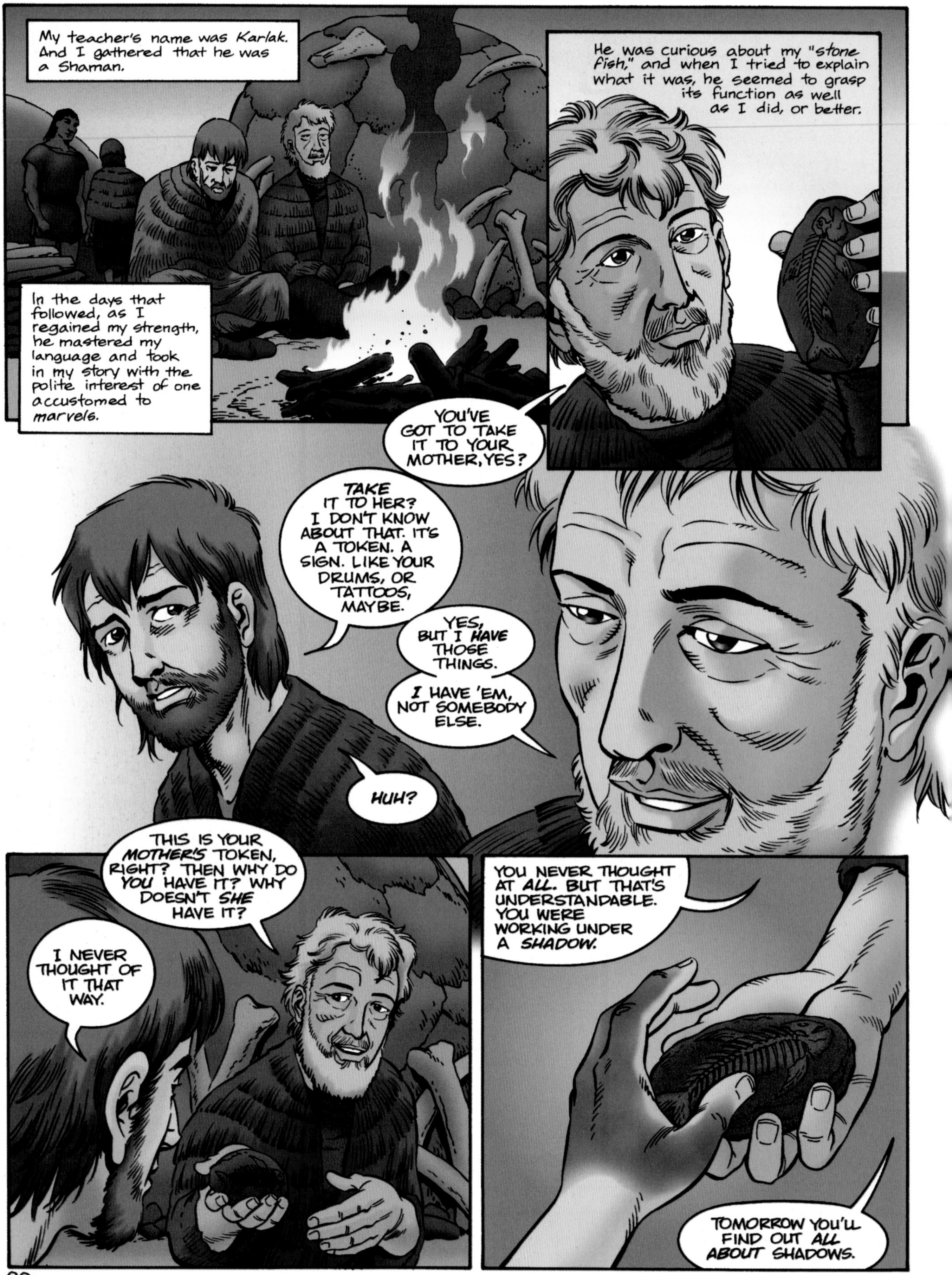
My teacher's name was Karlak. And I gathered that he was a Shaman.
In the days that followed, as I regained my strength, he mastered my language and took in my story with the polite interest of one accustomed to marvels.
He was curious about my "stone fish," and when I tried to explain what it was, he seemed to grasp its function as well as I did, or better.
YOU'VE GOT TO TAKE IT TO YOUR MOTHER, YES?
TAKE IT TO HER? I DON'T KNOW ABOUT THAT. IT'S A TOKEN. A SIGN. LIKE YOUR DRUMS, OR TATTOOS, MAYBE.
YES, BUT I HAVE THOSE THINGS.
I HAVE 'EM, NOT SOMEBODY ELSE.
HUH?
THIS IS YOUR MOTHER'S TOKEN, RIGHT? THEN WHY DO YOU HAVE IT? WHY DOESN'T SHE HAVE IT?
I NEVER THOUGHT OF IT THAT WAY.
YOU NEVER THOUGHT AT ALL. BUT THAT'S UNDERSTANDABLE. YOU WERE WORKING UNDER A SHADOW.
TOMORROW YOU'LL FIND OUT ALL ABOUT SHADOWS.

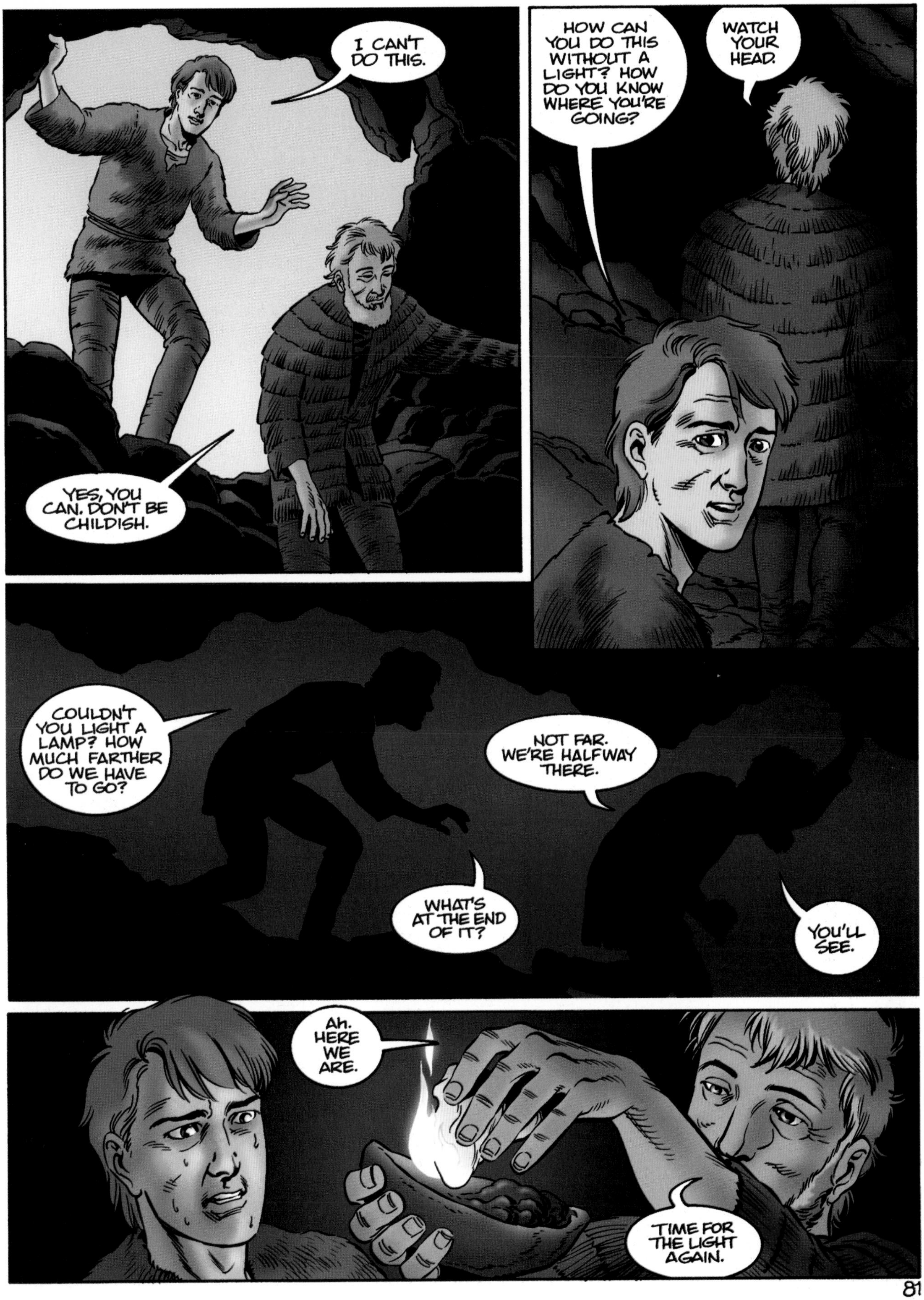
I CAN'T DO THIS.
YES, YOU CAN. DON'T BE CHILDISH.
HOW CAN YOU DO THIS WITHOUT A LIGHT? HOW DO YOU KNOW WHERE YOU'RE GOING?
WATCH YOUR HEAD.
COULDN'T YOU LIGHT A LAMP? HOW MUCH FARTHER DO WE HAVE TO GO?
NOT FAR. WE'RE HALFWAY THERE.
WHAT'S AT THE END OF IT?
YOU'LL SEE.
Ah. HERE WE ARE.
TIME FOR THE LIGHT AGAIN.

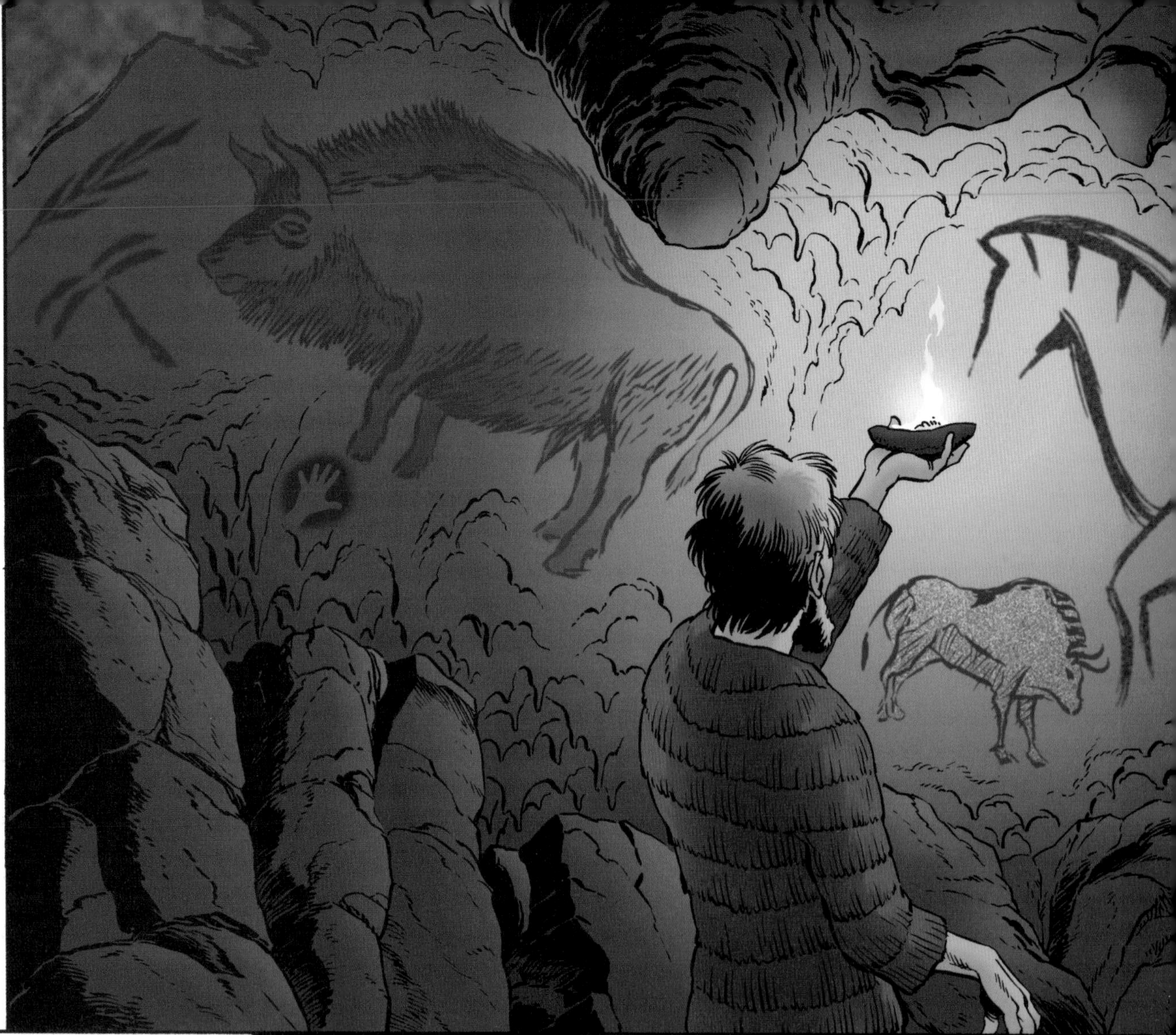

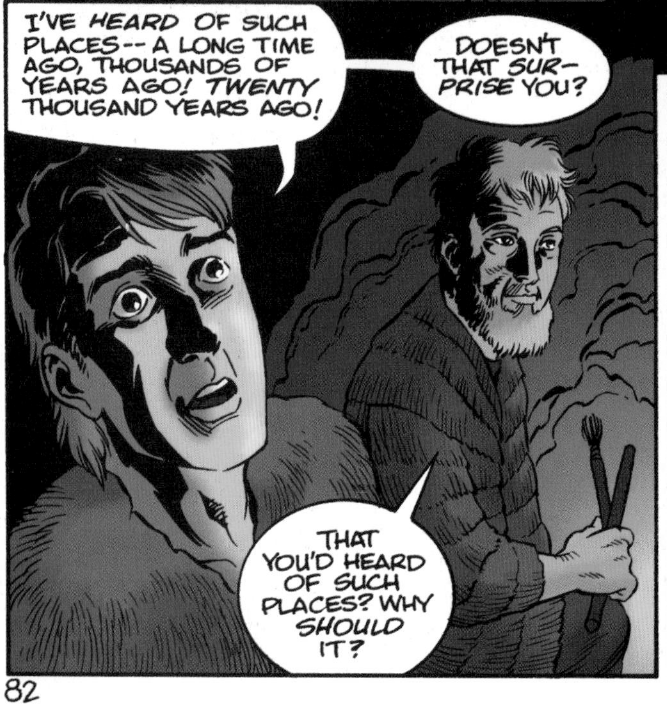
I'VE HEARD OF SUCH PLACES-- A LONG TIME AGO, THOUSANDS OF YEARS AGO! TWENTY THOUSAND YEARS AGO!
DOESN'T THAT SUR-PRISE YOU?
THAT YOU'D HEARD OF SUCH PLACES? WHY SHOULD IT?

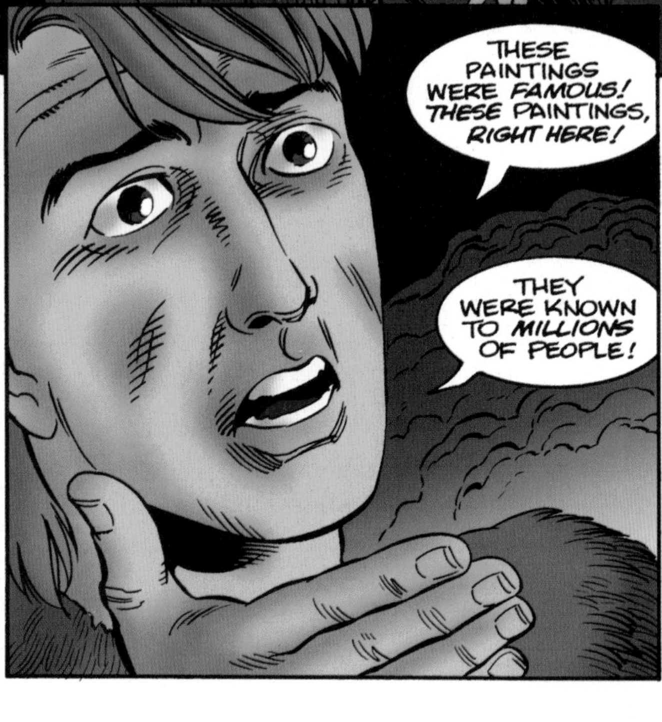
THESE PAINTINGS WERE FAMOUS! THESE PAINTINGS, RIGHT HERE!
THEY WERE KNOWN TO MILLIONS OF PEOPLE!

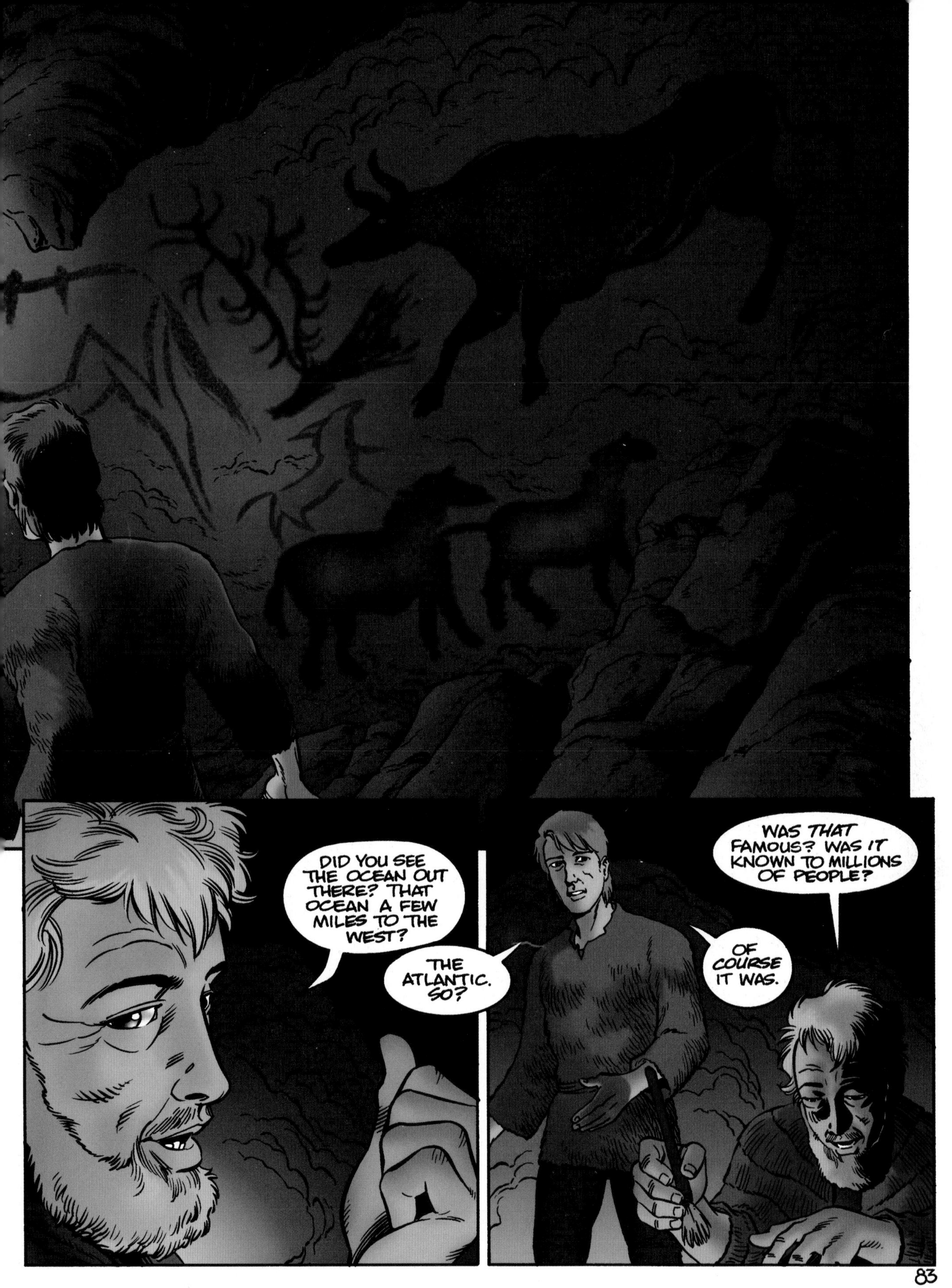
DID YOU SEE THE OCEAN OUT THERE? THAT OCEAN A FEW MILES TO THE WEST?
THE ATLANTIC. SO?
OF COURSE IT WAS.
WAS THAT FAMOUS? WAS IT KNOWN TO MILLIONS OF PEOPLE?

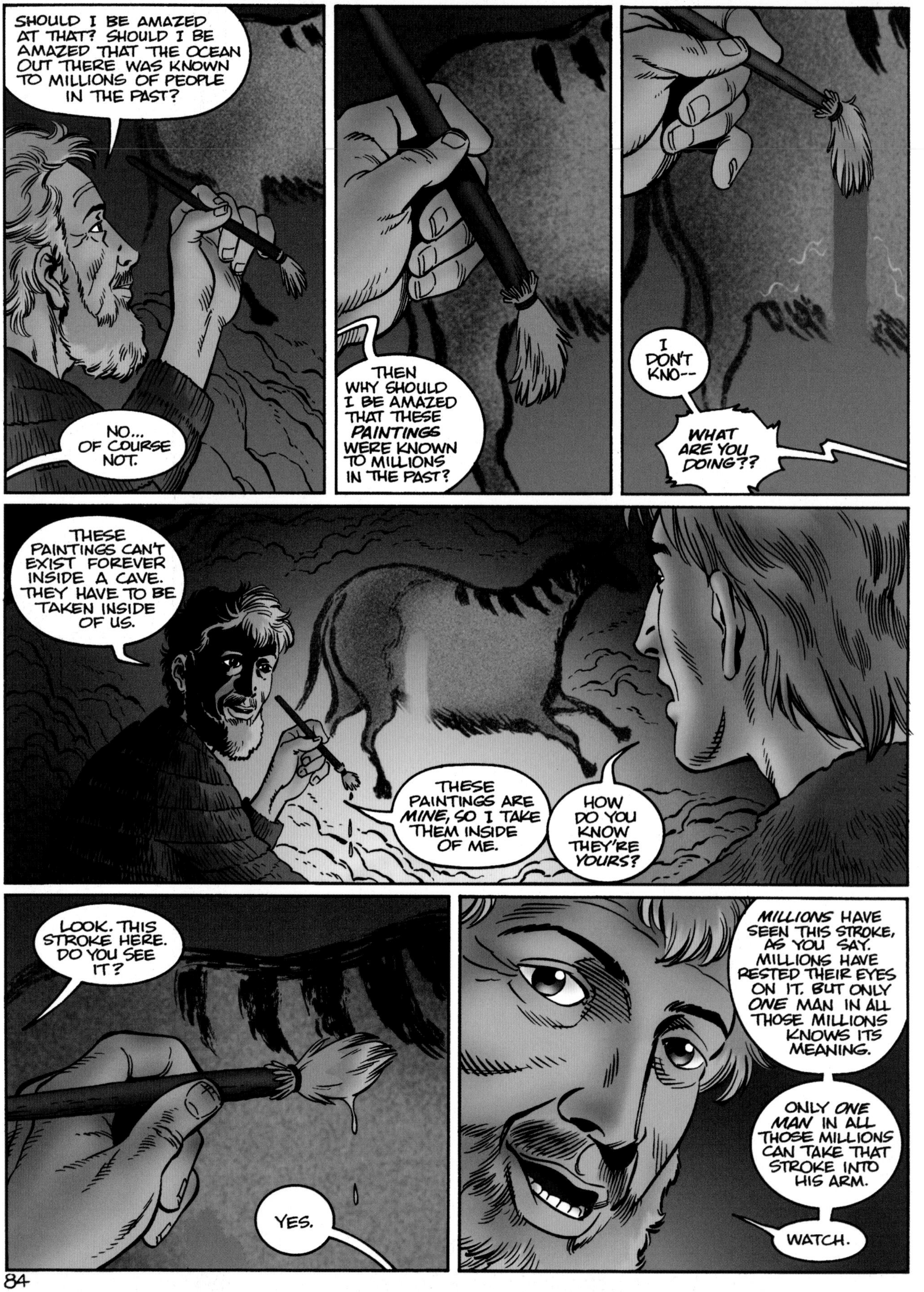
SHOULD I BE AMAZED AT THAT? SHOULD I BE AMAZED THAT THE OCEAN OUT THERE WAS KNOWN TO MILLIONS OF PEOPLE IN THE PAST?
NO... OF COURSE NOT.
THEN WHY SHOULD I BE AMAZED THAT THESE PAINTINGS WERE KNOWN TO MILLIONS IN THE PAST?
I DON'T KNO--
WHAT ARE YOU DOING??
THESE PAINTINGS CAN'T EXIST FOREVER INSIDE A CAVE. THEY HAVE TO BE TAKEN INSIDE OF US.
THESE PAINTINGS ARE MINE, SO I TAKE THEM INSIDE OF ME.
HOW DO YOU KNOW THEY'RE YOURS?
LOOK. THIS STROKE HERE. DO YOU SEE IT?
YES.
MILLIONS HAVE SEEN THIS STROKE, AS YOU SAY. MILLIONS HAVE RESTED THEIR EYES ON IT. BUT ONLY ONE MAN IN ALL THOSE MILLIONS KNOWS ITS MEANING.
ONLY ONE MAN IN ALL THOSE MILLIONS CAN TAKE THAT STROKE INTO HIS ARM.
WATCH.

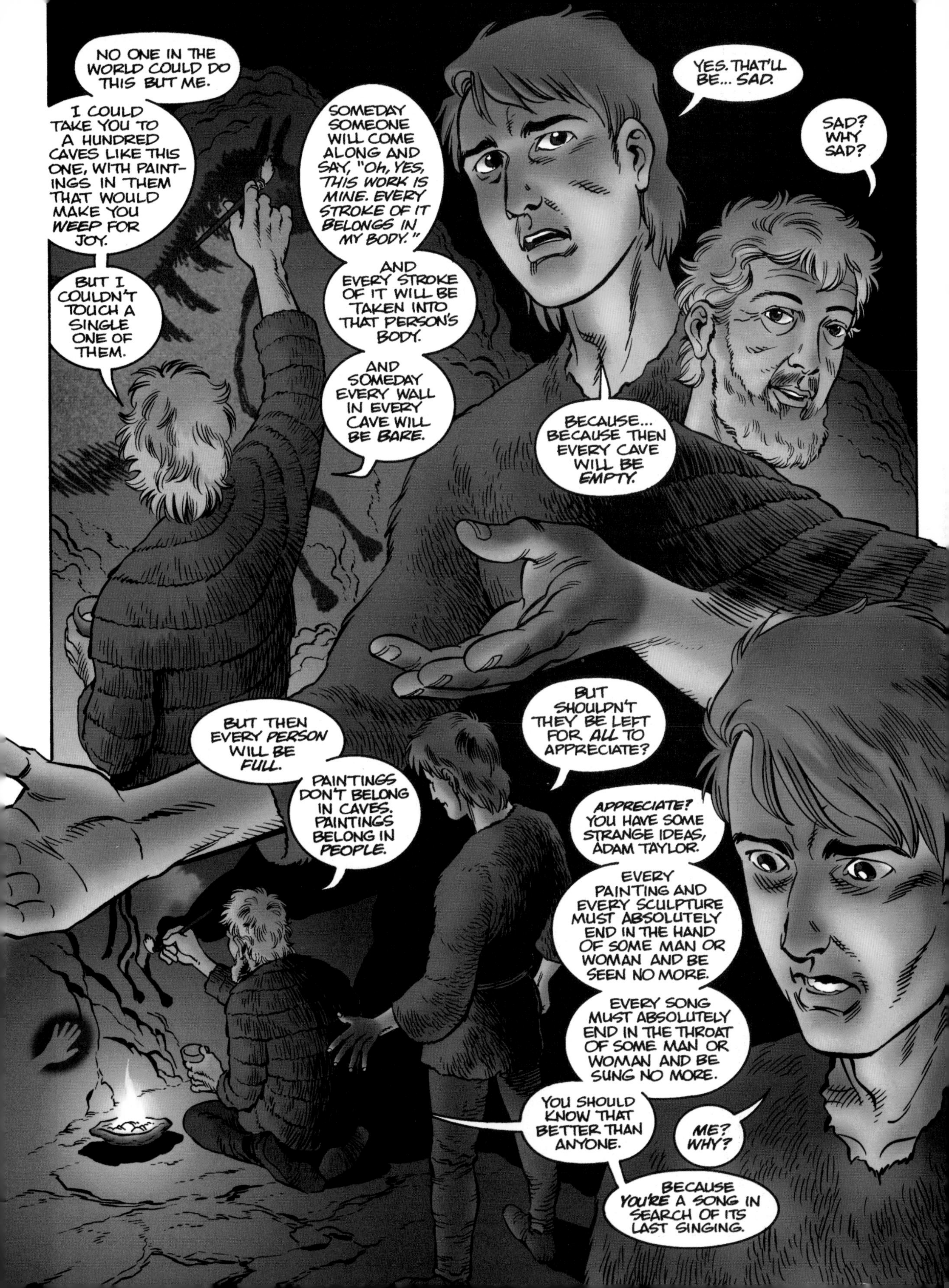

NO ONE IN THE WORLD COULD DO THIS BUT ME.
I COULD TAKE YOU TO A HUNDRED CAVES LIKE THIS ONE, WITH PAINTINGS IN THEM THAT WOULD MAKE YOU *WEEP* FOR JOY.
BUT I COULDN'T TOUCH A SINGLE ONE OF THEM.
SOMEDAY SOMEONE WILL COME ALONG AND SAY, "*Oh, YES, THIS WORK IS MINE. EVERY STROKE OF IT BELONGS IN MY BODY.*"
AND EVERY STROKE OF IT WILL BE TAKEN INTO THAT PERSON'S BODY.
AND SOMEDAY EVERY WALL IN EVERY CAVE WILL BE *BARE*.
YES. THAT'LL BE... SAD.
SAD? WHY SAD?
BECAUSE... BECAUSE THEN EVERY CAVE WILL BE *EMPTY*.
BUT THEN EVERY *PERSON* WILL BE *FULL*.
PAINTINGS DON'T BELONG IN CAVES. PAINTINGS BELONG IN *PEOPLE*.
BUT SHOULDN'T THEY BE LEFT FOR *ALL* TO APPRECIATE?
APPRECIATE? YOU HAVE SOME STRANGE IDEAS, ADAM TAYLOR.
EVERY PAINTING AND EVERY SCULPTURE MUST ABSOLUTELY END IN THE HAND OF SOME MAN OR WOMAN AND BE SEEN NO MORE.
EVERY SONG MUST ABSOLUTELY END IN THE THROAT OF SOME MAN OR WOMAN AND BE SUNG NO MORE.
YOU SHOULD KNOW THAT BETTER THAN ANYONE.
ME? WHY?
BECAUSE *YOU'RE* A SONG IN SEARCH OF ITS LAST SINGING.

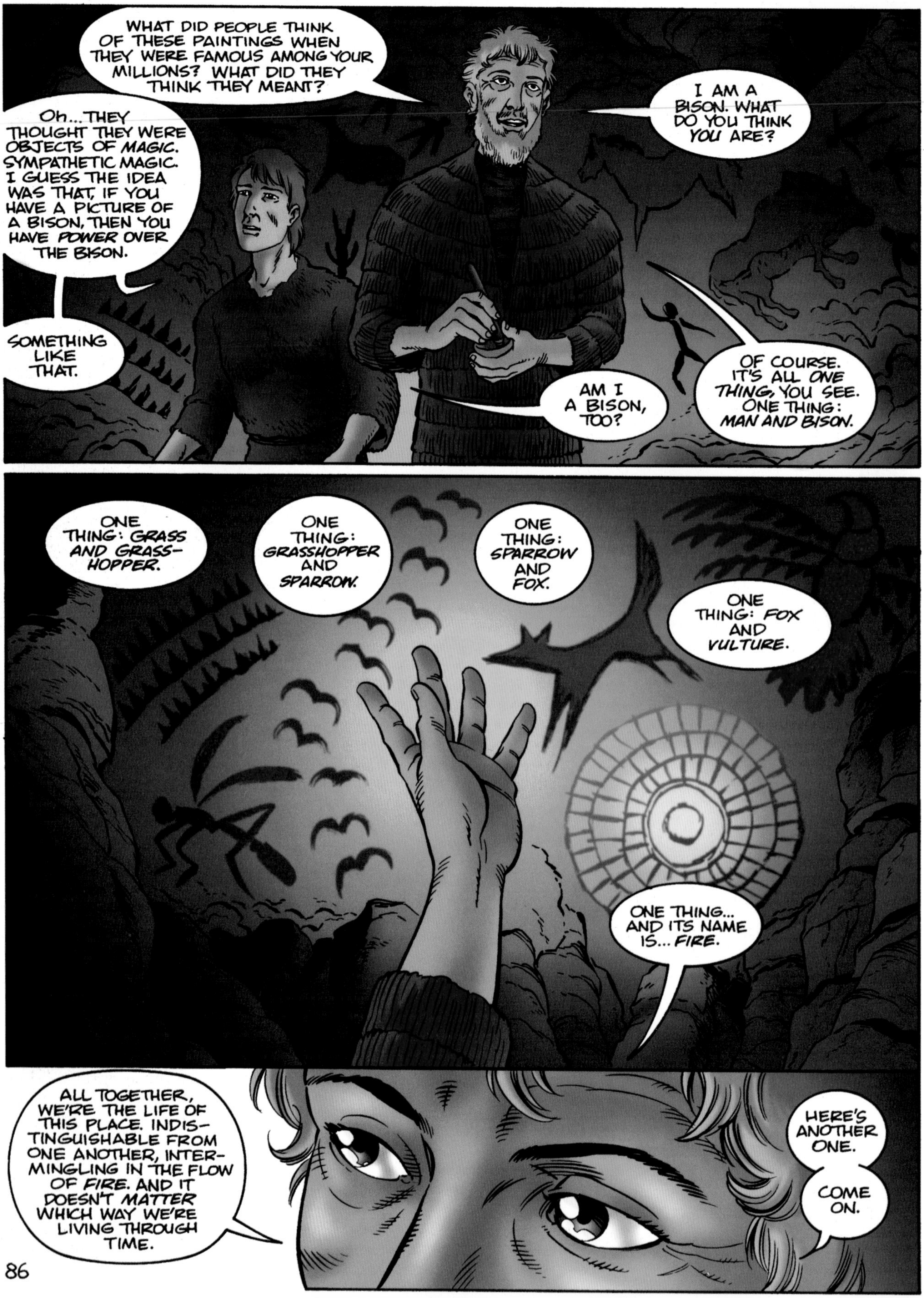
WHAT DID PEOPLE THINK OF THESE PAINTINGS WHEN THEY WERE FAMOUS AMONG YOUR MILLIONS? WHAT DID THEY THINK THEY MEANT?
Oh... THEY THOUGHT THEY WERE OBJECTS OF MAGIC. SYMPATHETIC MAGIC. I GUESS THE IDEA WAS THAT, IF YOU HAVE A PICTURE OF A BISON, THEN YOU HAVE POWER OVER THE BISON.
SOMETHING LIKE THAT.
I AM A BISON. WHAT DO YOU THINK YOU ARE?
AM I A BISON, TOO?
OF COURSE. IT'S ALL ONE THING, YOU SEE. ONE THING: MAN AND BISON.
ONE THING: GRASS AND GRASS-HOPPER.
ONE THING: GRASSHOPPER AND SPARROW.
ONE THING: SPARROW AND FOX.
ONE THING: FOX AND VULTURE.
ONE THING... AND ITS NAME IS... FIRE.
ALL TOGETHER, WE'RE THE LIFE OF THIS PLACE. INDIS-TINGUISHABLE FROM ONE ANOTHER, INTER-MINGLING IN THE FLOW OF FIRE. AND IT DOESN'T MATTER WHICH WAY WE'RE LIVING THROUGH TIME.
HERE'S ANOTHER ONE.
COME ON.

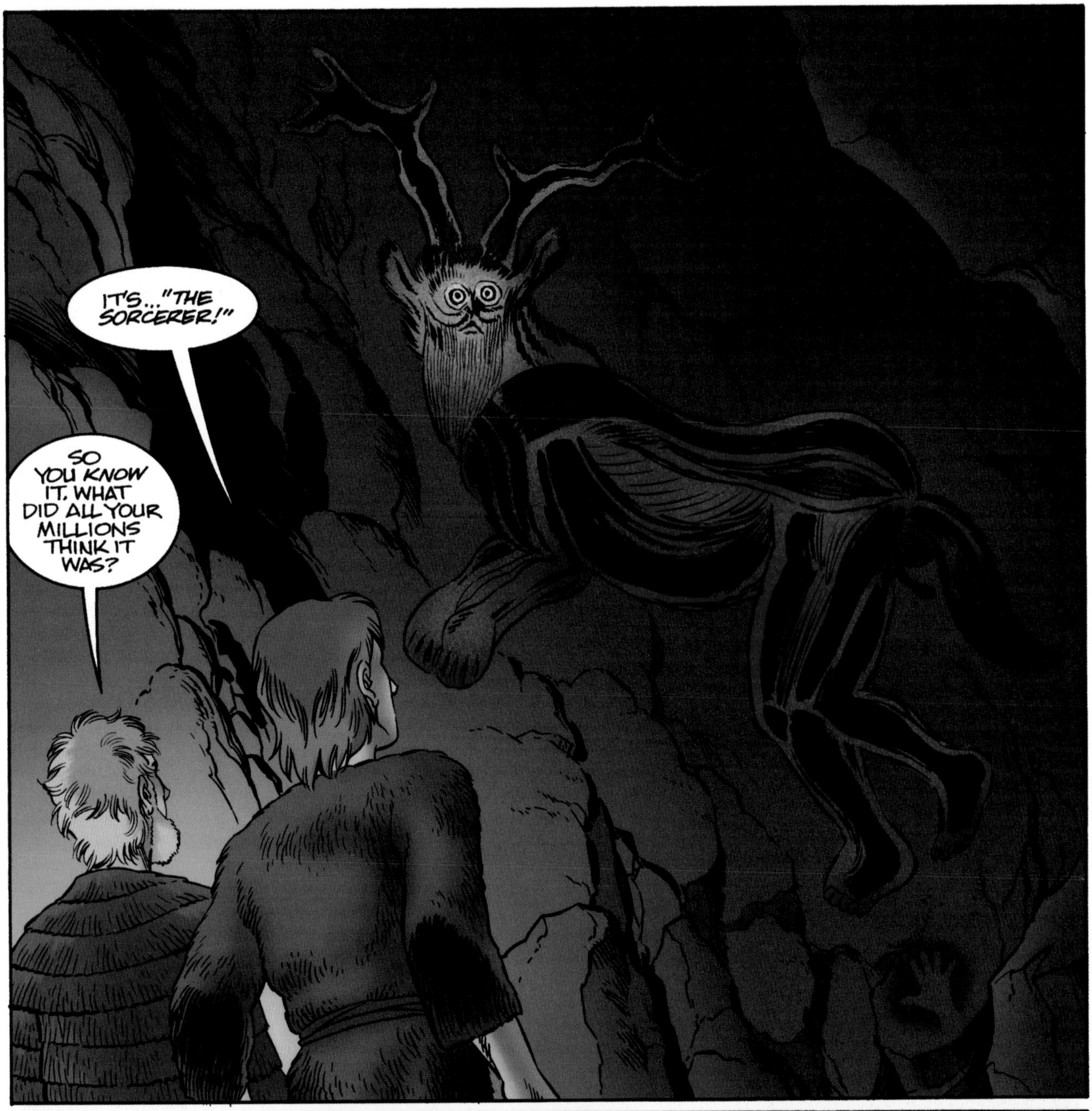
IT'S..."THE SORCERER!"
SO YOU KNOW IT. WHAT DID ALL YOUR MILLIONS THINK IT WAS?

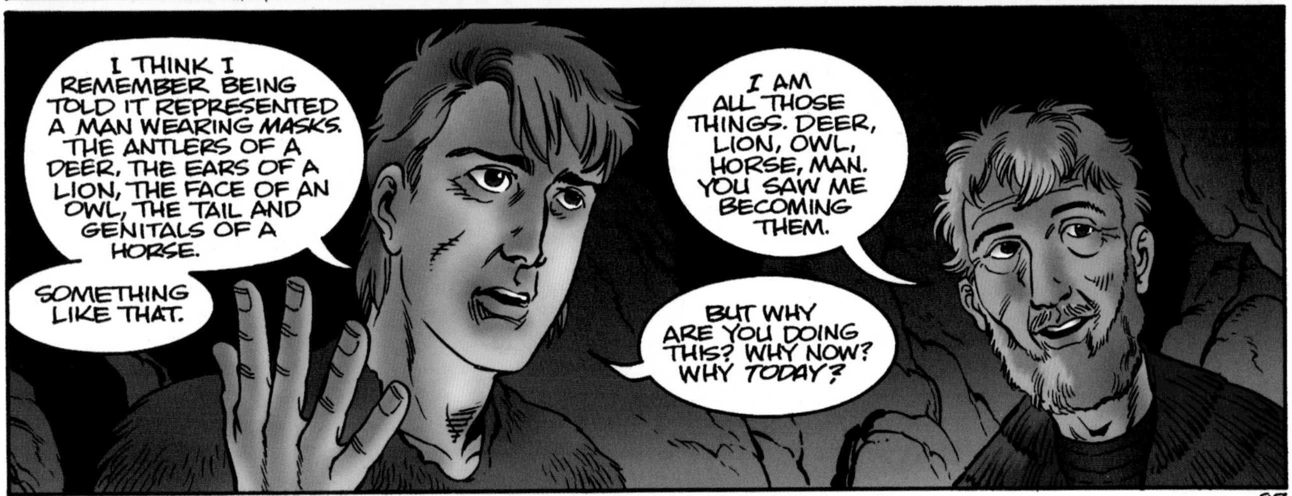
I THINK I REMEMBER BEING TOLD IT REPRESENTED A MAN WEARING MASKS. THE ANTLERS OF A DEER, THE EARS OF A LION, THE FACE OF AN OWL, THE TAIL AND GENITALS OF A HORSE.
SOMETHING LIKE THAT.
I AM ALL THOSE THINGS. DEER, LION, OWL, HORSE, MAN. YOU SAW ME BECOMING THEM.
BUT WHY ARE YOU DOING THIS? WHY NOW? WHY TODAY?

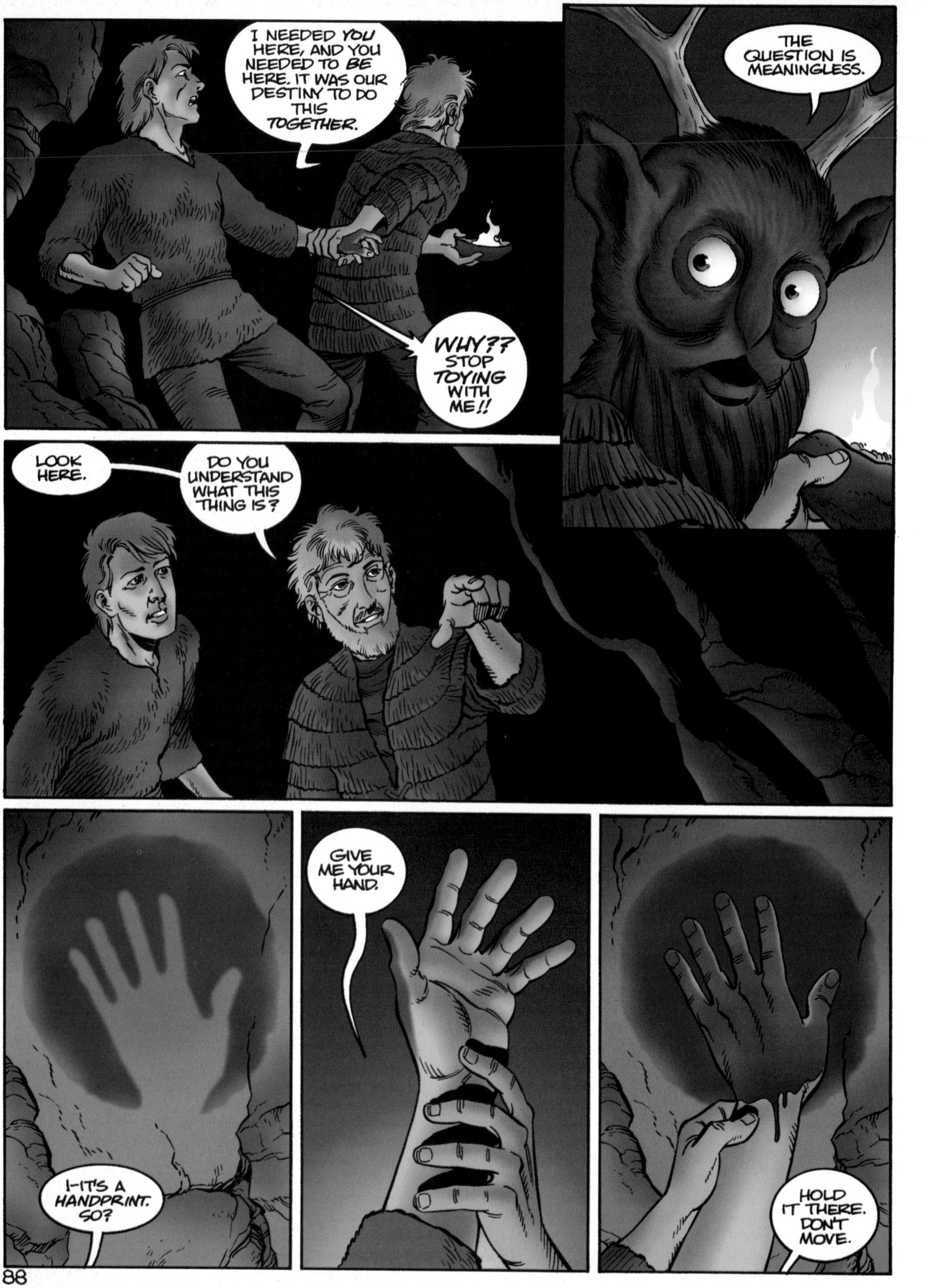
I NEEDED YOU HERE, AND YOU NEEDED TO BE HERE. IT WAS OUR DESTINY TO DO THIS TOGETHER.
WHY?? STOP TOYING WITH ME!!
THE QUESTION IS MEANINGLESS.
LOOK HERE.
DO YOU UNDERSTAND WHAT THIS THING IS?
I-IT'S A HANDPRINT. SO?
GIVE ME YOUR HAND.
HOLD IT THERE. DON'T MOVE.

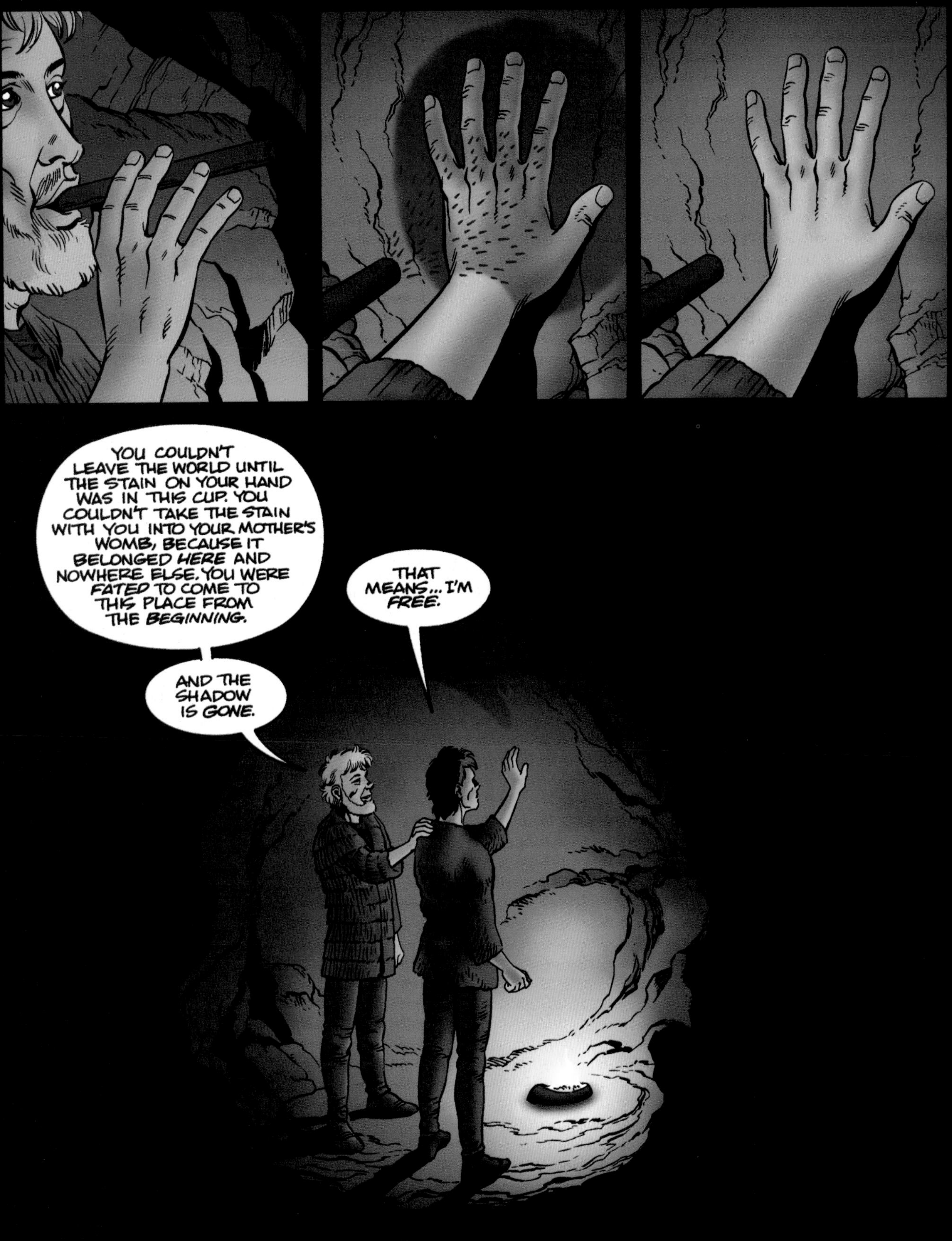

YOU COULDN'T LEAVE THE WORLD UNTIL THE STAIN ON YOUR HAND WAS IN THIS CUP. YOU COULDN'T TAKE THE STAIN WITH YOU INTO YOUR MOTHER'S WOMB, BECAUSE IT BELONGED HERE AND NOWHERE ELSE. YOU WERE FATED TO COME TO THIS PLACE FROM THE BEGINNING.
AND THE SHADOW IS GONE.
THAT MEANS... I'M FREE.

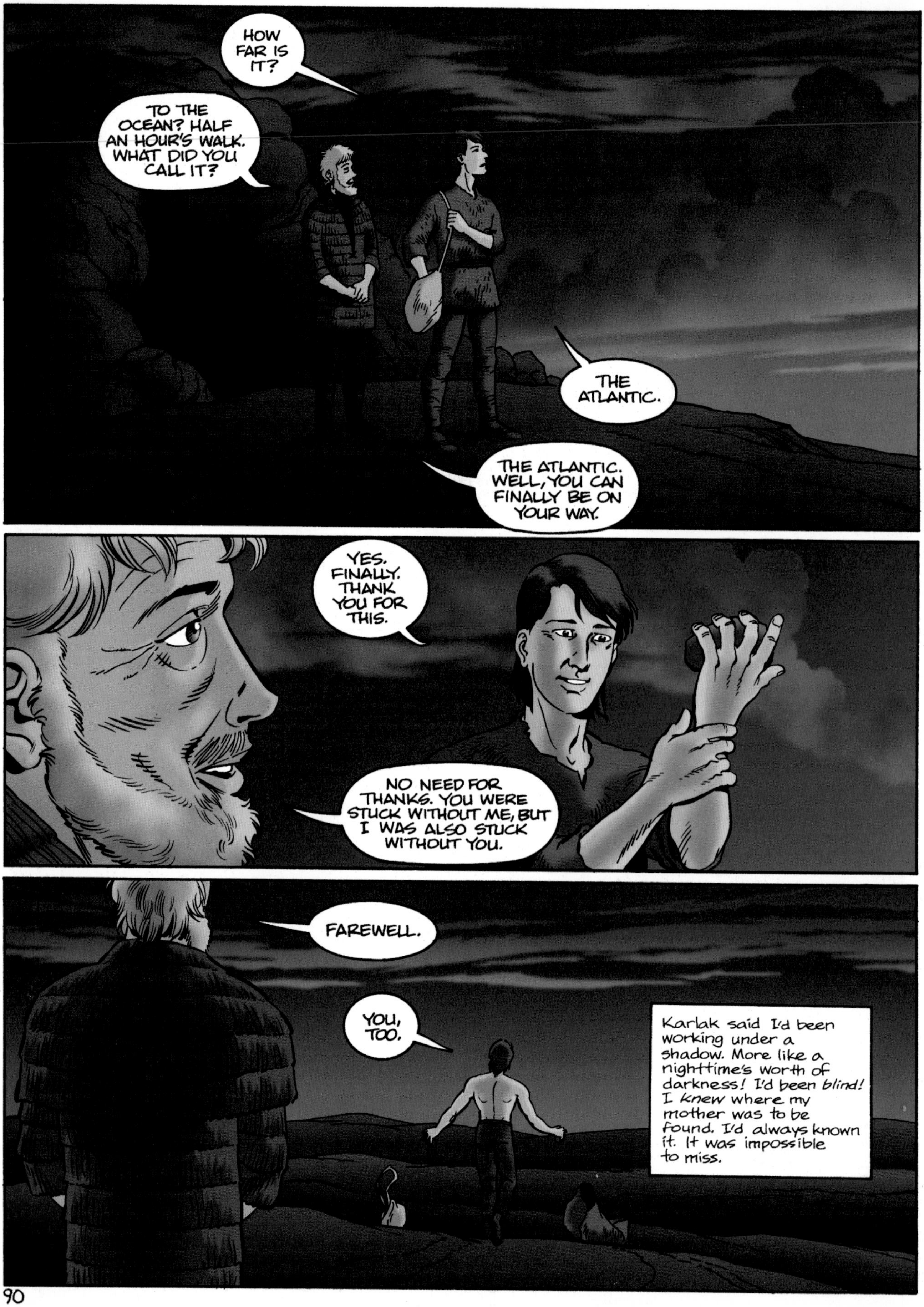
HOW FAR IS IT?
TO THE OCEAN? HALF AN HOUR'S WALK. WHAT DID YOU CALL IT?
THE ATLANTIC.
THE ATLANTIC. WELL, YOU CAN FINALLY BE ON YOUR WAY.
YES. FINALLY. THANK YOU FOR THIS.
NO NEED FOR THANKS. YOU WERE STUCK WITHOUT ME, BUT I WAS ALSO STUCK WITHOUT YOU.
FAREWELL.
YOU, TOO.
Karlak said I'd been working under a shadow. More like a nighttime's worth of darkness! I'd been *blind!* I knew where my mother was to be found. I'd always known it. It was impossible to miss.

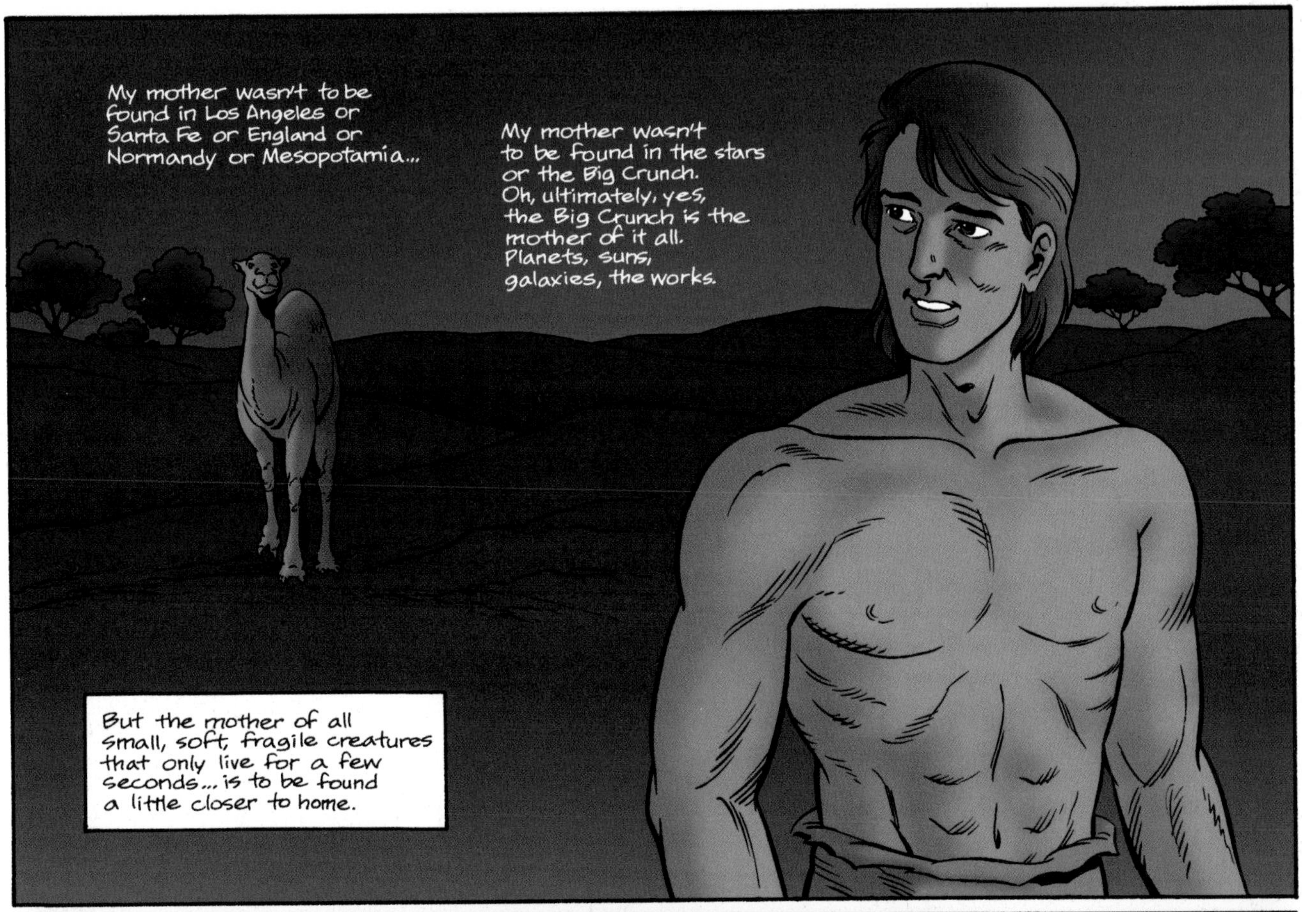
My mother wasn't to be found in Los Angeles or Santa Fe or England or Normandy or Mesopotamia...
My mother wasn't to be found in the stars or the Big Crunch. Oh, ultimately, yes, the Big Crunch is the mother of it all. Planets, suns, galaxies, the works.
But the mother of all small, soft, fragile creatures that only live for a few seconds... is to be found a little closer to home.

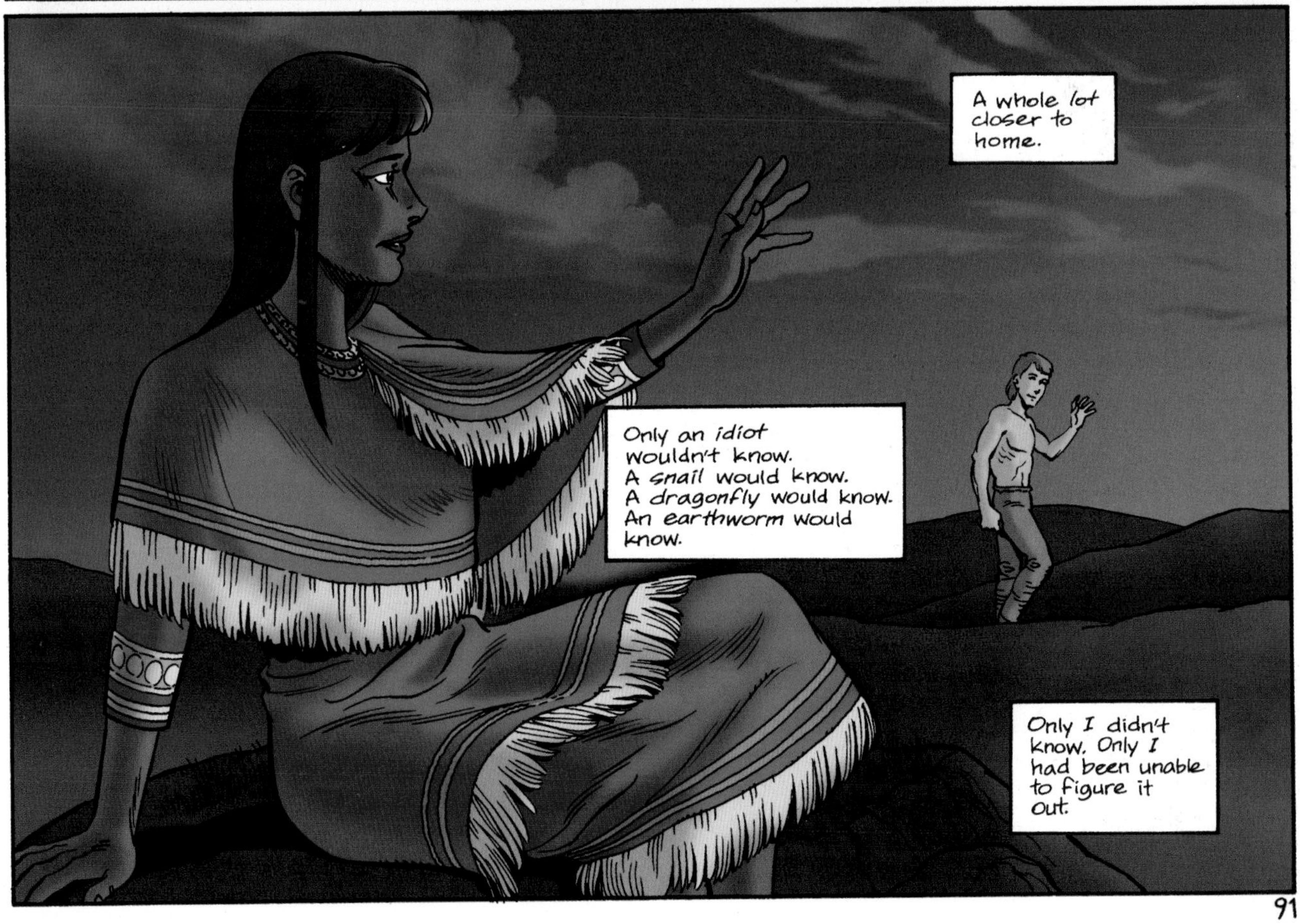
A whole *lot* closer to home.
Only an *idiot* wouldn't know. A *snail* would know. A *dragonfly* would know. An *earthworm* would know.
Only *I* didn't know. Only *I* had been unable to figure it out.

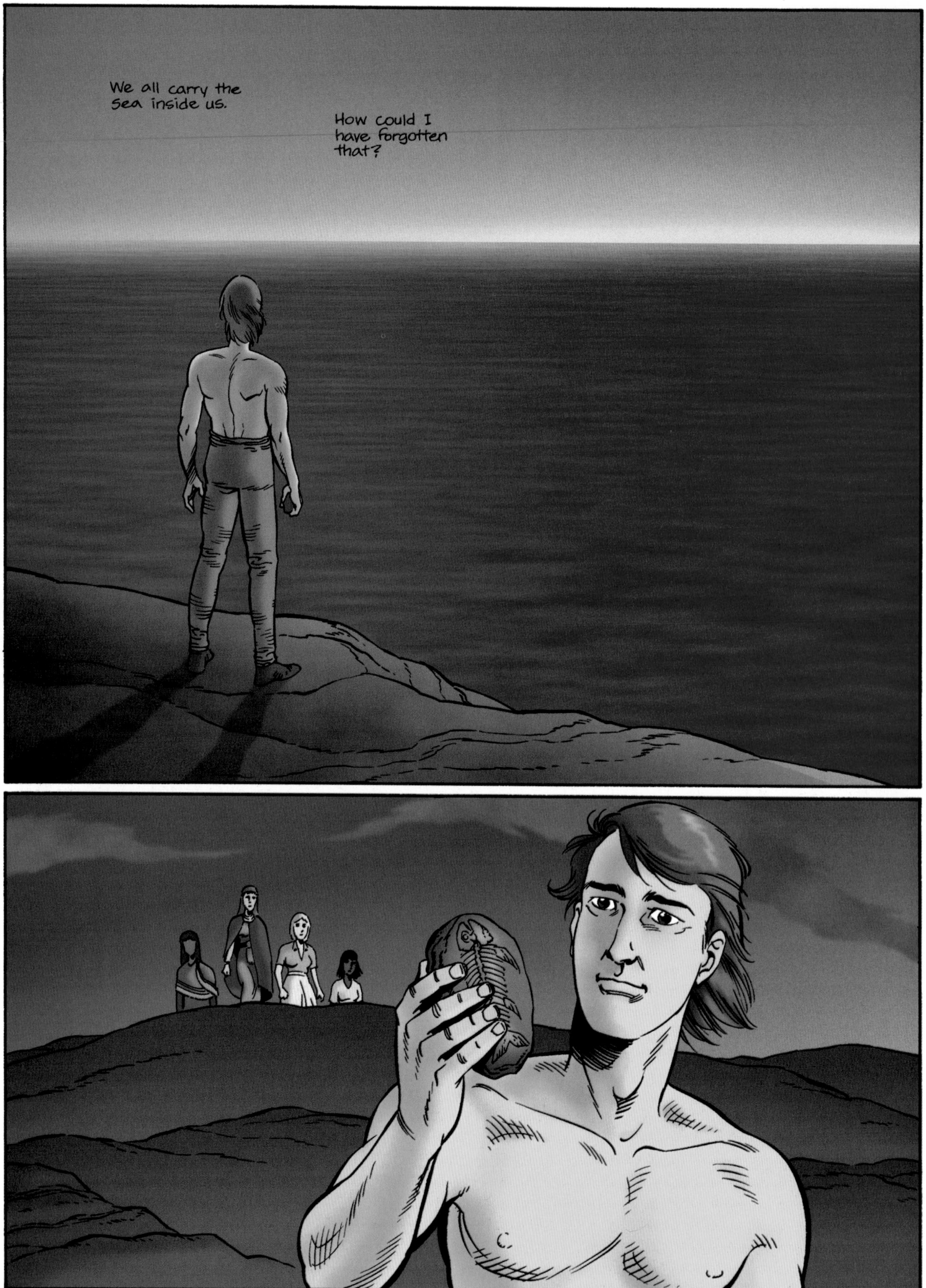

We all carry the sea inside us.
How could I have forgotten that?

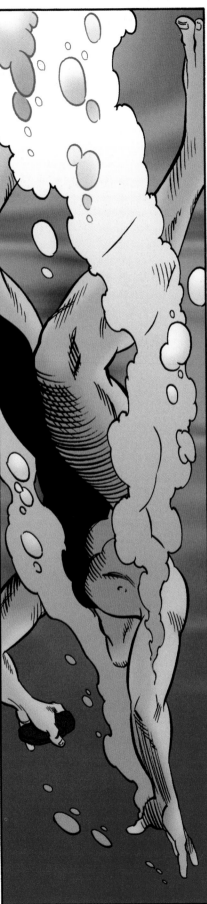

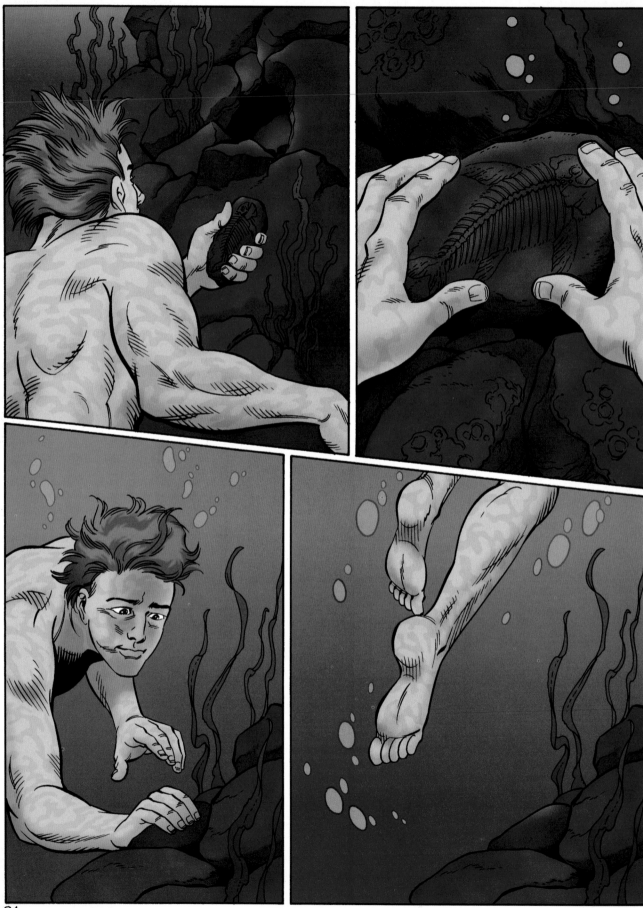

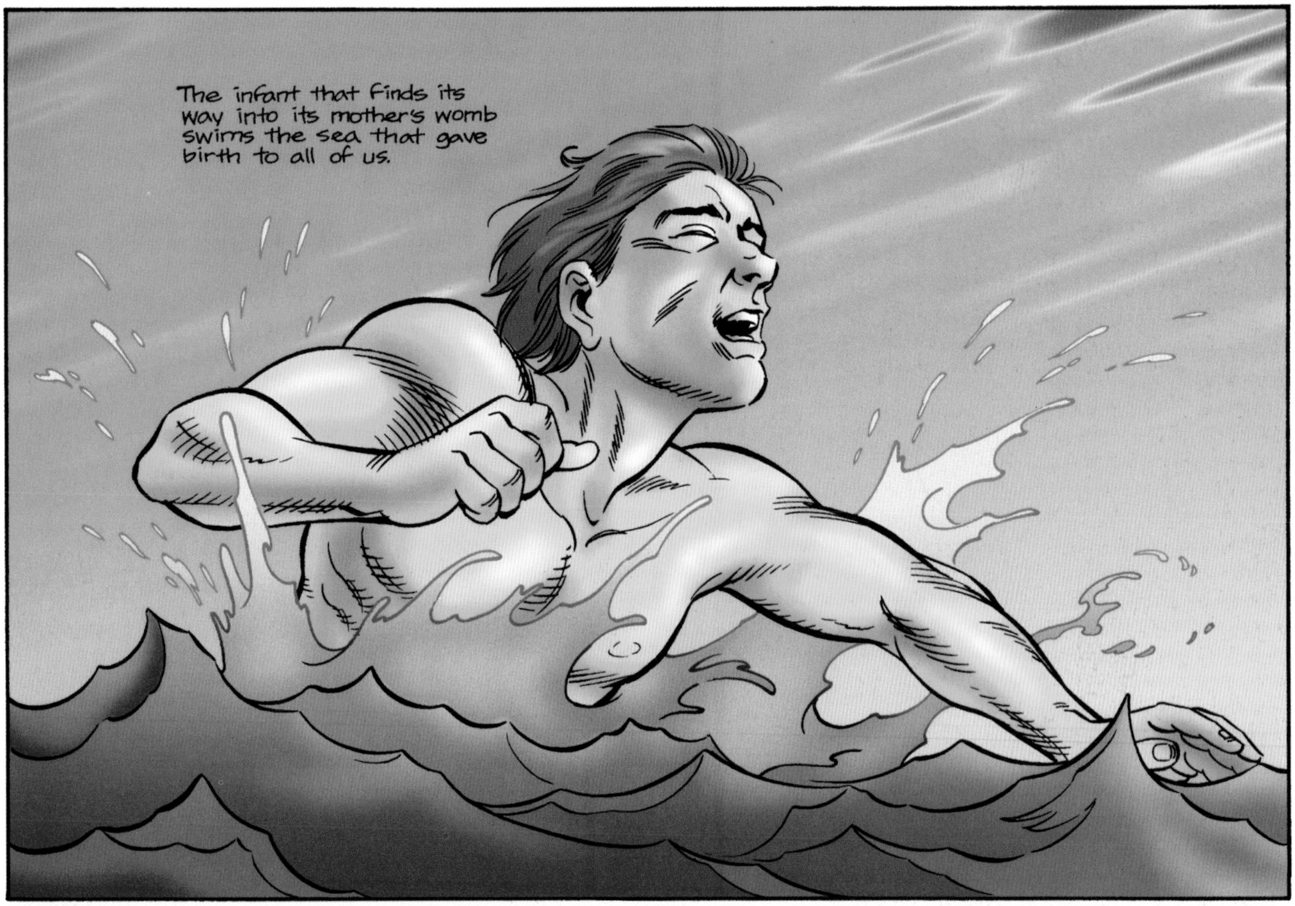
The infant that finds its way into its mother's womb swims the sea that gave birth to all of us.

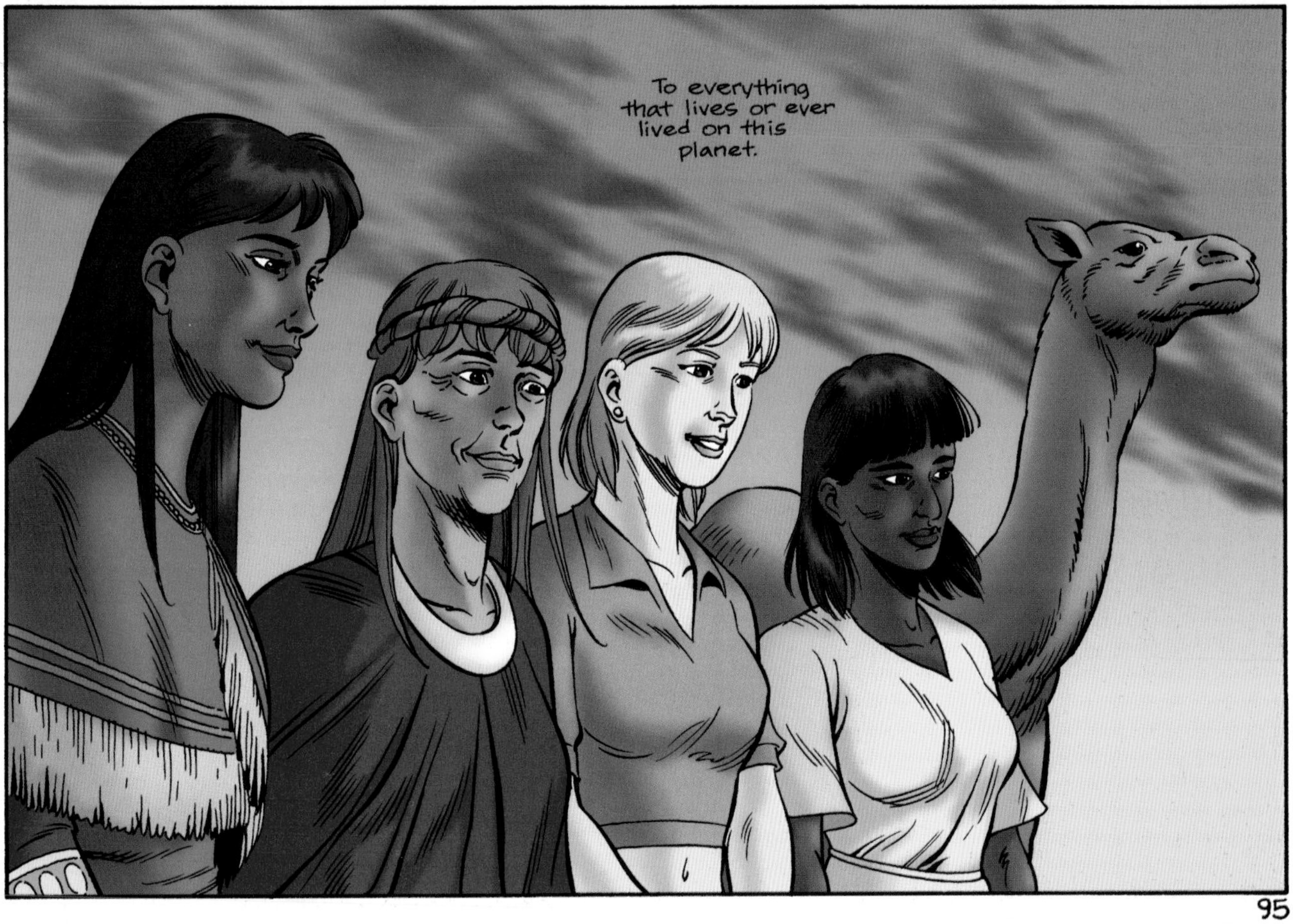
To everything that lives or ever lived on this planet.

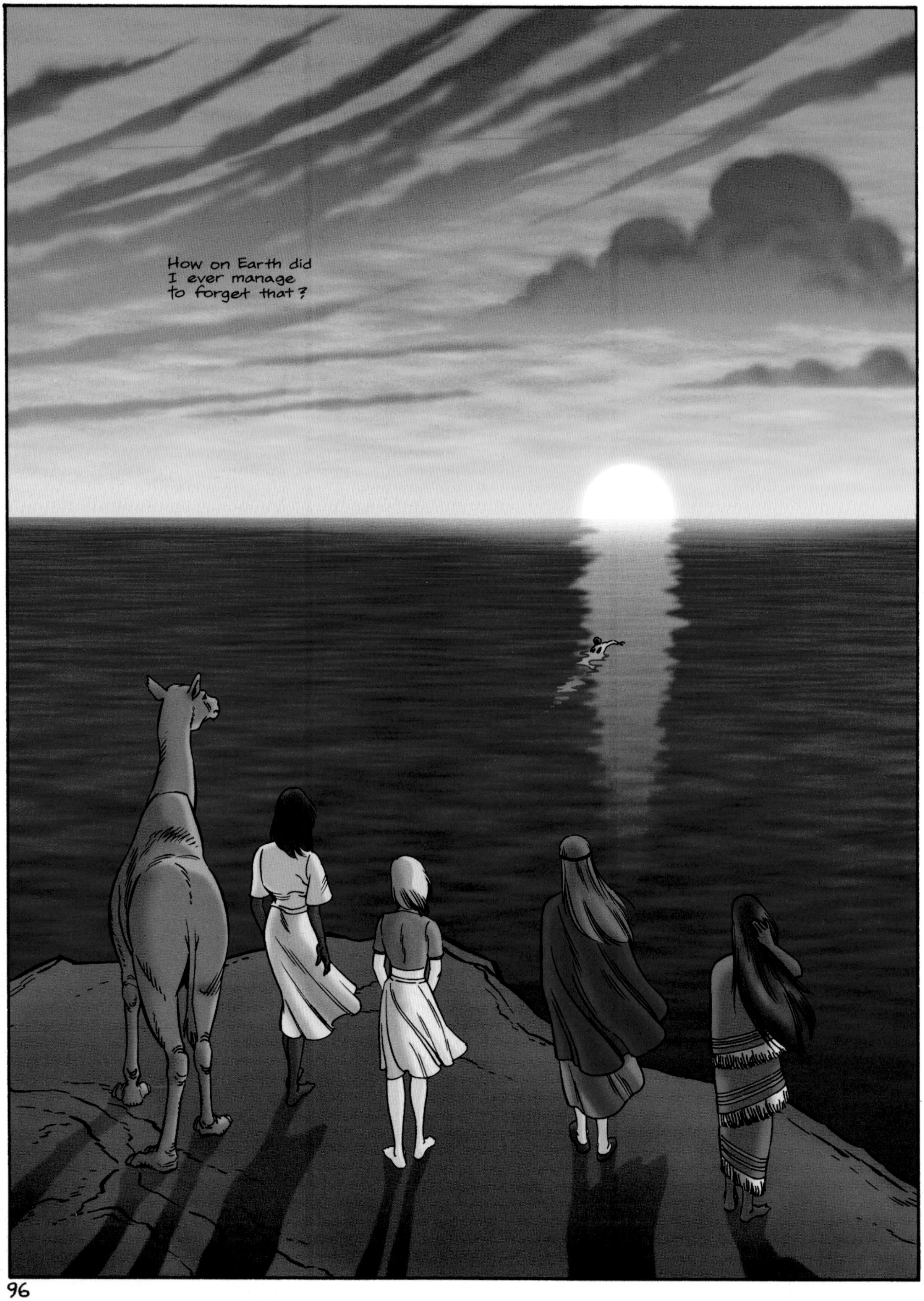
How on Earth did I ever manage to forget that?

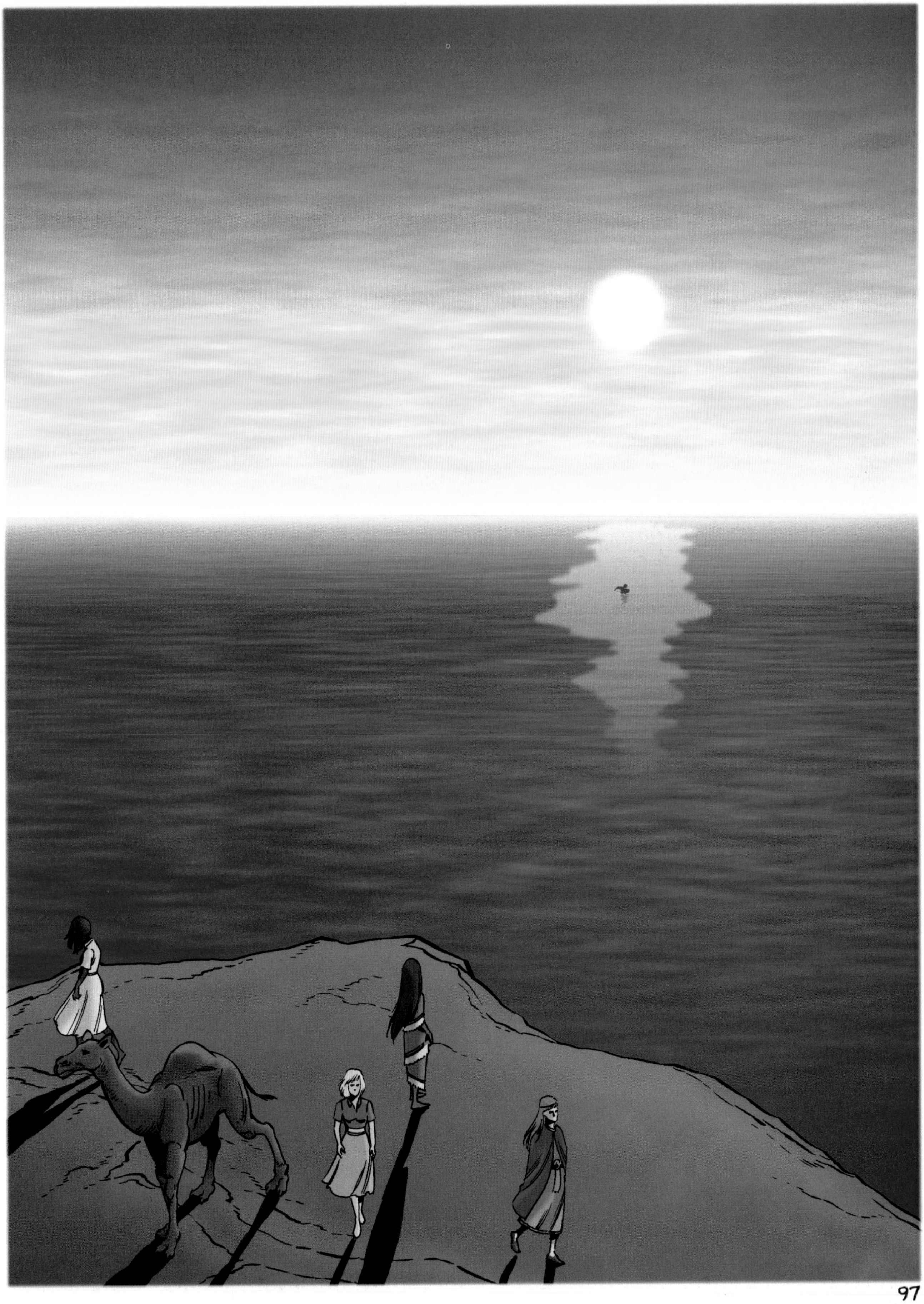

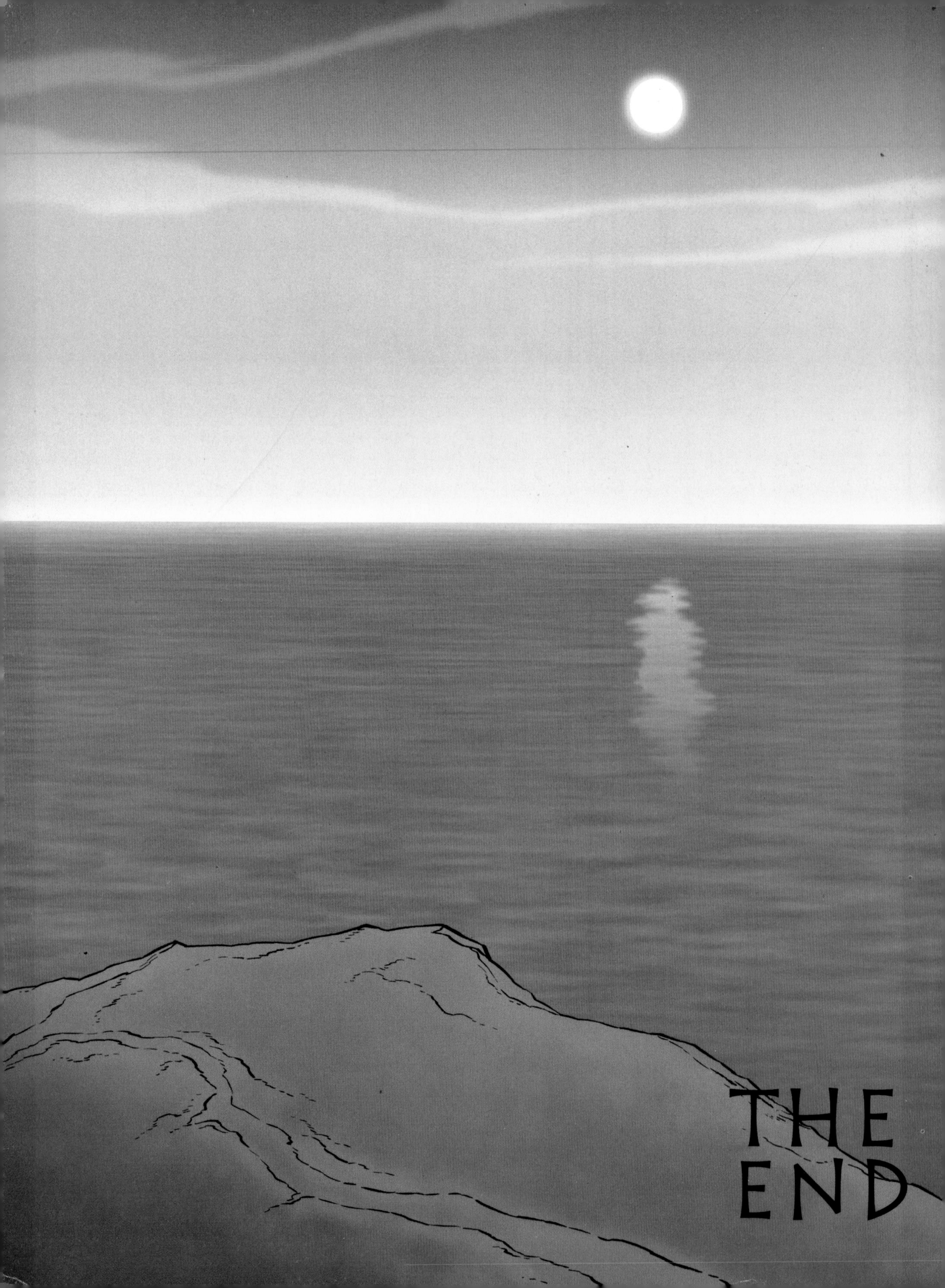
THE
END